Managing Changes
Exploring State of the Art

**MONOGRAPHS IN ORGANIZATIONAL BEHAVIOR AND
INDUSTRIAL RELATIONS, VOLUME 22**

Editor: Samuel B. Bacharach, *Department of Organizational Behavior, New York
State School of Industrial and Labor Relations, Cornell University*

Monographs in Organizational Behavior and Industrial Relations

Edited by **Samuel B. Bacharach**, *Department of Organizational Behavior, New York State School of Industrial and Labor Relations, Cornell University*

Volume 1, **Organizational Symbolism**

Volume 2, **The Organization and its Ecosystem:
A Theory of Structuring in Organizations**

Volume 3, **Military Leadership: An Organizational Behavior Perspective**

Volume 4, **Nationalizing Social Security in Europe and America**

Volume 5, **Absenteeism and Turnover of Hospital Employees**

Volume 6, **Industrial Organization**

Volume 7, **Structuring in Organizations: Ecosystem Theory Evaluated**

Volume 8, **Publish and Perish: The Organizational Ecology
of Newspaper Industries**

Volume 9, **Organizational Change in Japanese Factories**

Volume 10, **Strategic Management Frontiers**

Volume 11, **Organizational Issues in High Technology Management**

Volume 12, **Strategic Management in High Technology Firms**

Volume 13, **Issues in the Management of Human Behavior:
Analyses, Explorations, and Insights**

Volume 14, **The Environment/Organization/Person Contingency Model:
A Meso Approach to the Study of Organization**

Volume 15, **The Theory and Measurement of Work Commitment**

Volume 16, **Strategic Information Systems For Strategic,
Manufacturing, Operations, Marketing, Sales,
Financial and Human Resources Management**

Volume 17, **Corporate Environmental Policy and Government Regulation**

Volume 18, **Socioeconomic Change and Individual Adaptation:
Comparing East and West**

Volume 19, **Local Orders: The Dynamics of Organized Action**

Volume 20, **The Creativity Challenge: Management of
Innovation and Technology**

Volume 21, **Global Burnout: A Worldwide Pandemic
Explored By the Phase Model**

Managing Changes
Exploring State of the Art

by ELIZABETH MORE
Graduate School of Management
Macquarie University

JAI PRESS INC.

Greenwich, Connecticut   London, England

Library of Congress Cataloging-in-Publication Data

More, E. A. (Elizabeth A.)
    Managing changes: exploring state of the art / by Elizabeth More.
        p.   cm. — (Monographs in organizational behavior and
    industrial relations; v. 22)
    Includes bibliographical references and index.
    ISBN 0-7623-0415-4
    1. Organizational change. 2. Organizational behavior. 3. Work
environment. 4. Industrial management. I. Title. II. Series.
HD58.8.M637 1998
658.4'06—dc21   98-15098
                                                                      CIP

Copyright© 1998 by JAI PRESS INC.
55 Old Post Road No. 2
Greenwich, Connecticut 06836

JAI PRESS LTD.
38 Tavistock Street
Covent Garden
London, WC2E 7PB
England

ISBN: 0-7623-0415-4

Library of Congress Catalog Number: 98-15098

Manufactured in the United States of America

Dedication

For Professor Henry Mayer who said it was time to go it alone and who always believed in me; and for Professor Neville Wills who continues to make me laugh at the absurdities of managerial elitism and rigid mindsets, and who remains a friend through the good and the bad. I love you both.

CONTENTS

Acknowledgments   ix
Introduction   xi

I.   Managing In Today's Environment   1

The Changing Face of Managing and
   Organizing   1
Organization and Environment   4
Critical Stakeholders   9
Some Current Trends in Management
   Thought   12
Some Concerns   21

II. Managing Complexity, Ambiguity, and Change   25

Facing Uncertainty   25
Leadership   27
Managing Change   30

III. Managing Organizational Architecture   61

The New Versus the Old   61
Considerations in Designing and
   Building the Modern Organization   63
Collaborative Designs—Organizations
   Working Together   64
Understanding Interorganizational
   Cooperation   68
Finding the Right Partner   76
Managing Strategic Alliances   78
Benefiting from Cooperative Relationships   93

Real Problems in Cooperative Relationships   95
The answer?   97

IV.   Managing Mind-sets   **101**

New Mental Models   101
Organization Learning   105
Meaning, Creation, Interpretation,
   and Defensive Routines   111
Thinking Emotion   114
Thinking Intuition   117
Thinking Existentially   119
Thinking Funny   121

V.   Managing Knowledge   **135**

The Intelligent Organization   135
Organizational Knowledge   138
Contexts for Knowledge Management   143
Knowledge Management in Organizational
   Relationships   152
Some Possible Answers   155
Dilemmas   165

VI.   Managing Responsibly   **167**

The Organization in Society   167
The Question of Ethics   171
The Natural Environment   179
Sexuality, Gender, and Diversity   190

**VII.   Some Strategies and Techniques for
       Managing in a Changing Environment**   **197**

Managing Stakeholders   197
Managing the Environment   202
Issues Management   211
Managing Crisis   212
Managing Different   226

References   **231**
Author Index   **249**
Subject Index   **257**

Acknowledgments

The author is grateful to the *Australian Journal of Communication* for permission to draw upon work on humor and crisis management first published there as "Crisis Management and Communication in Australian Organizations," (22, 1, 34-47) and "Organizational communication—The Role of Humour," (20, 3, 45-70). I also owe a debt of gratitude to Isabelle Gakavian for wonderful administrative support and to Kelly Callaghan for her tireless and excellent research assistance, plus the ongoing friendship and patience on the part of both. Thanks also go to the many postgraduate management students on whom some of the ideas contained herein have been tried, and to Mark Tredinnick who prompted the writing of the work.

Special thanks go to my family for their ongoing love, encouragement, and technical support. Particular thanks to David for his technical support, to Lisa for being the best daughter, and to Purdy and Cassie who doggied their way trough the drafts, gave me perspective, and kept me company in the late evenings and early hours of the mornings.

Finally, I owe a debt of gratitude to all the researchers and authors whose work has provided the stimulus and basis for exploring state of the art.

Introduction

The future is not inevitable. We can influence it, if we know what we want it to be.... We can and should be in charge of our own destinies in a time of change.... The world of work is changing because the organizations of work are changing their ways. At the same time, however, the organizations are having to adapt to a changing world of work. It's a chicken and egg situation (Handy, 1990, pp. vii and 70).

You need to know *when* to play by the rules and *when* to change the game (Piasecki, 1995, p. 9).

Magic would be nice, but it is not easy to find (Levinthal & March, 1993, p. 95).

Given that managers and organizations, in both the public and private sectors, are in an age of uncertainty and complex, rapid change, it is imperative that we use that change to our advantage. This means being proactive rather than reactive, broadseeing rather than ostrich like.

Such behavior is difficult given that organizations are currently often caught up with internal wrangles and facing so many devleopments in the external world that quite frequently their only response seems to be to ignore the problems and dilemmas or muddle through in a state of bewilderment. Alternatively, unquestioning use of management guru recipes may often lead to exhaustion or cynicism.

Many writers have pointed out the erratic and discontinuous nature of contemporary change. Some suggest that the type of traditional corporate strategy and long-term planning of the past is not appropriate to our changed business environment, where futures are difficult to predict, where change will be qualitatively different and where changes come from many different directions simultaneously.

Faced with deep-seated uncertainties in an environment where the original complexities of corporate strategy are multiplied many times over, what might managers do and think, what might managing and leadership in a changing environment be really about?

Managers, significantly at all levels and functions, need to work proactively, setting the agenda, shaping the future, reexamining themselves and their organizations, the environment within which they operate, and at what resources and management strategies can be used to achieve their purposes within such a changing environment. In particular, they need to spend increased time on scanning and understanding environmental issues, which requires the development of skills and strategies relevant to this new dimension of the management role. That means, for example, the ability to understand the environment and to deal successfully with, and relate to, a range of critical stakeholders, both internal and external.

This is largely because the very world of work has altered: individual expectations and desires have changed; organizations themselves are transforming; but also the environment within which business functions has undergone dramatic shifts, including many which affect the very image of organization and society, in the closing decades of the twentieth century. No longer can the traditional view of the organization as a solely economic institution with economic responsibilities be upheld. Social, political, cultural, and other factors need to be part of organizational planning and operational processes. This, in turn, means changes in managerial knowledge, responsibilities, styles, thinking, and activities.

As the ambiguity of the title deliberately suggests, *Managing Changes* explores two critical issues—the changing nature of managing at the close of the twentieth century; and the real test of managing in our time—that of managing the complexities and opportunities abundant in change itself. It focuses, therefore, on the idea of managing in a way that is anticipatory and responsive, but also creative and imaginative, and in tune with changing environments in terms of proactive strategic processes involving a broader perspective than has often been the case in the past. It emphasises the need to understand the environment and use such understanding in devising ways of managing and organizing more suitable to our times and the future.

The importance of so doing is evident in the increasingly demanding and often hostile environment that organizations now face. This is evident, for example, in increasing regulation, global competition, examination of corporate governance, media portrayals of organizational life, the role of pressure groups, and the growing demand for more socially responsible and ethical organizational behavior.

Consequently, we confront and create environments that require new approaches to managing and organizing, new philosophies and paradigms, new strategies and, above all, newer approaches to understanding the world of work. This book takes such new approaches to heart and seeks to provide a basis for helping those heeding the call.

Managing Changes, therefore, chronicles and examines some of the transitions and challenges occurring in contemporary organizational life. Significant changes, opportunities and threats are occurring in the world of work in recent times and so the book is organized around some of these pointers. It does so by focussing not on the micro people dimensions of organizational life but rather the macro issues within which such dimensions are housed. The work does not provide a program, a ready prescription, or a 10-point plan for managers. Instead, it challenges traditional mindsets and approaches, and calls for renewed thought, emotion, and action. It asks the manager to balance between the old and the new, the simple and the complex, and to stay sane—indeed to revel in an environment of uncertainty, complexity, chaos, ambiguity, and paradox where there is no straightforward answer or one best way.

The book's central themes include:

- the need to be sceptical about the quick-fix recipe approach to contemporary management but to remain open to new ideas, explore and evaluate them;
- the capacity to understand and deal with both macro and micro perspectives of the environment, both internal and external, and to recognize the ongoing blurring of traditional boundaries between these divisions;
- to accept ongoing change, complexity, uncertainty and paradox, and, while revelling in this, also to understand the difficulties we humans face in managing within such an environment;
- the critical need to adopt new and diverse mindsets, but to retain the best of the old, and to develop competencies in individual,

group, and organizational learning and knowledge
management;

- to relish growing interdependency and relationships without
diminishing the quality of individual performance and effort;
and, finally,

- to embrace the need to manage responsibly and ethically in a
culture of ongoing individual and organizational renewal.

The organization of the work is as follows. Chapter 1 provides an
outline of some of the key challenges and solutions that have been
made by current management thought and practice. The chapter
traces the concept of organization and environment, explores the idea
of stakeholders, and overviews some current trends in management
thought. It demonstrates some of the flaws in the recipe approach
to current problems and the need for realistic time frames involved
in some of the changes urged upon confused managers. It points
forward to the need to really consider some key issues that are ongoing
and critical in order for us to better comprehend the overall
complexity and paradox of contemporary management in a
changing environment.

Chapter II examines the true difficulty of managing in times of
real uncertainty, paradox, and increasing complexity. It outlines a
variety of approaches to managing change itself in such a context.

Chapter III explores the necessity for moving beyond traditional
approaches to organizational structure to embracing the notion of
organization architecture. It particularly emphasises the growing
demands for relational competence, for understanding and managing
how organizations work together.

Chapter IV outlines some of the new mindsets required for
managing in a changing environment, and pays special attention to
questions of existentialism, gender, diversity, and humor in
organizational life.

Chapter V considers the developing interest in knowledge
management, recognizing the crucial competitive advantages to
organizations that reside outside bricks, mortar, and products.

Chapter VI investigates the rising interest in more responsible
management, acknowledging the growing nexus between business
and society, between business and nature, and the call for better
organizational practices in terms of ethics, values, and morality.

Finally, Chapter VII concludes the book by providing some ideas on strategies and techniques for better managing in a changing environment, extending the notion of stakeholder and environmental management mentioned in earlier chapters, and by stressing the need for creative and innovative new approaches to managing into the next century.

In so doing, the work offers a broad overview of some of the pivotal issues engaging management thought and practice today, helpful to those working in organizations now and trying to better grapple with what twenty-first-century management and leadership will demand. First, it provides an outline of new approaches to the work of organizations that impact most significantly on broad management roles and practice. Second, it offers comprehension of new competencies and mindsets required. Finally, it gives some insight to all those interested in the world of work, management thinking, and its implications for the broader social world within which we all live. It is based in a wealth of up-to-date international theory, research, and practice.

In order to do justice to these major concerns the book explores the many and varied responses available from current literature and research, thus making it a state of the art on contemporary management thought. Consequently it is heavily referenced to reflect the breadth of views and in order to allow the reader to follow up one or more of the fascinating trails left by thinkers in the specific subareas encompassed by managing changes. These subareas are, of course, the choice of the author and, in this sense, I have guided readers to the paths and trails I believe are most significant for us to traverse.

Chapter I

Managing in Today's Environment

Ultimately, there may be no long-term sustainable advantage except the ability to organize and manage (Galbraith, Lawler, & Associates, 1993, p. 3).

The future does not lie in old certainties or in the elimination of ambiguity and complexity. Rather the need is for approaches which see the steady state as the dead state, and which see dynamic instability both as a basic survival requirement and as the primary source of new possibilities and opportunities (Chattell, 1995, p. 3).

THE CHANGING FACE OF MANAGING AND ORGANIZING

The history of organizational life in recent times has been a fairly rapid progression through an agrarian to industrial to information/knowledge/systems age with a current volatility of environmental forces that has exceeded those in the past. Such volatility serves to emphasize the liability of our traditional organizational functions and core competencies to adapt or cope with the array of new problems emerging (Mitroff, Mason, & Pearson, 1994).

On top of increases in the amount and pace of environmental change the breadth of changes in the macro forces is impressive. We find, for example, challenges in the growing sophistication of information and communications technology; economic and industry restructuring; globalization; knowledge-based competition; changes and uncertainties in legal, political, and regulatory systems; managing diverse cultures and the growing demands of society. Furthermore, management itself in the modern era has emerged as the predominant and remarkable form of social control (Bergquist, 1993).

Such changes demand new approaches to managing and organizing per se. In response we have witnessed a variety of

1

developments to meet this demand. For example, the reorientation of reward systems from seniority to productivity and value added; emphasising education as well as training; focusing on customers rather than on employees and management; changing demands in roles and behavior of managers and executives; more permeable boundaries with traditional barriers between organizational functions and, indeed, between many organizations themselves being dismantled; flattening hierarchies or attempts to eradicate them altogether; greater concern for the external environment, and a growing realization of corporate social responsibility. Today the customer is all, sophisticated and educated, and demanding quality, responsibility, and timely and tailored services.

Even the basis for competitive advantage has changed. Kiernan (1993) shows how it has progressed through price and volume; quality; speed; and "mass customization." For our increasingly volatile and demanding environment into the twenty-first century, he advocates the following core elements as crucial for successful organizations:

- Organizational learning
- Innovation/experimentation
- Constructive contention
- Empowerment/shared leadership
- Optimized value potential
- Corporate sustainability
- Strategic reframing

In one American study of chief executives, Harper (1992) found the following critical attitudes concerning past and future challenges wrought by such an environment.

Categories in which the greatest changes to management have occurred:

- need for more participative management
- government regulations, rules, legislation, safety, EPA, and so on
- overall change in the marketplace
- leadership and building morale
- new breed of workers—day care, higher expectations, lower loyalty, lifestyles

- global markets and international competition
- productivity management and quality
- computer and information technology
- more intense competition
- increasingly tight supply of qualified management and labor.

Categories of greatest challenge in the 1990s:

- global competition and globalizing the firm's operations
- making sure the human side of the enterprise works at all levels
- keeping up with technology and implementing it in the workplace
- government relations, regulations, and welfare mentality
- improving every aspect of operations—reducing costs and improving quality and competitiveness
- transformational leadership: inspiring and energizing
- knowing customers and what they want
- implementation of participative management
- improving the ability to meet rapid and widespread change
- increasing productivity for blue- and white-collar personnel

The most frustrating response categories:

- dealing with regulatory bodies
- managing and motivating people
- difficulty in changing minds and ways of thinking; to accept change and embrace new ideas
- dealing with the rate of change
- finding enough motivated people to manage the company
- litigation and product liability issues
- getting managers to manage—to help their people, to improve their skills, and to take risks
- lack of appreciation by employees for their jobs and benefits
- the increase in required communication both inside and outside the company

The most rewarding response categories:

- discovering and advancing new talent; seeing people grow
- seeing what people are capable of accomplishing together

- the establishment of the essential balance among people needs, productivity needs, and profitability requirements to ensure the company's long-term competitiveness
- strategic planning and managing change
- the give and take with people in the company at all levels
- building new businesses by improving product value
- product development
- personnel—people
- developing and communicating the purpose or vision of the enterprise
- seeing the organization grow
- making profit for the shareholders: achieving ROI objectives
- working with the people in our company and taking care of our customers.

Of course, for our own particular society, and for us as individuals, there may be variations: but these findings do seem to ring true generally for many in contemporary organizations. In particular, we already know the central tensions and issues that confront the society of organizations today: the tension created by the community's need for stability and the organization's need to destabilize; the relationship between individual and organization and the responsibilities of one to another; the tension that arises from the organization's need for autonomy and society's stake in the common good; the rising demand for socially responsible organizations; the tension between specialists with specialized knowledge and performance as a team (Drucker, 1992).

Overall, however, the contemporary environment of ambiguity and rapid change requires far more supple and complex ways of thinking in contrast to some of the more simplistic textbook suggestions that abound (McCaskey, 1988). Nor are we always helped by the ongoing proliferation of paradigms (Pfeffer, 1997) in academic literature; or the difficulty of translating much useful theoretical work (e.g., Clegg, Hardy, & Nord, 1996) into improving organizational practice.

ORGANIZATION AND ENVIRONMENT

Emery and Trist (1973) alerted us to the variety of connections within an organization's environment—communication, processes, influences, transactions, and the like that determine the relationship between the two. They outlined four major environment types, suggesting that there is a general evolution toward the last mentioned, toward complexity and uncertainty—just the environment within which most of our current organizations exist:

- the placid, randomized environment—stable and unchanging with randomly distributed elements without relationships among them;
- the placid clustered environment—stable with resources concentrated in some areas;
- the disturbed, reactive environment—unstable and resources concentrated in different types of organizations; and
- the turbulent environment—dynamic with rapid change of relationships among elements.

The later, now classic, work of Pfeffer and Salancik (1978) emphasized the real significance of the internal-external interdependence and introduced the concept of boundary spanning as one critical approach to linking the organization to its environment. They argued that one must understand the ecology of the organization—the context for action—in order to comprehend the behavior of the organization as well as to manage and control such behavior. Organizations, inescapably bound up with environmental conditions, clearly engage in ongoing activities related to environment adjustment.

This view accelerated the long move from the early simplistic closed models of organizations isolated from their environments. Once organizational thinking accepted a more systems orientation it was clear that the organization was an organism that interacted with its environment, drawing on requisite resources, and communicating in the reception and sending of messages (see, for example, Katz & Kahn, 1978). Put simply, managing effectively today and into the future means managing the successful interaction of the organization's internal environment with that of its external environment, one of the key sources of uncertainty. In more complex terms, however, the boundaries between internal and external environments are not so easy to distinguish in a consistent manner, especially faced with the many intangibles today that make up the larger social and cultural domain.

We can, nevertheless, explore the environment from the perspectives of task/operation and remote environments. The former is the one most immediately relevant to the organization—its specific environment, the one with the clearest relationships, that most directly affects its ability to secure resources, and over which it generally has some degree of control. It also involves the organization's domain in the sense of its range of goods and services, and its customers and other stakeholders served. Included here are, for example, customers, distributors, competitors, suppliers, unions, and government (Jones, 1995).

The latter—the more remote or general environment, is a much broader context with forces and relationships over which the organization usually has very little influence or command, such as the economy, politics, sociocultural systems, technology, law and regulation, the environment, and global developments. Yet as this broader environment is potentially influential on the more visible task environment, it needs to be understood in some meaningful way.

While environmental complexity, dynamism, and richness (in terms of available resources) are important, a growing view is that the really critical dimension of the environment is uncertainty. Duncan (1972), early on, classified such uncertainty as follows:

- Uncertainty in dynamic environments is the result of a high rate of change, or the frequent introduction of new factors in decision making.
- Uncertainty in complex environments emerges from the variety of environmental factors involved for decision makers to consider or the breadth of environmental sources involved.

He found that it was environmental change, rather than environmental complexity, that individual decision makers found the most threatening.

Writing later, Stoffels (1994) also divides the uncertainty in an organization's environment into two dimensions: turbulence, or the frequency and extent of change; and the strength of signal or how "visible" is the change or impact. He suggests that some strategies of insulating against turbulence are concentric diversification, conglomerate diversification, or forming coalitions. Turbulence-reducing strategies include vertical and horizontal integration. Moreover, reducing the larger organizational environment into more manageable units, also aids understanding. These include the following:

- Operation: governments, economies, control, productivity, capacity, resources.
- Financial: governments, economies, capital markets, money markets.
- Technological: applied, developed, emerging, in process, conceptualized, boundaries of knowledge, governments.
- Competitive: governments, economies, industries, markets, products.
- Stakeholders: employees, shareholders, customers, suppliers, community, society, governments.

Pettigrew and Whipp (1993) also emphasize the requirement for organizations to understand their environments, pointing to the need for them to become open learning systems in order to better deal with the challenges that changing environments produce. The activity is not the sole function or responsibility of one or a few individuals but must be organization wide and strategic. For them, there exist four conditioning features that reveal how open an organization is to its environment and the changes therein:

1. the extent to which there are key actors within the firm who are prepared to champion assessment techniques which increase the openness of the organization;
2. the structural and cultural characteristics of the company;
3. the extent to which environmental pressures are recognized and their associated dramas develop; and
4. the degree to which assessment occurs as a multifunction activity which is not pursued as an end in itself but which is then linked to the central operation of the business.

Moreover, they emphasize that:

- analysis, judgment, and action combine in order that the organization understand and assess its environment;
- the dominant logics of an industry and the internal features of the organization both shape the process;

- we must recognize environmental assessment as occurring across the whole organization; and that
- the process is not simply a straightforward orderly procedure.

Environmental pressures—at local, national, and international levels—in conjunction with internal variables and industry characteristics, also significantly influence the types of organizational structures or architectures that emerge. Besides, as political, social, and cultural systems, environments also define and legitimate organizational boundaries, structures, managerial systems, and processes, and play a critical part in their creation and maintenance. As Meyer and Scott (1992) suggest, they both construct and constrain the very nature and shape of contemporary organizations.

Others take a somewhat different view to this rather macro institutional environment approach. Some see environment and its impact on organizations in terms of a population or organizational ecology perspective with organizations competing for diverse resources (Hannan & Freeman, 1989). In this perspective interest centers on the way organization structures are formed over a long time and on a population of organizations rather than individual ones. The theoretical frame suggests environmental selection in terms of organization forms fitting certain niches, and offers this as the basis for change rather than strategic management decisions or adaptive strategies. It tends to be a fairly deterministic and nonliberal view for management.

The resource dependency approach explores the interdependencies of organizations with different resource arrangements in their environment. Given the uncertainties of resource dependence, organizations can choose their operational environments and strategic approaches to relationships and processes, managing in a more active sense than that suggested in the ecological framework. As such, organizations try to limit dependency by acquiring control of critical resources and simultaneously trying to maximize the dependency of other organizations on them by having control of key resources (Evan, 1993). This emphasis on interorganizational relationships is growing in importance as interdependency increases in our complex organizational environment. Not surprisingly, then, discussion of such relationships forms a major part of a later section of this book, namely in chapter III.

Finally, some writers (for example, Pfeffer & Salancik, 1978; Weick, 1979; Stacey, 1993) have stressed the way in which environments are actually socially constructed or invented, based on perceptions rather than on scientifically observable facts. This provides us with a much more active and seminal role for contemporary organizational managers than do some of the other perspectives described above.

CRITICAL STAKEHOLDERS

In order for management to be more effective, understanding of the players in the environment is critical. Today the modern organization is increasingly affected by numerous forces, many of which appear outside the normal range of control that traditional organizations believed they possessed. What we find is organizations being more and more regarded as being accountable to numerous "investors" (Deetz, 1993).

We can conceive of such forces or "investors" in terms of stakeholders, those affected by or who affect the organization's actions, behavior, and politics (Mitroff, 1983). Stakeholder attitudes, interests, and activities can have a significant impact on an organization. Stoffels (1994, pp. 48-49) provides a useful definition:

> A stakeholder is an entity with which the firm has a mutual relationship, or interdependence. Some sectors of the stakeholder dimension consist almost exclusively of people, but the term also includes the social systems and agents that represent the interest of people, and the infrastructure which surrounds and supports people...the state of being of the stakeholder entity influences the organization, and that of the organization influences the entity. The same can be said of changes in the state of being....The stakeholder dimension reflects both trends and abrupt shifts in societal norms and values; personal preferences and life styles; community attitudes and support; customer tastes; suppliers' business practices; shareholder risk/reward expectation; and employee health, safety, morale and commitment.

Although the concept of stakeholders can be found in the literature of the 1960s (Freeman, 1984) over the last decade it has captured the attention of the management discipline in a variety of subfields, including organizational studies and ethics. The core of the approach is that individuals or groups—internal, external, or interfacing— have a stake (that range from an informal interest to a financial commitment or a formal legal claim) in what the organization does through being able to affect or being affected by an organization's operations. These can be considered in terms of primary stakeholders with formal, official, or contractual relationships and a direct and necessary economic impact on the organization; and secondary ones who are much more diverse and not directly engaged in the organization's economic activities but who are influential or affected by the organization (Savage, Nix, Whitehead, & Blair, 1991). Stakeholder management thus entails, firstly, strategic stakeholder analysis—who they are and what are their needs, interests, and capacities, and their willingness and opportunity to cooperate or threaten the organization. Secondly, it involves managing relationships that range from ones of cooperation to those of threat, and ranking claims and relationships for maximum effect. This is rather a daunting task given the complexity of actually managing as the term implies what is often the unmanageable, and what may be increasingly difficult to map per se (Savage et al., 1991; Arlow, 1992).

The organization's publics consist, for example, of employees, government, financial communities, customers, potential customers, distributors, consumer groups, suppliers, unions, office and plant communities, media, opinion leaders, educational bodies, and the like. Because of the constant interplay between external and internal stakeholders, an organization is affected across numerous dimensions—economic, social, political technological, managerial, to mention just a few. More recently we have witnessed the growth of powerful opponents—advocates, dissidents, activists, zealots, and even fanatics (Freeman, 1984; Arlow, 1992). Management then must develop defensive, offensive, and, ideally, proactive strategies for dealing with such stakeholders, explore interdependencies and continuously work with the organization's many publics.

Such stakeholders also include an organization's shareholders, and many, such as Friedman (1985), avoid a general stakeholder view and espouse the neoclassical economic view that it is this group whose interests management must serve, above all else, in a strictly "bottom line" approach to organizational life. This enforces an economic rather than social or political view of an organization's role.

Indeed, Hill and Jones (1992) suggest a combination of agency and stakeholder theory. The former is where one or more individuals (the principal[s]) engage with another (the agent) to perform some service on the principals behalf, involving delegation of some decision-making authority to the agent. The assumption here is that there is a divergence of interests between principals and agents. The stakeholder view, as mentioned earlier, involves groups of constituents who have claims on the organization. Here, then, we can see managers making decisions and allocating resources consistent with stakeholder group claims and, therefore, being agents of other stakeholders. In other words, we can have the general class of stakeholder-agent relationships subsuming the more particular principal-agent relationships.

One stakeholder theory of the organization (Brenner & Cochran cited in Hosseini & Brenner, 1992, p. 102) offers the following fundamental propositions:

1. Firms and/or organizations must fulfill some set of their various stakeholders' needs in order to continue to exist.
2. One way for firms and/or organizations to understand the relevant needs of their stakeholders is to examine the values and interests of their organization's stakeholders.
3. Managing firms and/or organizations involves structuring and implementing choice processes among various stakeholders.
4. The identification of an organization's stakeholders, their various values and interests, the relative importance of each value for each stakeholder, the relative influence of each stakeholder's value position, and the nature of the value trade-off processes used, provide information useful for understanding the behavior of and within the firm and/or organization.

Morgan (1988) argues that the need to manage multiple stakeholders or multiple interests is a critical competence in our organizations, related to a move away from a shareholder to a stakeholder organizational concept; the move from discrete organizations to networked organizations; and the move from highly integrated businesses to potpourri collections of very differentiated units. He suggests the following as ways of managing this diversity of interests:

- recognizing the "stake" and potential contributions of stakeholder groups;
- adopting stakeholder perspectives in the planning process; and
- developing stakeholder concepts of accountability.

However, perhaps these approaches are too narrow and it is more realistic to admit that neither stakeholders nor management alone control the organization. What we have, rather, is a shifting coalition of interests that affect organizational decisions and processes in a diversity of ways, occurring in an environment full of conflicting demands (Marcus, 1996).

SOME CURRENT TRENDS IN MANAGEMENT THOUGHT

...reality is not only what we see on the surface; it has a magical dimension as well and, if we so desire, it is legitimate to enhance it and color it to make our journey through life less trying (Allende, 1988, p. 21).

Given such a turbulent environment and the increasing force ·of stakeholders, it is not surprising that managers at all levels continue to demand radical solutions to the myriad of organizational problems they face.

In response, management theory has tried to devise such solutions and claims to have discovered the, or an array of, magic bullet(s), supposed revolutionary innovations to finally ensure perfect and easy management. The Price Waterhouse Change Integration Team (1996, p. xiii) has called this "a virtual feeding frenzy of programmatic change." The hype surrounding such innovations varies in terms of time frame and extension but it is always there in some form or another. Frequently, the meeting of organizational challenges has been the bandage and quick-fix approaches—downsizing, outsourcing, and the like—often without adequate analysis of underlying problems, complexity, and ambiguity, and searching for long-term solutions.

Yet fundamental solutions and strategies demand radical rethinking and redesign of many aspects of current organization life. Indeed it is argued (Stacey, 1993) that a fundamental paradigm shift is required that moves us away from an organizational dynamic of regularity and consistency to one that regards irregularity, contradiction, creative tension, and the capacity not only to adapt to but also create its environment, as the very foundation for the successful organization.

Many solutions seem to be forthcoming from an array of management gurus, such as Michael Porter, Rosabeth Moss Kanter,

Tom Peters, and John Harvey-Jones, who circle the globe and promise the latest panacea for organizational ills. Their performances may be seen as "strenuous efforts, by one device or another—to reawaken; to generate fundamentally transformed 'consciousness' of self, organization and priorities; to see new patterns and new possibilities, which ordinary life, before the performance, had not made available or obvious" (Clark & Salaman, 1996, p. 103).

Such gurus have an influential effect on current management thinking and they often set agendas for organizational reform from TQM to restructuring. Some of their thinking has emerged from studies of successful organizations, individual managers, leaders, teams, and the like. *In Search of Excellence* (Peters & Waterman, 1987) is, perhaps, the most well known of this genre.

Structure As Solution

> Despite the emergence of the myriad new organizational forms we read so much about, the boxes and lines on an organization chart are a poor match for the dilemmas raised by eroding industry barriers, increasing commoditization, and simultaneous pressures for centralization and decentralization (Liedtka, 1996, p. 23).

Many still believe that structure is the most powerful tool for an organization and that the essence of solving organizational problems lies in restructuring. This is not surprising given that many of our traditional organization structures have focused on systems devised to ensure control and conformity and, therefore, have served merely to inhibit much needed creativity and initiative (Bartlett & Ghoshal, 1995).

Yes, we do need to create new organizational architectures flexible enough to adapt to change. Such architectures must enable organizations to evolve and modify as technology, skills, competitors, and the entire business change (Howard, 1992).

A myriad of organization design solutions have been offered to increasingly bewildered management in recent years—restructuring focused on manipulating units on the organizational chart (downsizing, rightsizing, and delayering); and reengineering, which revises organizational processes per se (process management, process innovation, and process redesign) among them (Keidel, 1994).

Dess, Rasheed, McLaughlin, and Priem (1994) suggest that fundamentally there are three major choices in contemporary organization structure:

- the modular structure where the organization outsources many parts of its value chain in order to reduce costs and increase quality;
- the virtual structure where the organization engages simultaneously in multiple alliances, taking advantage of developments in technology and allowing penetration of new markets; and
- the barrier-free structure where flexibility is enhanced through breaking down barriers within the organization.

Most recent emphasis has been on the third of these options. But more and more organizations are using outsourcing and some are considering the virtual option. Of course an organization may choose to adopt more than one of these options and, indeed, Apple Computer has chosen all three.

Unfortunately, choice is no simple matter. For instance, only some "designers" recognize that organization architecture is affected by the context provided by institutional environments and interorganizational relationships. Others fail to really consider the ways in which organizational architecture can meet the major challenges of our times. For example, Mitroff, Mason, and Pearson (1994) propose organizations need to meet the major challenges of crisis management, issues management, global competitiveness, total quality management, environmentalism, and ethics through five innovative organization entities: a knowledge/learning center, a recovery/development center, a world service/spiritual center, a world-class operations center, and a leadership institute. However, even they understand that such an ideal might be a long time coming.

Reengineering. Increasingly, however, management is admitting that structure can be a major impediment to meeting the corporate challenges in the 1990s and beyond. So, if reorganization tends to focus on organizational structure per se, more is needed. We have to change the fundamental processes and behaviors by which an organization operates. The fundamental question of how the organization runs must be asked (Howard, 1992).

Consequently, instead of structures and roles alone, management thought now emphasizes exploring the very nature of organizational processes. Reengineering has been a very visible part of this exploration.

In the 1990s business process reengineering was the latest in a long line of fads. It claims to reverse the industrial revolution and advocates annihilation, starting afresh as the solution to management ills (Hammer & Champy, 1993). Its prime concern is on developing systems structured around teams, designed to mirror the processes the organization actually works around, instead of functions it uses in executing such processes. Reengineering shifts emphasis away from vertical functions to horizontal processes, from producer to consumer, stresses the macro over the micro, and reorients toward the team rather than the individual as the building blocks of the organization. Supposed benefits include shorter time frames, reducing costs, and gaining competitive advantage.

Organizational Cooperation and Collaboration. One answer is organizational cooperation and collaboration, not only the increasing tendency of cooperation across organizations but also that within organizations, across lines of business. What we have here is committed, interdependent entities jointly making and owning decisions and taking collective responsibility for outcomes. Such processes work through the ability of individuals, within and across organizations, to build meaningful relationships. Key advantages are that they allow for more flexible working and learning across traditional barriers. Many also consider the capacity to build and sustain collaborative relationships as the basis for new types of competitive advantage and the cornerstone for contemporary and future organizational success (Liedtka, 1996).

The Virtual Organization. More radical options involve those of disposable or virtual organizations. The growing army of virtual organization champions emphasize the key advantages of incentives and responsiveness. However, there are difficulties in such designs and the key is to match the right structure to what one is doing. Chesbrough and Teece (1996, p. 67) outline the issue as follows:

> Some innovations are *autonomous*—that is, they can be pursued independently from other innovations...some innovations are fundamentally *systemic*—that is, their benefits can be realized only in conjunction with related, complementary innovations....The distinction between autonomous and systemic innovation is fundamental to the choice of organizational design. When innovation is autonomous, the decentralized virtual organization can manage the development and commercialization tasks quite well. When

innovation is systemic, members of a virtual organization are dependent on the other members, over whom they have no control. In either case, the wrong organization choice can be costly.

Aside from matching structure with function, two other major dilemmas, according to Handy (1995), confront such radical architecture. One is the critical question of trust, based in some sense of mutuality and reciprocal loyalty. The other is how to create a sense of belonging, a sense of community in the virtual organization, without which this new architecture looks very precarious.

People as Solution

More and more we recognize that structure is not all, and that knowledgeable, qualified, competent people can be our most priceless weapon in organization competition (Drucker, 1992). The changes mentioned above, including structural ones, have meant that there has been a concomitant revolution in organizational relationships, now much less well defined and more ambiguous than in the past.

Today, the organization man has given way to the development of organizational members, tapping into their talents and uniqueness, and encouraging diversity instead of conformity—in other words, creating an individualized organization. In such an organization traditional systems, policies, and processes must be redefined in order to unleash the best of human assets.

Control. Critical among concerns with solutions focused on people is the issue of control. Although efforts to develop self-controlling and self-monitoring systems go back a long time in management history, as is evident in the earlier, classic work of Herzberg (1968) and Maslow (1954), today management is, more than before, being exhorted to influence people without directly controlling them (Grint, 1994).

As Simons (1995, p. 80) puts it: "A fundamental problem facing managers in the 1990s is how to exercise adequate control in organizations that demand flexibility, innovation, and creativity." His solution is a system of four levels of control:

- diagnostic control systems that overcome a lack of focus or of resources by building and supporting clear targets;

- belief systems that overcome uncertainty about purpose by communicating core values and mission;
- boundary systems that overcome problems of pressure or temptation by specifying and enforcing the rules of the game; and
- interactive control systems that overcome problems of a lack of opportunity or fear of risk by opening organizational dialogue to encourage learning.

Hirschhorn and Gilmore (1992) rightly argue that traditional organizational maps are outmoded, describing worlds that no longer exist. Yet, while traditional boundaries of hierarchy, function, and the like have been erased, they point out that boundaries are still required. What has replaced the outmoded is an array of psychological boundaries, invisible to management, but needing to be recognized and used productively for the effective flexible organization of the 1990s and beyond. These they call:

Authority boundary—"Who is in charge of what?"
Task boundary—"Who does what?"
Political boundary—"What's in it for us?"
Identity boundary—"Who is—and isn't—us?"

For them the boundaryless organization has an authority that is not about control but more about containment of those variables that disrupt productive work. Moreover, their solution to managing these more ambiguous relationships and boundaries is to become much more aware of one's own and others' feelings. This enables management to understand the boundaries people require in relationships in order to do their best.

As Ghoshal and Bartlett (1996, p. 23) emphasize, in successful organizational transformation managers understand that "transformation is as much a function of individuals' behaviors as it is of the strategies, structures, and systems that top management introduces." They stress four elements of the transformational behavioral context—discipline, support, stretching individuals through enhancing expectations, and trust.

Empowerment. However, today much concern about control really incorporates consideration of the issue of "empowerment," a term much bandied about and often without specific guidelines to assist the perplexed manager. Essentially, as Ford and Fottler (1995) suggest, it is about encouraging and rewarding employees exercising initiative and imagination—a process of directed autonomy in which employees can choose how to go about following overall directions concerning work. In order for functional empowerment, employees require information and knowledge for understanding and contributing to organizational performance; a reward structure based on organization performance; and authority to make decisions affecting organizational outcomes. Yet empowerment occurs within some organizational limits and it is choosing such limits where the real challenge in using such a strategy lies.

For them, the critical point is to choose what approach to adopt and, where possible, to gradually implement more and more empowerment. This is done on the basis of understanding a job as having two dimensions—content (tasks and procedures) and context (rationale, the fit with the overall organizational goals, setting, etc). The recipe to follow then becomes:

- no discretion—the job is designed and monitored by someone other than the employee, with no decision making concerning job content or context (traditional);
- task setting—employees given much decision responsibility for the content but little for context;
- participatory empowerment—employees given some decision-making power over both content and context;
- mission defining—employees empowered only to decide on job context; and
- self-management—employees have total decision-making authority for both content and context (ultimate but rare).

What is the most suitable level of empowerment has to be decided, and then implementation strategies devised in order to reach such targets. Indeed, a variety of levels of empowerment may be suitable, both across the organization and in terms of what to extend to individuals. Of course it is critical for managers to evaluate not only their employees but also themselves and their organizations when considering empowerment, assessing, for example, the readiness of management to give up decision-making authority, the readiness and willingness of employees to participate in empowerment, and the culture of the organization overall to engage in such an approach to managing people.

Intangibles As Solution

Structure and human resources are, however, not the only arenas of solution offered by management thinking in the 1990s.

Learning and Knowledge. The learning organization is built on the solid foundation of appropriate culture, the embrace of change, functional mind-sets, structures, and flexible boundaries both within and outside the organization in order to tap knowledge and ideas from suppliers, customers, partners and other stakeholders, technology and performance management systems (Kiernan, 1993).

In the information age an organization's survival and competitive advantage has moved toward reliance on its ability to capture information, mold it into useable knowledge, embed it as organizational learning, and communicate it speedily throughout the organization (Bartlett & Ghoshal, 1995). Indeed, "Organizational learning will replace control as the dominant responsibility and test of senior management and leadership" (Keirnan, 1993, p. 9).

Developing techniques and measurements for knowledge management is at the forefront of much contemporary management thinking, including the work of many management consultancy groups around the globe. Growing areas of interest are:

- organizational memory and how that is affected by downsizing in particular;
- ways of unlearning; and
- emotional intelligence as the capacity to move beyond a simple image of the rational organization—to read and manage the emotional dimension of organizational life.

Culture. But many are not merely calling for changes in organizational practices and processes. They are calling for the reinvention of organizations themselves. This requires, first, uncovering the organization's hidden context—its underlying assumptions, premises that guide decisions, action, and the culture of the organization. Reinvention demands the creation of a new context, the foundation upon which all changes can be sustained. In other words, "given an organization's being determines its context, its possibilities. Remarkable shifts in context can happen only when there is a shift in being" (Gross, Pascale, & Athos, 1993, p. 101).

For reinvention, what management and others in the organization are doing is merely one aspect of gaining a competitive edge. The real foundation is something much more intangible—being within a context—who you are versus what you do. This is true of the individual as well as the organizational level (Gross, Pascale, & Athos 1993). Identity is emerging as a critical management concern.

One solution lies in that very intangible entity—culture. While there is little detailed consensus about organizational culture, there is certainly keen interest in what Bloor and Dawson (1994, p. 276) describe as "a patterned system of perceptions, meanings, and beliefs about the organization which facilitates sense-making amongst a group of people sharing common experiences and guides individual behaviour at work."

Two critical concerns here are with (a) professional culture and (b) national culture in a global economy. Given the growing influence of professionals it is important to consider the interaction of professional and organizational cultures:

> At its simplest, professional subcultures are often stronger than other groupings within an organization in the sense of having extra-organizational associations and peers to aid them in shaping new cultures and codes of conduct, and resisting the imposition of other cultural values and practices. In other words, professional cultures, which reside outside organizations are central to sustaining professional subcultures within organizations. Thus, whilst professional subcultures conflict, coincide and interlock with each other, they each have the potential to redirect and shape organizations (Bloor & Dawson, 1994, pp. 286-287).

Managing across cultures is a significant issue also to be understood in the global environment. One approach has been provided by the work of Hofstede (1993). In over a decade of research he has accumulated data to suggest five major variables in national cultures, which need attention by management in their international dealings:

- power distance—the degree of inequality considered normal;
- individualism—the degree to which people prefer acting as individuals or members of groups (collectives);
- masculinity—the degree to which traditional masculine attributes (e.g., success and competition) win out over

traditional feminine ones (e.g., caring and warmth of relationships);

- uncertainty avoidance—the degree to which individuals prefer structured over unstructured situations; and
- long-term orientation—concern with the future over short-term values.

Corporate Image. Finally, the critical capacity to manage the organization's image and reputation is increasingly recognized as a key to competitive advantage in the global marketplace. That is one reason for the growing attention to crisis and issues management. The other concern is with the role of the organization in society and the question of organization and industry ethics. Certainly the increased emphasis on information, ideas, and intelligence emerging in management thinking can offer a solution to the tug-of-war between material growth and damage to the environment (Handy, 1995).

Undoubtedly, organizations are responsible for the effect they have on employees, customers, other stakeholders, the environment, and the like. But whether or not they should and can tackle major social ills, as many are increasingly demanding they do, is more complex. As Drucker (1992, p. 99) warns: "good intentions are not always socially responsible. It is irresponsible for an organization to accept— let alone to pursue—responsibilities that would impede its capacity to perform its main task and mission or to act where it has no competence."

SOME CONCERNS

Given our unpredictable and chaotic environment, and our newfound "appreciation for the power of randomness and change" (Freedman, 1992, p. 30), it seems the search for the magic bullet, for miracle solutions to organizational problems, will escalate. Unfortunately, all that glitters in management thinking turns out not to be the gold that we seek, not the ultimate solution for making our journey through organizational life much less trying as we would wish. Furthermore, fundamental shifts in management thought are difficult to achieve, both in theory and practice.

Grint (1994) argues that many such solutions, throughout management history, are not novel but rather become popular because they are made plausible to target audiences through capturing the "spirit of the times." Moreover, Clark and Salaman (1996), in a serious but very unflattering critical analysis, emphasize the very real similarities between management gurus and witchdoctors.

Solutions based on studying successful organizations are also fraught with problems. There is danger in following such recipes for success, not only because some of the analysis on which some of these studies are based may be problematic (including the fact that they don't survey unsuccessful organizations) but also because one cannot simply transport what works in one situation to another with a 100 percent guarantee of similar success. Only a few years after the publication of *In Search of Excellence* (1987), many of the excellent organizations cited had fallen from grace and others were being excellent without complying with the success rules outlined in the book. Besides, other companies following success recipes have actually found their efforts have failed, such as Volvo and Saab when using "team concept" ventures (Vedder, 1992).

Even structural solutions are not as miraculous as first believed. Delayering organizations, the drive to replace hierarchies with teams, is not without difficulties, especially when rather than thinning managerial cohorts, the organization takes them out entirely. Chief among a wide range of problems is the loss of expertise, loyalty, and an array of proving grounds for junior managers (Grint, 1994).

Furthermore, when closely examined, reengineering does not appear to be the radical innovation it claims (Grint, 1994) and most efforts fail, similar to the failure rate of total quality management efforts. Even reengineering's pioneer, Hammer, estimates that 50-70 percent of all reengineering efforts fail to achieve their objectives (Keidel, 1994).

Moreover, the much touted collaborative solution to problems and increasing competitive advantage turns out to be hard to achieve in a status quo climate of turf protection and where the skills required are rarely rewarded. Most organizations don't have the requisite qualities such as developing new skills, mind-sets, and organizational architectures. Often, to time-stressed, meeting-saturated managers the risks and effort involved in collaboration can appear to outweigh the benefits (Liedtka, 1996).

So, much of what have been offered as magic bullet solutions are problematic. The end result is that we are forced to rethink the very nature of organization and organizing, changing our fundamental mental models, maps, and assumptions as we go toward the twenty-first century.

Bolman and Deal (1997) call for "reframing" so as to tame and befriend our organizational beasts. Reframing demands seeing events through multiple lenses so as to prevent conceptual and psychological blindness. They advocate the integration of previously distinct major theoretical perspectives and isolated traditions—the four frames of structural, human resources, political, and symbolic—as a solution to better professional practice.

Keidel (1994, p. 17) offers a complement to this in terms of "rethinking" as an alternative approach to the solutions offered in much recent management thought. It is targeted at individual and collective mind-sets, on sense-making, it is conceptual, and a source of strategic advantage. He describes it as conceptualizing so as to "incorporate organizational identity, or *character*—who we are and what we stand for; organizational purpose, or *constituencies*—for whose benefit we exist; and organizational methods, or *capabilities*—how we satisfy customers/consumers." He argues that rethinking organization cognition, by changing patterns of understanding, can lead to efficiency, customer satisfaction, and employee development.

Along with rethinking goes the challenge of shaping the organization's behavioral context and of creating an environment in which people can exploit information more effectively, take initiative, cooperate, and learn (Bartlett & Ghoshal, 1995). This cannot be achieved through structure or any single management magic bullet alone.

With increasing globalization—the need to manage across domestic, international, multinational, and transnational boundaries—new approaches to human resources must be developed which are appropriate to each level of management. Especially significant is the need to have a holistic view of the worldwide business environment, to understand the issues of national cultures, and employ effective cross-cultural interpersonal competencies and the like (Adler & Bartholomew, 1992).

In the past, solutions heavily pointed to structure and people. Today there is more emphasis on solutions lying in the realm of intangibles such as culture, power, and knowledge. The truth, however, is that we need solutions combining all three. And solutions that are not one of magic bullets or panaceas, but are undergirded by a deeper, longitudinal approach that questions simplistic assumptions and solutions and explores the very nature of organizing into the twenty-first century.

At the heart of our dilemmas lies strategic thinking in a global sense, not the past myopic strategic planning that has essentially been about articulating and elaborating existing strategies and visions. As Mintzberg (1994) suggests, we need more than just planning. We require strategic thinking that synthesizes learning and knowledge into a vision of the direction an organization should follow. This requires intuition, creativity, and reinvention, a more complex process than much of what has been offered in contemporary management thought and practice.

Chapter II

Managing Complexity, Ambiguity, and Change

...companies that fail to manage change will, in time, be managed by change (Want, 1993, p. 28).

Companies that succeed are those that—as individuals and organizations—become change-capable. Change-capable organizations recognize change as a constant element of the landscape, and stability as the exception. They define changes as opportunities, rather than threats. They work to turn change to their advantage. In many cases, they actively and deliberately create change so that they can then capitalize on it. Their strength lies not in order and structure but in responsiveness and flexibility (Nadler, Shaw, Elise Walton, & Associates, 1995, p. xiv).

The new science of complexity leads us to see organizations as complex adaptive systems. Such systems are creative when they occupy a space at the edge of disintegration, and here their specific futures cannot be foreseen. The price we pay for creativity and free will is an inability to foresee and intend future outcomes (Stacey, 1996, p. 182).

FACING UNCERTAINTY

Managing change—creating, responding, and using it—is now considered perhaps the most critical competency for long-term organizational survival and prosperity (Moss Kanter, Stein, & Jick, 1992; Mink, Esterhuysen, Mink, & Owen, 1993; Stace & Dunphy, 1994). Proficiency in managing proactive change is requisite for organization success and for leading industry change in a broader sense (Strebel, 1994).

Given our current environment, some suggest that organizational success is not about choosing between stability and instability but rather from choosing both: we are constantly on the edge between order and chaos—stability for pursuing current business efficiently and chaos necessary for stimulating dynamic strategic issue agenda formation (Stacey, 1991; Bergquist, 1993). Consequently, it is not surprising that much change management reveals inconsistencies, paradoxes, dilemmas, and contradictions (McWhinney, 1992). Moreover, it may be that what we see as organizational complexity and chaos is not a wholly new, permanent context, but rather something that has characterized organizational operations for at least the past two centuries and which we are only now truly recognizing in postmodern terms (Bergquist, 1993).

Organizations in the past were considered the bringers of order, controllers of their own destiny, and living in a relatively simple and stable environment. That reality is altered now and complexity, turbulence, instability, increasing risk, unpredictability, and paradox replace simplicity and stability. While short-term outcomes are predictable, this is more unlikely with long-term outcomes. Strategic planning today must, therefore, be more in tune with managing the control parameters of containing anxiety, using power, the law of information, ensuring tolerable degrees of difference, and having connections across organizational networks (Stacey, 1996).

So in the postmodern organization we confront chaos—both order and disorder in contemporary organizational life. Given such dynamics, no longer do we have the stability of traditional practices of organizational analysis; contingency; long-term planning, forecasting, and simulation; visions; consensus and strong cultures; measures of probability. Instead we will need contradiction, conflict, dialectics, learning, dynamism, and self-organization (Stacey, 1993).

The complexity that organizations face involves more entities in the environment (e.g., competitors); growing diversity through increasing knowledge; and growing interdependence among organizations. Such environmental changes (Huber & Glick, 1993) require changes in organizational processes such as decision making and implementation, information acquisition and distribution, and a heavy emphasis on better management of organizational learning.

Today, we recognize more clearly the chaos underlying apparent order and accept that disorder and chaos, in the form of unpredictability and complexity, both affect and are affected by the contemporary postmodern organization. Such an organization, often troubled by ambiguity of identity, exists, Bergquist (1993) argues, on the edge between order and chaos, with no going back, and the way

Pre-modern	Modern	Postmodern
small and simple	large and complex	small - moderate
unclear mission	unclear mission	clear mission
unclear boundaries	clear boundaries	diffuse boundaries
paternal/charismatic leadership	systematic leadership	leadership versus management
communication oral and face-to-face	communication formal and written	communication oral / electronic
capital as land and reputation	capital as money, buildings and machines	capital as information/expertise knowledge
manual labor for food, shelter and security	labor for wage and salary	labour for meaning in addition to sustenance

Figure 1. Different Ages of Organizations (after Bergquist, 1993).

forward across a tilted, warped plane. He characterizes the different ages of the organization in Figure 1. What is clear from Bergquist's (1993) discussion, is a change from objectivism to constructivism. That is, the past perspective assumed an external reality and universal truths that could be known and articulated. Nowadays we find reality as socially constructed (at both a social and personal level), without universal truths or principles to guide us. We have, therefore, moved away from a facts and figures emphasis to that of story and performance. Yet the world in which organizations exist is not one or the other but, rather, is simultaneously premodern, modern, and postmodern. Furthermore, for the postmodern manager chaos is neither good nor bad—it merely is as it is. Out of it emerges the positive richness of the modern organization—a hybrid entity, characterized by differing forms and dynamics. Such fluidity and shifting boundaries (epitomized by the reality of the mobile office), while increasing complexity, ambiguity, and confusion, is also critical for the flexibility and responsiveness required for survival in the current environment.

LEADERSHIP

Given such uncertainty and chaos, it is not surprising that the contemporary leader is required to do more. Leaders are called upon to be "genetic architects of the biological corporation" (Gouillart & Kelly, 1995, p. 3). Moreover they are required "to have the existential and political courage to address issues such as concreteness, morality, responsibility, and commitment; and to become a role model for others. However, the problems involved in finding such leaders and in their ability to effect change are substantial" (Pauchant & Associates, 1995, p. 120).

It is clear from research and experience that complex organizational environments and the management of change demand effective leadership at all levels but particularly at the executive level. Such senior personnel affect organizational change in a variety of ways but we can summarize these as the following activities (Huber & Glick, 1993):

- sources of change—through their values, ideologies, mental frameworks, and belief systems determining their desired strategies, structures, and cultures;
- inhibitors of change—through beliefs and competencies constraining change;
- interpreters of the organization's environment—through shared understandings, conceptual schemes, labeling of environmental stimuli as problems or opportunities; and
- manipulators of the organization's environment—through influencing the environment by lobbying, advertising, and similar activities.

Traditional approaches to leadership are today called into question in an era that clearly reveals a leadership of both chaos and order, yet which emphasizes collaboration rather than control by authority as in the past. Critical dimensions to managing contemporary and future complexity and ambiguity are those of managing multiple stakeholders, managing a myriad of things simultaneously, and being able to manage transition and change (Morgan, 1988). Importantly, leadership perceptions stamp their mark on organizational life and so one of the major challenges for leaders today is to choose actually what they want to see and why, in this work environment of order and chaos (Bergquist, 1993).

The postmodern leader moves away from the idea of the great figure and more toward situational or contingent models with a focus on the spiritual rather than purely secular approach. Indeed, we have shifted from a rather sacred view of the leader in premodern times; through the modern divorce from the sacred and an emphasis on the secular, professional, systems, planning, and management; and back to a postmodern blend of both sacred and secular. Flexibility in style and a strong commitment to learning are critical. As Bergquist (1993, p. 13) puts it:

> Leaders of this edgy postmodern world must somehow navigate a turbulent "white water" environment, one filled with unpredictability and requiring both short-term survival tactics and long-term strategies based on broad visions and deeply embedded values. Leaders must be sources of integration in postmodern organizations. They perform this integrative role through the creation and sustenance of community and through acting in the role of servant to those with whom they work. The notions of community and servanthood, in turn, lead us away from the traditional (both pre-modern and modern) notions of a society based on dominance to a society based on partnership and collaboration.

He indicates that continuing problems for contemporary leaders reside in:

- group collusion in a leader's incompetence;
- inadequate feedback to reveal leadership differences between theory and practice and resulting in leaders having little personal insight;
- the issue of control in this turbulent environment—the apparent contradiction between growing benevolence and responsiveness while often being more subtly repressive and controlling; and
- the need for diverse traits for success—mastering the unexpected, and often unwanted; tolerating ambiguity; coping and anticipating rogue events that often substantially impact the life and dynamics of the leader and the group.

Others (Nadler & Tushman, 1990, p. 87) maintain that two different yet complementary styles of leadership are required for successful change:

> ...effective re-orientation requires both charismatic and instrumental leadership. Charismatic leadership is needed to generate energy, create commitment, and direct individuals towards new objectives, values or

aspirations. Instrumental leadership is required to ensure that people really do act in a manner consistent with their new goals. Either one alone is insufficient for the achievement of change.

This is taken up by Kets de Vries (1994) who emphasizes the two roles of leadership, focusing on the charismatic one involving how leaders envision, empower, and energize to motivate followers; and the instrumental in terms of designing, controlling, and rewarding organizational behavior appropriately. He does, however, point to the way that the very personality of senior executives—the inner theater—has a major influence on strategy, culture, and even organizational structure. The irrational as well as the rational dimensions of such leadership need to be understood—by leaders and others—in order for the organization to perform successfully.

Furthermore, given different types of change, and varying situations, variable leadership styles are required for change management and that includes leadership across the organization not merely at its helm.

MANAGING CHANGE

Pettigrew and Whipp (1993) regard strategic change and competition, occurring at multiple levels over time, as joint and inseparable processes. The research undertaken by Stace and Dunphy (1994) has led them to believe that successful organizations are those that initiate change, respond to change, plan change, and implement change as an ongoing way of life.

So change in organizational life today is a necessary constant. While in the past the status quo provided an adequate approach to organizational life, today success goes to those organizations that effectively encompass change and manage it for competitive advantage. The real challenge of the decade and beyond is to understand and manage change proactively rather than reactively. This is increasingly difficult given that much of the change in our postmodern era, as discussed earlier, is variable and unpredictable in specific terms (Bergquist, 1993). Being catalysts for change is also significant—waiting for a crisis to occur to precipitate change is a dangerous strategy because of the damage done to the organization during the delay.

It is important, however, to demystify the change process insofar as this can provide us with some measure of control and resilience. Losing control and the ambiguity are difficult to deal with and threaten effective management of change.

Reframing the process of change can make it more manageable. Yet there is no template, no uniform blueprint, that guarantees successful change. While we can learn about general elements that guide a successful change program it is clear that what works for one organization does not necessarily work for another.

Crisis as a basis for major change is useful because it presents a basis for changing the status quo and creates an immediate sense of urgency as a key motivating force. But we cannot always wait for a crisis to facilitate our organizational change processes.

Traditional wisdom, founded in the work of Lewin (1951) suggests that the effective change process consists of unfreezing present behavior, altering it and then consolidating or freezing the new. This is useful in some senses but suggests a steady state for the altered organization, which does not accord with much of contemporary sentiment concerning change. Rather we find the process is constant, continuous, and requires more than contentment with the status quo for any lengthy period. Newer thinking (McWhinney, 1992), instead, points out that change today does not follow a smooth, determined, consistent path. Furthermore, it is also variable in accord with the differing beliefs about reality that feed into individual understanding of change.

Forces for Change

As discussed in the first chapter, there are a variety of sources for change. Moss Kanter, Stein, and Jick (1992) emphasize environmental shifts (macroevolutionary), organizational growth (microevolutionary), and power and politics (political). More specifically, and foremost among these, are the variables involved in the organization's external environment—social, political, cultural, technological, regulatory, competitive, and the like. Second, are change factors within an organization itself that may range from new leadership, change agents, to power and political behavior. Alongside these, the following factors are suggested as important: more demanding customers; increases in productivity, quality, responsiveness, and product differentiation (customization); greater speed of response;

continuous innovation, and demands for a higher quality of work life (Stace & Dunphy, 1994).

Types of Change

Bergquist (1993) characterizes different eras of change as follows:

- the premodern organization usually changed in terms of simple expansion in size of number of elements;
- the modern organization, affected by difference in the rate and nature of change itself, focuses on structural growth incorporating size extension but also modification of how things are done in the organization; and
- the postmodern organization, buffeted by accelerating and unpredictable change, alongside gradual or nonexistent change, is a hybrid of forms, functions, and change rates and types.

Consequently, we end up with a variety of approaches to change—the major large-scale transformational organizational change or the more micro incremental fine-tuning approach emphasizing improvement. It can be discontinuous or continuous. In terms of the time dimension, change can be reactive or anticipatory. We can demand change in the individual, team, or overall organization; in the structural or cultural dimensions of the organization, or, sometimes, in all three.

Sensitivity to different types of change and tailoring individual strategies to suit is a vital aspect of organization change management. What are some of these change varieties? Moss Kanter, Stein, and Jick (1992) focus on three forms of change:

- changes in the organization's relationship with its environment—identity;
- changes involving the internal array of organizational parts—coordination; and
- changes emphasizing the political dimension—control.

In order to cope, organizations can change their relationships to markets and major stakeholders (creating a new image, restructuring, alliances, etc.); change organizational operations (culture and structure); and change control structures.

A further range of change alternatives is provided below (Want, 1993):

- Operational change necessary for improving or altering operations within the organization and dissent within the business' culture. Here strategies employed include new technology, developing the work climate, improving productivity, and promoting work-unit effectiveness.

- Directional change required where an organization's business strategy is starting to fail in the marketplace or where there are major deficiencies within the organization preventing it from implementing its business strategy. Here, along with planning for change and appropriate restructuring to support strategy, directional change demands the promotion of research and development, enriching the work climate, encouraging feedback, redirecting human resource support, and appraising management control systems.

- Fundamental change is precipitated by business failure due to leadership or mission problems. Here the issue of changing organizational culture, including rethinking the organization's mission itself, is critical.

- Total change arises from problems of alienation and business failure or from a decision to completely turnaround the business.

Nadler and colleagues (1990, 1995) outline the ways in which organizational change may vary along two key dimensions:

1. Incremental and strategic changes

- Incremental changes occur within the current organizational system and processes in order to enhance the effectiveness of the organization. They generally affect only selected parts of the organization.

- Strategic changes affect the whole organization and basically redefine the nature of the organization or alter its basic framework, including its key components of structure, strategy, human resources, processes and, possibly, its core values.

2. Reactive and anticipatory changes

- Reactive changes occur as a result of the need to respond to some external event that is forced upon the organization.

- Anticipatory changes occur because senior management sees competitive advantage in anticipating events to come.

In combining these dimensions, they describe a basic typology of different changes as follows:

- Tuning—change that is incremental and anticipatory, initiated in anticipation of future events, and focused on modifying specific organizational components.
- Adaptation—incremental change that is initiated reactively.
- Reorientation—strategic change that is initiated in anticipation of future events.
- Re-creation—strategic change provoked by immediate demands.

The major distinctions, then, are that we can have first-order change where organizations can learn and adjust. Second-order change occurs where the organization can no longer adjust but must change in a profound and irreversible manner as in an avalanche (Bergquist, 1993). Meyer, Goes, and Brooks (1993) also use the concept of first-order and second-order change but extend this to differentiating between firm and industry levels. At the firm level they suggest: adaptation as first-order change involving incremental change; or metamorphosis as second-order change involving frame-breaking organizational change. At the industry level they outline evolution as incremental change within established industries; or revolution as emergence, transformation, and decline of industries.

From the research covering the life cycles of organizations it is possible to summarize (Nadler & Tushman, 1990; Nadler et al., 1995) key findings concerning strategic organizational change. First, that strategic organizational change, environmentally driven, is a vital part of contemporary organizational life. While not a guarantee of success, organizations failing to make the requisite system-wide changes, generally die. Second, because they are based in crisis conditions, require changes in core values, and suffer from severe time constraints, re-creations are more risky than reorientations. Changing core values leads to heightened resistance to change and escalating political behavior. Third, if more time is available to shape the change, structure coalitions, and empower individuals, reorientations appear to be more frequently successful, although the requisite for visionary executives makes this a risky approach.

Risky or not, what constantly emerges is just how different is contemporary organization change when compared to earlier decades. Particularly significant is the issue of discontinuous organization change, a process that is accelerating and that demands more than the traditional incremental or evolutionary organization development approach.

Consequently, while incremental change will always be a requisite of organizational life, today revolutionary, radical, and large-scale speedy transformation is more common. Here we find the clear inadequacy of a purely structural approach to organizational change that has characterized modern organizational life. Instead, we need postmodern organizational efforts that change that focus on process and attitude (embedded in organization culture and climate) as an alternative or complement at least. The unique challenges of the postmodern era require we better understand and address the more intangible components of change—such as the attitudinal and cultural ones. Second-order, major transformative change simply demands different perspectives for understanding the nature and purpose of organizations (Bergquist, 1993).

Transformation of organizations means challenging everything. It also means having sound leadership; appropriate organizational structure; developing an appropriate vision and direction; communicating that vision; clarifying issues of accountability; changing the behavioral context of the organization; and empowering individuals to think and act, guided by a set of agreed organizational values and principles. Such change is on the grand scale involving, for example (Gouillart & Kelly, 1995):

- reframing—changing the organization's conception of itself and its potential;
- restructuring—changing the organization's structure to ensure competitive performance;
- devitalization—driving growth through linking the organization to its environment; and
- renewal—ensuring effective people management and the spirit of the organization.

This type of transformation, it is argued (Ghoshal & Bartlett, 1996), is best achieved by the following sequential process, necessary to destroy the forces of organizational inertia:

- simplification—building front-line initiative, supported by instilling appropriate discipline and support;
- integration—realigning cross-unit relationships, supported by building stretch (enhancing expectations) and trust; and, finally,
- regeneration—ensuring continuous learning, supported by balancing discipline, support, stretch, and trust.

Moreover, it is important to maintain a dynamic imbalance that prevents the rigidity of success and institutionalization of knowledge, for example, by challenging conventional wisdom. One must also mirror intellectual understanding of what such change requires with emotional commitment to action.

Allied to the alterations in type of change—continuous or discontinuous, incremental or transformative, is the issue of timing, the actual speed of change required. Time frames are different in the 1990s and beyond—the luxury of drawn out years for a change process are rarely available today. Yet the issue is not clear—there are pros and cons to evolutionary and revolutionary change. Not surprisingly, some, like Stace and Dunphy (1994) suggest a situational approach and a flexibility in management behavior as ideal. They emphasize the following four categories of successful change:

- Developmental transitions—constant mid-range change, using collegial, consultative strategies with the leader as coach, team leadership, and emphasising the change of dominant values and mind-sets.
- Task-focused transitions—a relentless mid-range change process directed by executive leadership as a captain, but with a more consultative style at the business unit level and an emphasis on improving structures and systems.
- Charismatic transformations—revolutionary change engendered and led by a charismatic executive, a charismatic leader, who is able to engender staff support, emphasizing a new corporate vision, image, and strategy.
- Turnarounds—radical change focused on reshaping strategy and structure, led by a strong leader, a directive commander, and a strong senior team with centralized decision making.

Others (Reger, Mullane, Gustafson, & DeMarie, 1994) argue that while there is a place and time for incremental and revolutionary approaches to organizational change, what is most effective for the majority of contemporary organizations is a more moderate, proactive, mid-range process that they call "tectonic." The context for such change is a turbulent external environment and an internal objective of ensuring significant change but one that builds on existing elements of organizational identity rather than completely replacing it. Within such a perspective, incremental change, focused on minor adjustments can work in stable environments but this is not the current norm nor does it overcome internal organizational inertia. The revolutionary approach often fails because of internal conflict and the assumption that one can start from scratch as reengineering and total quality management often demand. So change must be sufficiently large to overcome inertia without being large enough to create catastrophic conflict, destructive of positive organizational attributes.

The following nine distinguishable conditions point to the feasibility of rapid change (Eccles, 1994):

- organizational crisis
- irresistible external pressure
- action by a major stakeholder leading to an unintended effect that may jeopardize the organization's future
- the buy-out or spin-off from an organization
- setting up a novel kind of operation in the organization or entering a new market
- the introduction of a new CEO, or a visionary, power-holding, new top management team
- power concentrated in the hands of a decisive individual or small coterie in an entrepreneurial organization
- appropriate changes in an organization's structure and in its reward motivators
- people rearranging their perspectives and their behavior because of a persuasive new vision.

However, these approaches really reside in considerations of the difference between change in predictable and unpredictable environments. Stacey (1993) makes this point in terms of exploring change in equilibrium and nonequilibrium dynamics:

- closed change (the system in equilibrium)—in which one can perfectly predict the future behavior of a system within clear-cut linear connections between a cause and an effect;
- contained change (the system close to equilibrium)—in which we can forecast the system's behavior by using the laws of probability; and
- open-ended change (the system far from equilibrium)—in which we cannot forecast the long term at all as it is impossible to predict in a situation where the connections between cause and effect are lost.

Given what has been said earlier in this chapter, it is the threat of these that confronts and troubles most contemporary organizations and managers.

Resistance to Change

Humans generally possess tendencies both toward change and risk-taking and against them. Both external and internal organizational stakeholders who wish to maintain the status quo for varying reasons resist change requirements. They are also troublesome because the emotional side of change is often disregarded—issues such as the potential for and threat of loss (of jobs, status, colleagues, etc.), frustration, and dealing with uncertainty and ambiguity (Marks & Shaw, 1995).

Frequently change programs fail (Fry & Srivastva, 1992, p. 3) "because they are too disruptive, threatening, or confusing to those who actually need to change." Not surprisingly, in a chaotic environment we tend toward the familiar. We eschew change as increasing our vulnerability and making us lose control. Resistance itself can be conceptualized in terms of a natural behavioral response to perceived threat; as politically motivated in power plays; as a constructive counterfoil to problematic organization change; and as manifesting the real problems of restructuring culture, mind-sets, and the like within the change process (King & Anderson, 1995). These different motivations are important considerations.

It is important to analyze resistance in terms of its intensity, source, and focus and to understand which of the many varieties of resistance one is confronting. For example, we may group these in terms of (Leigh, 1988):

- cultural—when inbuilt organizational values and traditions are affected;
- social—when established relationships are threatened;
- organizational—when status quo formal arrangements, or individuals' established power and influence are endangered; and
- psychological—when selective perception regards change as wholly detrimental and reinforces conservatism and conformity.

Strebel (1994) complements this approach, delineating resistance in terms of the following, moving from the easier to the more difficult sources of resistance to alter:

- rigid structures and systems reflecting organizations, business technology, and stakeholder resources that are not consistent with the forces of change;
- forces of closed mind-sets reflecting business beliefs and strategies that are oblivious to the change;
- entrenched cultures reflecting values, behaviors, and skills that are not adapted to the forces of change; and
- counterproductive change momentum driven by historical or other change drivers that are not relevant to the most urgent forces of change.

Others (Moss Kanter, Stein, & Jick, 1992) emphasize that tensions in many organizational change programs occur because of the differences among change strategists, change implementors, and change recipients—differences relating to roles, levels, and particular orientations toward change per se. Moreover, they link some difficulties with not understanding the change process in terms of an organization's life cycle. In addition, with ongoing change, not surprisingly, there is often escalating cynicism about organizational change (Reichers, Wanous, & Austin, 1997).

It is unlikely that only one source of resistance will be met by those planning and implementing change, but it is the case that some forms of resistance are easier to deal with than others. Changing mind-sets and behavior are clearly more difficult than altering structures and systems—perhaps this is the reason that restructuring per se seems to be the most popular form of organizational change.

There are a variety of combinations of strong/weak forces of resistance, and change and the tension between the old and the new are the basis for the type of change that occurs. As Strebel (1994) argues, radical corporate reorganizations result from breakpoints in rigid organizational systems. But radical or not, it is those change processes that allow the organization to adapt to its environment that prove most viable. He offers a useful outline of a change path diagnostic that assesses the relative strength of the forces of change and resistance, essentially distinguishing between reactive change where the organization is already affected by forces for change; and proactive change where the organization is healthy and its performance is not yet affected by the forces for change. One can choose from eight different change paths:

1.   Reactive Change Paths:

- resistance where the change force can be rolled back and represents threat—there is no internal change;
- renewal where the change force can be rolled back but offers an opportunity—change is limited to parts of the organization;
- revitalization where the change force can't be rolled back but time is available—there is ongoing change throughout the organization; and
- restructuring where the change force can't be rolled back but there is little time available—intense change occurs on a few dimensions.

2.   Creating Proactive Change:

- corporate realignment where the change force is easily identified but the organization is closed to change—organizational contrast with another approach;
- cascading implementation where the change force is easily identified and the organization is open to change—progressive adaptation to the change forces;
- focused reengineering where the change force is difficult to identify and the organization is closed to change—benchmarking, explicit focused comparisons; and
- bottom-up experimenting where the change force is difficult to identify but the organization is open to change—learning by example from successful internal change.

Proactive change is often the most difficult to engender when things are going well for the organization. Then it is hard to move from an intellectual understanding that something more is required than the status quo to stay ahead of the competition, to actual action in that direction. Whatever the precise change strategy, however, continuous attention to and activity in dealing with change forces is vital to the ongoing success of organizations as recent history at IBM clearly demonstrates.

Reger, Mullane, Gustafson, and DeMarie (1994), mentioned earlier, argue that, "Overcoming resistance can be accomplished by linking change initiatives to valued elements of organizational identity." However, one should also acknowledge that resistance can be functional, that it has a more positive aspect through its capacity to challenge assumptions, plans, rationales, and protect what may very well turn out to be vital dimensions of the status quo in the process of change management. One should consider what useful purpose organizational resistance is actually serving. If, instead, one wishes to deal with resistance, it is important to identify and analyze it; clarify the change's real or perceived negative consequences and then seek to weaken the apparent link between the two; and reduce resistance by a range of measures that might include adequate communication in order to avoid surprises, ensure top management support, and appropriate participation (Leigh, 1988).

Four steps that can help move change processes from resistance to motivating change are recommended by Morris and Raben (1995, p. 64):

- surface dissatisfaction with the present state;
- promote participation in change;
- give rewards for behavior in support of change; and
- provide time and opportunity to disengage from the present state.

They also offer the following as critical ways of managing transition:

- develop and communicate a clear image of the future;
- use multiple and consistent leverage points;
- develop organizational arrangements for the transition; and
- build in feedback mechanisms.

The following approaches are also suggested—restoring individual faith and confidence; constructing effective and supportive work teams; ensuring effective organizational dialogue; and building a culture of innovation and learning (Marks & Shaw, 1995). These are, though, goals to which most organizations should be working, not only those confronting major change.

Leading Change

One of the potent factors in change management is that of leadership. As Mink, Esterhuysen, Mink, and Owen (1993, p. 24) argue:

> ...strong leadership is a critical ingredient in transformation. Leadership is needed to gain widespread commitment to a shared purpose, to communicate about and persuade others of the need for change, to motivate and align people to work toward a shared purpose, and to build systems that support change; without these ingredients, no change effort can succeed.

The mutating face of leadership is well described by Bergquist's (1993) analogy with nature: the premodern leader living in a world of potential (the cocoon); the modern leader in a world of daily work (the silkworm); and the postmodern leader in a turbulent environment (the butterfly). There is also a choice of approaches that range from the military models, reflected in the current revival of interest in the ancient strategist Sun Tzu and the lessons learnt from Desert Storm, through to the more humanistic approaches advocated by Kouzes and Posner (1990) and Covey (1992).

Today there is growing agreement on some of the critical competencies required of effective leaders: vision, managing complexity, industry and business insight, a general management perspective, drive for success, personal integrity, flexibility, self-awareness, active learning, influencing without authority, developing talent, and teamwork (Ketterer & Chayes, 1995). We recognize the mythical status of the omnipotent leader, yielding instead to a view that leaders don't have all the answers but, rather, must ask the right questions (Heifetz & Laurie, 1997).

Yet more is required of change leadership in contemporary and future times. For leadership in change management is no simple matter—no magic prescriptions or road maps are available. As

Pettigrew and Whipp (1993, p. 145) emphasize, we need leadership of change that is appropriate to its contexts and which does not necessarily focus on a single leader at a single level. They propose that:

> Leading change in order to compete is not understood by reference to universal principles carried out by an exceptional individual. More effective in leading change appears to be: the use of varying leadership approaches over time; a combination of practices to address shifting competitive circumstances; the recognition that leader and context will affect each other reciprocally; and the use of operational leaders at all levels in the firm.

Change leadership, therefore, requires multiple skills:

- understanding how people and organizations learn and adapt to change;
- perceiving people as strategic assets for competitive advantage, emphasizing the need for nurturing and development;
- focusing on the future, closing the gap between what is and what could be;
- aligning organizational realities with the external environment;
- setting high performance standards and making all accountable for their achievement;
- emphasising individual, team, and organizational learning;
- believing in the value of distributed leadership; and
- fostering a culture where all can assume ownership of the change process (Ketterer & Chayes, 1995).

So we need much more than a simplistic approach to the question of change leadership, more than a reliance on a heroic visionary CEO leading the charge in the 1990s and beyond.

The point that is being argued is that incremental change is generally managed within an organization's current structures and process and consequently a variety of leadership styles may suffice, in accord with the normal management and leadership of the organization. Strategic change, however, requires the fundamental change of the existing management processes and structures themselves and means leadership becomes even more critical. The leadership role, in this situation, moves from building clarity and support for the status quo into one that builds tolerance for ambiguity and confidence in the advantages of change. It moves beyond mere improvement to questioning the validity of historical performance and the very structure of the organization (Elise Walton, 1995).

But what type of leadership? Nadler and Tushman (1990, p. 87) summarize the issue well:

> It appears that effective organizational re-orientation requires both charismatic and instrumental leadership. Charismatic leadership is needed to generate energy, create commitment, and direct individuals towards new objectives, values or aspirations. Instrumental leadership is required to ensure that people really do act in a manner consistent with their new goals. Either one alone is insufficient for the achievement of change.

For Nadler (1995) charismatic leadership may then be seen as sufficient but not necessary for major change. This type of leader is strong in the following characteristics:

- envisioning—setting out a persuasive vision; setting high expectations; providing consistent models of behavior;
- energizing—showing personal excitement and energy; displaying personal confidence; celebrating progress through finding and using organizational success; and
- enabling—empathizing; voicing personal support; communicating confidence in people.

Furthermore, it is argued that such leadership needs complementing by an instrumental leadership that manages environments in order to ensure the right conditions prevail for motivating desired behavior. The key functions of this instrumental leadership are as follows:

- structuring—creating the appropriate structures and building the teams and human resources planning that will allow for the requisite behavior the change necessitates;
- controlling—devising systems and processes for measuring, monitoring and assessing behavior and results, and administering corrective action; and
- rewarding—administering rewards and punishments according to the type of behavior that is appropriate to the requirements of the change.

While such leadership styles may reside in one individual, this is not very often the case. In addition, major organizational change, especially of the reorientation type, actually requires more than the individual leader. It requires leadership being institutionalized at the senior management level and beyond, developed throughout the organization as a whole. What our environment demands, in terms of complex change management approaches that are not once off but ongoing, cascading, overlapping series of changes, are a diverse range of flexibly minded leaders managing flux in an organic way (Moss Kanter, Stein, & Jick, 1992).

Others emphasize the need for adopting the servant-leader approach in contemporary organizations, one that was originally postulated by Robert Greenleaf in the 1950s. Spears (1995) outlines the characteristics of such leadership for the turbulent 1990s in terms of: listening, empathy, healing, awareness, persuasion, conceptualization, foresight, stewardship, commitment to the growth of people, and building.

Culture and Change

Culture is a critical determinant of how well an organization is able to deal with change. It is through culture, largely in terms of attitudes, values, beliefs, and patterns of behavior, that we can transform an organization to better deal with its environment. Given that the question of organizational culture—its guiding beliefs, assumptions, and behaviors about organizational practices—is critical to successful change, we need to consider the issue of organizational culture and subcultures when faced with the management of change.

Culture itself is both visible and invisible. It is visible in the behaviors and artifacts that reflect what is unseen—the unspoken rules that frame an organization's self-image and, in turn, provide the basis for individual identity and meaning. It is also myriad in the sense that in any organization we find more than one culture.

In order to have better future strategies we must use past knowledge to enhance our understanding of the present. Organizational history, how consistent the change process is with the current culture, the relative strength of the culture in terms of its rigidity or resilience, the leadership philosophy, and the emphasis on individual versus teamwork during the change process, are all critical issues for consideration.

A culture that encourages innovation, risk-taking, and appropriate action is vital to an organization's capacity to deal with the change processes required for it to challenge the status quo and improve continuously. By contrast, a complacent culture, one that feels comfortable and harmonious, and that attempts to avoid conflict at all costs, is also a problem according to Pascale (1990). For him, "Running scared seems to keep a company on the edge of performance (1993, p. 38)." Or, as Eisenhardt, Kahwajy, and Bourgeois (1997, p. 77) put it: "The absence of conflict is not harmony, it's apathy." Therefore, an organization needs contention to keep itself vital and major breakthroughs are unlikely to be achieved without the conflict involved in breakdowns of some sort.

Clearly, then, there is some element of culture change in strategic organizational change. Different strategies have been adopted and yet, as Eccles (1994) points out, what we find is that changing organizational behavior is more effective in changing attitudes than vice-versa. This is largely because it is harder to change the value component underpinning people's deeper attitudes, than altering the behavioral component of culture through incentives. In other words, he argues, rather than the sequence of (a) altering attitudes, culture, behavior, performance and then rewards; we need to (b) alter incentives and accountabilities (rewards and structures), behavior, performance, attitudes, and then culture.

Elise Walton (1995) emphasizes culture change in terms of:

- content of the change—the vision of the new culture (focused on identity and values);
- leverage points for change—what and how to change (focused on the diverse areas of structure, process, and the management of hardware and software); and
- tactical choices—when and where to change (focused time considerations within the broad organizational change and preference for a multi-perspective that is top-down, bottom-up, and lateral).

Communication and Change

Alongside leadership and culture, the pivotal role played by communication in change management cannot be overstated. There is a growing consciousness of the primacy of manipulating information and communication activities for organizational processes. Increasingly now, organizations are conceived, not in solid and structural terms, but more as process and relationships. The emphasis on communication, consequently, makes great sense.

Even in normal times there are usually problems with organizational communication but certainly these escalate during periods of ambiguity and change. The trend today is away from limited need-to-know restricted approaches to communication to much more open, honest, timely, and proactive communication based on a real understanding of the needs of varying stakeholders both within and external to the organization. Some guidelines for such communication include:

- identifying an organization's concerns and priorities and indicating what management wants to do about them;
- focusing on the significance of events—what they actually mean;
- providing a frame of reference within which particular events can be placed and explained;
- foreshadowing subsequent change and providing justification for it;
- matching words with actions;
- a hands-on leadership approach, communicating vision, mission, and goals, what is known and unknown, including the bad news; and
- encouraging hope and optimism in the organization (Marks & Shaw, 1995).

A different approach is argued for by Larkin and Larkin (1994) who stress that successful communication during change management involves:

- communicating directly to supervisors (with employees receiving information from supervisors rather than from the head office);
- using face-to-face communication rather than print; and
- communicating the relative performance of the local work area instead of information about the organization as a whole.

Key questions Stace and Dunphy (1994, p. 130) pose instead are:

- What are the goals of the communication?
- Who is to be involved in the communication process?

- What kinds of issues are to be addressed in the communication process?
- Through what channels will communication messages flow?
- What will be the balance of power and influence between the parties to the communication?

While these exist in the routine daily operations of an organization, the challenge of change focuses attention on such concerns. This is not surprising given that much of the basis for organizational change resides in the very alteration of relationships among organizational members (Bateson, 1979). Given such tensions, and, as mentioned earlier, the tendency toward cynicism about change management, it is crucial that effective communication involving credible, appropriate, and well-timed information (Reichers, Wanous, & Austin, 1997) is at the heart of change management approaches.

In organizations, as Bergquist (1993) reasons, there exists a blend of truth and lies, often focused on fiction people know is untrue but which they are supposed to accept as true. Oftentimes reality, once released, forces some sort of change. Such reality can emerge more effectively if we make better use of the more irreversible informal communication that really provides organizational order, including the much maligned use of rumor and gossip, to get at the truth. We need to better blend the formal with informal communication in order to raise credibility and trust in organizations when communication mainly consists of a blending of truth and lies.

Deconstructionists, as he points out, argue that conversation is the essence of organization and that the broader perspective of information is the product of all organizations. Conversational rules are intertwined with organizational relationships. Consequently, our postmodern leader, recognizing conversation as a form of integration, must be primarily a conversationalist, and one who can manage, be sensitive to, and influence organizational conversations. He or she must understand that relationships and organization communication processes involve the creation and re-creation of diverse organizational meanings and stories that become foundational in devising institutional visions, identifying dominant cultural themes, and generating appropriate solutions to long-standing organizational problems.

Yet this is no easy task. For example, distinctions are made by a growing number of writers (Argyris, 1982; Senge, 1990) among types of conversation—debate characterized in win-lose terms; discussion focused on arriving at consensus; and dialogue, concerning our sense of truth and reality, as a basis for proceeding with other types of communication. Moreover, the current emphasis on formal, written organizational communication, belies the real desire for oral communication, especially storytelling and myth making (Kaye, 1996).

Our postmodern era thus recognizes the pivotal nature of verbal communication and storytelling for the organization. This concurs with understanding the way social construction of reality erodes boundaries between fiction as art and fiction as reality. With organizational life as basically extended conversations, organization reality is conveyed primarily through the conversations—stories, memos, and so on—about the organization. These lie at the heart of the organization's culture and are pivotal in change processes, aided and abetted by the complementary gossip network (Bergquist, 1993).

For others such as Foucault (1980) and Lyotard (1984), the emphasis ought be on the way in which the powerful in the organization construct social reality through the use of language. That is why they often seek to oust the more uncontrollable informal communication where the less powerful can bypass them more readily.

Change, Power, and Politics

The whole issue of power is vital in organizational life overall, an indisputable part. Certainly it is integral to organizational change processes because the change process is at heart a political one. Managing change means understanding, diagnosing, and managing the organizational dimensions of power and politics—bargaining, negotiation, persuasion, and the like. Resistance is, therefore, not a surprising aspect of the process as mentioned earlier in the chapter.

Much has now been written on the issue of organizational power, although the topic itself lay dormant until fairly recently. Today political competence is recognized as part and parcel of management and leadership competence.

Power affects organizational outcomes and organizational politics is about using power. It is central to change processes and management. Power resides in the system, in the control of resources, in organizational processes, and in the management of meaning. Power in all these aspects, and crucial to collective action and exploiting vested interests, needs to be mobilized in order to implement organization change. It is often conceived in terms of the negative and coercive, as self-interest; but it can be used creatively and constructively to benefit a diverse array of people in the organization or, indeed, the organization as an entity itself (Hardy, 1994).

Some (Gergen, 1992) have characterized power in organizational settings along differences in terms of historical eras:

- romanticism often equates power with the personal—with personal capabilities such as drive, determination, intelligence, inspiration, insight, charisma, and so on;
- modernism associates power with structure—with machine functioning, giving those who occupy certain organizational positions in the structure possession of more power than others; and
- postmodernism suggests that we are empowered only through the actions of others as social interdependence.

One's historical perspective of power, then, is important in how one approaches power issues in managing change.

Certainly today, in open-ended change, the role of politics is even more critical than before. Stacey (1991) outlines the way in which there is a pull toward four different directions—equilibrium states—for an organization's political system:

- a high degree of consent through a strong sharing of culture;
- a high willingness to apply power with concentrated power and a clear hierarchy;
- a low degree of consent with no sharing of culture; and
- a low willingness to apply power with widely distributed power and a complex structure.

He argues (p. 361) that what is required now, in the dominating environment of open-ended change, is a particular type of political system, one enabling people to cope with open-ended change, allowing and encouraging questioning, and exposing new perspectives:

Clearly, people are not open to persuasion and new perspectives when they strongly share a wide range of cultural norms and when they share none at all. They are also clearly not open to persuasion when power is so highly concentrated that those at the top do not need to listen, or when it is so widely distributed that there is not much they could do even if they did listen. Cultural difference and differences in power distribution therefore create the conditions in which people influence and are influenced. In other words, power is not continuously applied as authority or force, and continuous power vacuums and impotence are also avoided. It is in the border area between the equilibrium states of authority, force, power vacuum and impotence that we find power in its form of influence and that is what change requires.

Consequently, the political systems necessary in change situations involve managing those that ensure:

- differences in culture, avoiding both the strong sharing of cultural norms over a wide range and a situation where they are hardly shared at all; and
- difference in power distribution, avoiding both widespread distribution of authority over strategic resource allocation as well as a confusion of hierarchical structures.

Morris and Raben (1995, p. 64) offer the following pragmatic steps to help manage the political dynamics of change:

- Assure the support of key power groups.
- Use leader behavior to generate energy in support of change.
- Use symbols and language.
- Build in stability.

While in the past power has often received a bad press, almost reluctantly, perhaps, some such as Eccles (1994, p. 43) are now suggesting that there is sometimes too high a price to pay for egalitarian approaches, especially in time frames for change management. He argues that the need for leadership does not evaporate with empowerment and participation, stressing:

…rapid strategic change can occur in an organization, particularly when its leaders use their power and influence to orchestrate the forces that press upon the firm. They cannot duck or delegate that responsibility if they want to implement strategy effectively. Delegation can only work in a context where top management remains symbolically and practically involved, championing the change process and encouraging those below.

On the other hand, power ought be used for the good of the whole rather than in a negative self-aggrandising manner. Ideally, the leader as politician is about the positive use of power, balancing individual interests with that of the whole and emphasising win-win relationships overall.

Change and Continuity

Of course one of the initial critical questions is whether or not change is actually required, that is, we must avoid change for change's sake and eschew a modernist predisposition to change whatever the need or costs. Moreover, given the need to change, it is vital to emphasize a sense of continuity, preserving the functional bonds that unite organizational members and the best of what has gone before in terms of organizational characteristics and culture. What is emphasized here is the interrelationship among transition, novelty, and continuity, the need to manage the organization in both continuous and discontinuous perspectives. As Fry and Srivastva (1992, pp. 1 & 24) point out:

> ...while the management of novelty and management of transition form two major executive agendas in all of today's social systems, it is a third agenda— the management of continuity—that provides for meaningful and purposeful change and that brings value to new ideas....[It is critical to] preserve the past to ensure the future; conceive the future to enact the present; and transform the present to provide linkages that hold together the past, the present, and the future.

They argue that continuity is the key to organizational health and that we must explore continuity, what holds organizational members together, in order to increase our understanding and our capacity to guide organizational change more effectively. Consequently, it is as important to affirm what has been valuable in the past experiences and identity of organizational life as it is to introduce innovative change. Such practice provides a vital key in getting around the natural tendency to resist organizational change.

Other writers echo this nowadays, such as Eccles (1994), emphasizing the need to cherish an organization's best assets, to maintain and develop them. Preserving and valuing the essential, and still relevant and successful dimensions of an organization's heritage, is crucial—the trick is to know just what this or these are in reality!

Solutions and Strategies

> The message is clear: one-stop change interventions, panaceas, the latest "buzzologies," and change Band-aids, are rarely successful. Change agents need to aim for change interventions which are targeted and focused on critical variables, but which are comprehensive enough in their scope and depth to achieve results. Change agents must build confidence that change, however painful it might be, is an ongoing journey rather than a one-intervention event, and involves changes in strategies, systems and structures as well as behaviours (Stace & Dunphy, 1994, p. 202).

The ability to cope effectively with change throughout the organization is critical. The classic Lewin (1951) model of change, mentioned earlier, is not necessarily always viable in the 1990s environment. What we have, then, in addition, is a range of scenarios or different "recipes," some of which are outlined below as a guide to managing change.

As Pettigrew and Whipp (1993) assert, strategic change rarely moves neatly across a succession of stages from analysis to implementation, essentially because of the potent forces within an organization. These, often relating to the economic, personal, and political imperatives driving the change, tend to produce dilemma and the need for continuous assessments, ongoing diverse adjustments, and repeated choices. In their detailed research across a variety of industries, high performing organizations displayed five factors critical to success: environmental assessment, leading change, linking strategic and operational change, seeing human resources as assets and liabilities and, overarching these, maintaining coherence in the management of change.

They suggest, however, that no simple formulas will do. Stace and Dunphy (1994) echo this sentiment against quick-fix formulas in the previous quotation, arguing that many change formulas apply only to specific situations and that the complexity of real organizational life is often ignored by simple solutions. This is true even for the four dilemmas they highlight in change management, suggesting that one should not consider them purely in either/or ways:

- rational or adaptive strategy development?
- structural or cultural change?
- continuous improvement or radical transformation?
- leadership and command or empowerment?

In one survey of over 100 chief executives and top managers from America's largest organizations (McKenna, 1993, p. 50), the key factors for successful change management were outlined as:

- effective change leadership;
- communicating the purpose and change plan;
- management agreement on the business strategy;
- ensuring understanding and securing commitment for the change; and
- having an appropriate culture supporting the change process (aided by mission statement, training, and education, and appropriate changes in the reward and recognition systems).

Clearly the bottom-line performance is affected by employee stress resulting from organizational change, particularly the uncertainty that generally accompanies such processes. The outward manifestations of such stress include a breakdown of trust and loyalty, absenteeism, unproductive work patterns, and increased turnover. One approach to dealing with such difficulties is provided by Smith Kline Beecham, an American health-care company where successful change management was partly based in the inclusion of training and development strategies in the organization's change management plans. A one-day training program, "Managing Change" was offered, on a voluntary basis, to all employees, grounded in the idea that employees must believe in their ability to make the best of change. As described by McKnight and Thompson (1990), the key goals of the program were fourfold:

- providing a useful basis for discussing the psychological dimensions of managing transition;
- providing employees with the requisite skills for coping effectively with change;
- helping employees understand how they as individuals actually manage change (e.g., basis for resistance, etc.) in order to raise awareness of the emotional aspects of change and allow individuals to better choose their responses to the change; and
- instead of merely informing staff about changes, emphasizing how best to help employees cope gracefully with the changes.

The team utilized two conceptual models to guide their work. First, they focused on three ways that individuals respond to change:

- As victims, facing a situation they believe they cannot handle. Panic, fatalism, pessimism, cynicism about management intentions, and complaint are the most visible signs of this least-effective response. The response is essentially reactive, with victims waiting for change to overtake and crush them.
- As survivors, buoyed by the view that they are at the mercy of a situation they cannot change. Clinging on or becoming competitive for information, positions, or currying favor with senior management are some ways in which the survivors see themselves living through the changes. This response is about sensing what is coming and behaving accordingly.
- As navigators, the most useful and proactive approach to change, facing the trauma of change but being able to pursue a creative vision of a desired future. Such individuals are able to manage stress, essentially by believing in their own capacity to deal competently with the situation.

Second, they stressed that employees need to work through the three zones of transition from the old to the new—the ending, the neutral zone, and a new beginning. A critical belief was that the majority of people have a tremendous capacity for dealing with reality, adapting to it, and coping with it—when presented with what reality is. Rather than reality, it is uncertainty that causes people to struggle.

However, clearly outlining expectations, realistic ones, of change for all involved in the process is vital. Also critical is ensuring accountability that extends throughout the organization, not one that just resides in the top levels.

From case studies of three major American organizations, De Meuse and McDaris (1994) found employees believed that the change process could be improved by ensuring that employees were involved in the change process early on; that they were given a meaningful say in the type of changes that would occur and their timing; that communication about the changes was frequent; and that managers be highly visible, acting as role models for change.

Strebel (1993) suggests that, if corporate change is to proceed, explicit and implicit individual organizational contracts held by its stakeholders must be altered. He emphasizes the "corporate contract" encompassing the shared understanding of changed rules—what the company values, how value is created and distributed among stakeholders. Clearly successful change is founded in adequate value being created to the benefit of all critical stakeholders, value greater than their individual switching costs.

It is, therefore, vital to identify the key stakeholders at an early stage. Some sort of stakeholder analysis identifying the major players, exploring how their particular interests are to be affected, and what that implies for the change management process, is a crucial foundation. For him the successful change process incorporates:

- creating discontent with the current contracts;
- finding a new value creating idea;
- developing a new corporate contract as a basis for commitment to the change process;
- facilitating individual contract revision; and
- ensuring that the change process is supported by the contract mix.

Given the political dimension of organizational change processes, those managing the change need to have the requisite political skills. They need also to be able to use the services of multiple roles—change sponsors, change champions, change agents, change advocates, and change managers.

We even have a Ten Commandments guideline for managing change (Moss Kanter, Stein, & Jick, 1992, p. 383):

1. Analyze the organization and its need for change.
2. Create a shared vision and common direction.
3. Separate from the past.
4. Create a sense of urgency.
5. Support a strong leader role.
6. Line up political sponsorship.
7. Craft an implementation plan.
8. Develop enabling structures.
9. Communicate, involve people, and be honest.
10. Reinforce and institutionalize change.

These guidelines need to be fleshed out in terms of following steps in the change management process: to build coalitions (assemble backers and supporters); articulate a shared vision; define the guidance structure and process; ensure communication, education, and training; undertake policy and systems review; enable local participation and innovation; ensure standards, measures, and feedback mechanisms; and provide appropriate symbols, signals, and rewards.

Stace and Dunphy (1994) emphasize the following key themes of change in their most recent work:

- renaissance in the midst of revolution;
- beyond continuous improvement to "permanent revolution";
- living with the tension of change;
- situational and countercyclical change strategies;
- permanent change as deep change; and
- intelligent learning, not fads.

They outline different approaches to managing change:

- soft approaches incorporating adaptive strategy, cultural change, continuous improvement, and emphasizing empowerment; and
- hard approaches incorporating rational strategy, structural change, radical transformation, and an emphasis on leadership and command.

Their research (p. 197) demonstrates that successful change interventions:

- are linked to, and promote, the vision and emergent strategy of the organization;
- are focused at an appropriate level of intervention (does the whole system need change, or only particular elements of it?); and
- have longer life and greater effect if they have "depth" rather than mere surface appeal and are clustered into groupings to form a blend of related practices or methods—they have an intellectual coherence.

By contrast we have the argument (Eccles, 1994) that there are essentially four categories within which successful change programs require consideration of multiple questions:

1. Purpose and initiative.

   Have we a champion?
   What dedicated group will drive this through?
   What are we trying to achieve?
   Where are we trying to get?
   Why are we doing this?
   Is the logic clear?

2. Concordance and trust.

   Are we together on this?
   Have people bought in to the plan?
   Is there enough trust and shared agreement?
   How much dare we spell out?
   Do we talk and listen to each other fruitfully?
   Do people understand?

3. Leadership, capabilities, and structure.

   Are we ready and willing to lead?
   How much do we help people to act responsibly?
   Is it clear who is to be responsible for what?
   Are we organized sensibly to pursue our goal?

4. Building on action and success.

   Do we reward commitment, success, and meritorious failure?
   How shall we show that it works?
   How shall we gain momentum and enthusiasm?
   How can we best make speedy progress?
   How shall we treat the injured?
   Can we adapt and learn?
   How shall we cope with contingencies?
   How resilient and flexible are we?

Some, such as Mink, Esterhuysen, Mink, and Owen (1993) maintain that, in the majority of cases, failure in change programs occurs because of problems in introduction and management rather than in the plan per se. They propose that the key focus should be on change as a process, not an event; as accomplished by individuals; as a highly personal experience; as involving developmental growth, both in feelings and in skills; and as best understood in operational terms. In addition, individuals, innovations, and the context, in that order, ought be the focus of facilitation.

For Kotter (1995) the major errors in change management are:

- not establishing a great enough sense of urgency;
- not creating a powerful enough guiding coalition;
- lacking a vision;
- undercommunicating the vision by a factor of 10;
- not removing obstacles to the new vision;
- not systematically planning for and creating short-term wins;
- declaring victory too soon; and
- not anchoring changes in the corporation's culture.

Another mistake is forgetting that, for successful change management, there must be some characteristic(s) of the organization that do not change (Goodstein & Burke, 1991). The emphasis here is on the need for some stability amid the chaos of major and complex organizational change. This is mirrored in the following recommendations for change management (Reger, Mullane, Gustafson, & DeMarie, 1994):

1. Conduct an organizational identity audit before undertaking any major change.
2. Tailor the change to fit the organization.
3. Present the change as significant (to overcome organizational inertia) while tying it to valued aspects of organizational identity.
4. Introduce change in a series of mid-range steps.
4a. Use sense-giving opportunities to widen the identity gap.
4b. Use outsiders to make your case.
5. Take the path of least resistance.
6. Know how much change your organization can handle.

Bergquist (1993) also suggests the need to consider stabilization, remarking that it is, of course, far less glamorous than change itself. Yet stabilization helps us learn from the past and provides us with time to consider our assumptions about change. He proposes the formation of temporary systems and sanctuaries in the postmodern organization. In addition, he urges:

- identification and nurturing of different attitudes to organization life and leadership;

- development of a new sense of collaboration and community; and
- finding our intrapersonal internal sanctuary.

Overall, however, the major imperative is that successful organizations must become effective learning entities in an era of uncertainty and increasing complexity. The organization must see change itself as an opportunity to learn and grow.

Chapter III

Managing Organizational Architecture

...organizations are best conceived not as static structures but as complex, ongoing processes (Bergquist, 1993, p. 242).

Handling the changing configurations of flexible structures is the greatest challenge that management faces (Cohen, 1993, p. 222).

As industry structures evolve to constellations of regular dancing-partners, no firm can afford to be completely alone ever again (Harrigan, 1995, p. 20).

THE NEW VERSUS THE OLD

Given the many forces challenging traditional management practices and organizations it is not surprising that the very notion of organization design and structure has come under scrutiny. Not that old forms disappear but rather they coexist with new creations designed to better match changing organizational environments and strategies. Indeed, Ghoshal and Bartlett (1994) emphasize the need to move from the current reliance on a strategy-structure-systems doctrine, emphasizing structure as allocation of resources, responsibilities, and control, to another more flexible approach. This is what they call "the purpose-process-people doctrine" designed to shape behaviors and provide an environment in which people can take initiative, cooperate, and learn. In other words, structure is only one of many tools available to management in a changing environment.

The concept of organization structure and design has been expanded or, indeed, altered to incorporate newer dimensions—the notion of architecture seems more appropriate. Inflexibility and rigidity are too costly to allow survival and the organization to

61

prosper in a global competitive environment. New approaches are required as organizations redefine and reinvent themselves in the 1990s and beyond, seeking new ways of managing and new forms of organization to match them.

Traditional control mechanisms are in decline, replaced by alternate "controls" that are bounded by the dictates of empowerment and self-management. These work not only at the individual level but also at the critical group or team level—with self-directed work teams, and more broadly to that of organizational partnering on the larger scale. Indeed, we can characterize the change from the old to the new style of organization as follows (Galbraith & Lawler, 1993, p. 298):

New	Old
Dynamic, learning	Stable
Information-rich	Information-scarce
Global	Local
Small-and-large	Large
Product/customer-oriented	Functional
Skills-oriented	Job-oriented
Team-oriented	Individual-oriented
Involvement-oriented	Command/control oriented
Lateral/networked	Hierarchical
Customer-oriented	Job requirements-oriented

Such differences require alternatives to traditional ways of managing and organizing. They also demand more than what might be offered by restructuring or reengineering alone. As Keidel (1994) outlines:

- restructuring focuses on organization units in changing boxes and lines and emphasizing efficiency;
- reengineering targets organization processes in changing work systems, stressing efficiency and customer satisfaction; and
- rethinking, concentrating on organization cognition, attempts to change patterns of understanding and is the only approach that can encompass efficiency, customer satisfaction, and employee development.

Of the three, the first is usually used when there is little choice and the organization has to reduce its costs rapidly, the second is a sort of in-between position, and the third is more likely used by organizations able to financially and culturally defer their return on investment. The latter does, however, tend to reap more long-term benefits finally.

In summarizing current trends, it is clear that organization design today is emphasizing hyperflexibility, adaptability, continuous improvement and innovativeness, and a global and stakeholder focus. There is a trend to flatten traditional hierarchies and to ensure permeable boundaries both within the organization and between the organization and its external boundaries. Technology developments, helping to overcome barriers of time and distance, and allowing for the rise of electronic commerce, have enabled many alterations in traditional organization design. Moreover, job design in conjunction with such organization design innovations now focuses on different areas. It explores increasing individual and group empowerment (through self-control and responsibility, cross-training, and continuous learning); and leadership without traditional control (with management moving from planning, directing, evaluation, rewarding, and organizing as traditional activities, to establishing values, facilitating, structuring processes, communicating, and networking) (Lewin & Stephens, 1993).

Nevertheless, while there are ongoing experiments in new forms of work and organization design, it is also clear, as Zuboff (1995) argues, that the real possibilities of transformation are constrained by ongoing traditional assumptions and imaginations centered on industrial-era notions, and the ongoing practice of control and hierarchy. Instead of fundamental change and reinvention, we have often witnessed the reengineering, downsizing, and efficiency drives in what is, essentially, a repackaging of the old rather than a real move to an information economy overall. She argues that we have seriously underestimated the moral, social, and emotional requirements of adapting to an information economy; and calls for a new social contract in which who people are at work, what they can know, and what they can do is radically redefined.

CONSIDERATIONS IN DESIGNING AND BUILDING THE MODERN ORGANIZATION

As indicated previously, management attitudes now are moving beyond the traditional emphasis on controlling, directing, and setting priorities toward encouraging more participation, self-reliance, and distributed leadership across flattened structures. The focus is on ways of empowering individuals and organization groups, the sharing of information, and increasing involvement and accountability throughout the organization structure. Having effective and efficient internal environments and ensuring these are appropriate to position the organization for competitive advantage in the external environment is critical.

Congruence among the various facets of the multiple systems comprising organizations is important, with information technology supporting structure, structure supporting human resources practices, and the like. For the increasingly high involvement organizational model, what is required is for information, power, knowledge, and rewards to be located at the lowest practical organizational level, with congruence arising from having these factors located together. It is characterized by an emphasis on teams and task forces, a flat and leaner structure overall, and a focus less on functions than on products, services, and customers. Actual physical layout supports managerial ideology, attitudes toward jobs per se, and the support provided by information technology (Lawler, 1993).

Collaboration and autonomy at individual, team, and organization-wide levels are rapidly escalating in importance. Such autonomy and collaboration is fundamentally enabled by developments in computing and telecommunications technology, allowing for the wide distribution of information and for work to become independent of location. Organizations are relying on internal and external networking in order to meet the demands of increased flexibility, speed, quality, and efficiency. Structures to match such demands must be very fluid, flexible, and highly responsive to change. They will intensify the emphasis on teams, cooperation, and collaborative designs (Cohen, 1993).

COLLABORATIVE DESIGNS—ORGANIZATIONS WORKING TOGETHER

The traditional approach to organization design has very much focused internally on the single organization itself. But gradually the boundaries have been fading and the concept of design has looked further afield, to incorporate external stakeholders, including relationships with other organizations themselves. This has included efforts after:

- modular organizations that outsource non-vital functions but retain full strategic control;
- virtual organizations that consist of an evolving network of independent but linked organizations working together to achieve common strategic objectives; and
- barrier-free organizations that avoid boundary mind-sets by devising deliberately ill-defined tasks and roles and bridging differences in culture, function, and goals to facilitate cooperative behavior (Dess, Rasheed, McLaughlin, & Priem, 1995).

One difficulty, however, has been that, until recently, organization strategists and scholars have emphasized competition above all else in organizational relationships. Now, however, there is a growing body of thought and evidence that displays a different perspective— one that recognizes organizational cooperation as a critical weapon in the global competitive game.

With such growing recognition and the almost exponential growth of such cooperative relationships, one would imagine a much better comprehension of the organizational cooperative entity than appears to exist. While understanding is growing, there seems a lot of room for its increase and for overall improved management of such relationships.

Following the example of others, such as Badaracco (1991) and Lynch (1993), it is argued that, despite differences in the specific forms of cooperative relationships, the strategic and operational management principles governing them are similar. Therefore, the term "alliance" (alliances being perhaps the most fundamental of all such collaborative relationships) is used to cover the widest possible array of cooperative relationships. The approach is designed to be general, broad, and encompassing, in order to better outline critical aspects of organizational arrangements that move away from our traditional perceptions of distinctive entities with strict boundaries.

Few organizations are self-sufficient or flexible enough today on their own to survive in the competitive global landscape of the late twentieth century. Mergers and acquisitions as a solution to this dilemma distinguished the 1980s. Now, the particular emphasis on internationalization and the need for cooperation to access complementary assets, makes partnership agreements of some sort a natural and logical option.

Consequently, today, the more prevalent topic of interest in theory and practice is that of "partnering" or organizational alliance relationships. Such relationships differ from other organizational forms through being characterized by members retaining substantial independence, a nonhierarchical structure, a collaborative culture, and relative equality in power and authority (Bergquist, Betwee, & Meuel, 1995).

While competitive strategy alone may still be the norm, a growing body of research and literature suggests that best-practice organizational strategy and competitive advantage today is enhanced by cooperative or "collaborative advantage" (Moss Kanter, 1994). Increasing interest is an outgrowth of escalating risk emerging from rapidly changing markets, technologies, competition, product life cycles, the failure of many mergers and acquisitions, and unstable strategic environments generally (Lynch, 1993). Moreover, while alliances are not a new phenomenon as such, the ways knowledge and alliances are interacting and altering the terms of competition, organizational strategies, and management work is new (Badaracco, 1991).

Park (1996) suggests the following more specific economic and organizational impetus for strategic alliances:

- changes in international political economy—intense world-wide competition, increasing protection and political intervention, institutional responses to global competition, and insufficient innovation at the macro level;
- changes in industry-level competitive structure—market maturity and diversity of consumer demand, and a shortened product life cycle;
- changes in modern technological structure—the importance of speed and information, imitation and risks of R&D, and dispersed technological expertise; and
- changes in organizational operation—limitation in large-scale organizations, organizational complexity, and requisite flexibility.

Collaborative partnerships, then, including those with competitors, in some organizational form can represent a better, more mutually advantageous way of doing organizational business than the adversarial relationships or predatory competition characteristic of the past. The current trend, therefore, is to pool optimal resources, use the global marketplace, and add value in unfettered enterprises (Bergquist, Betwee, & Meuel, 1995).

Some claim that few are aware of the full scope and significance of such relationships (Lessem, 1992). Certainly, understanding them is critical to both managers and policymakers alike, as the new types of alliances differ from earlier organizational cooperative ventures. They contrast with previous versions in their increasing international dimensions; rising competitive collaboration; and expanding cooperation across apparently unrelated industries (Yoshino & Rangan, 1995). Additionally, given that they involve innovation, they call upon different approaches to organizational processes and managerial competencies—the basis for both the success and failure of these new structures.

Understanding of such relationships has spanned a variety of disciplines, with a heavy emphasis on economic theory initially. Aside from a few recent industrial sociology and psychological efforts, such organizational relationships have mostly been explained by:

- transaction cost economics—firms choosing alternative arrangements for minimizing the sum of production and transaction costs;
- organization theory, specifically the resource dependence approach mentioned earlier, where organizations are interdependent with other organizations for necessary resources; and
- the competitive strategies of firms, emphasizing the perspective of competitive advantage.

These have been considered inadequate, especially in terms of ignoring process (Ring & Van de Ven, 1994), and so richer explanations are being sought today (Culpan, 1993). Comprehension of organizational relationships must recognize both their complexity and evolution over time, and that there is no one "typical" relationship per se. Yet, while each cooperative relationship is unique in some respect (Hakansson & Snehota, 1995), there are some generalizations and guiding principles that practice and theory can yield to assist us in better management of such ventures.

Unfortunately, the whole definitional area of interorganizational relationships is somewhat confused. We have a multiple range of terms employed from collaboration, cooperation, coordination, coalition, alliance, partnership, and network used most commonly (Huxham, 1996). Here the following general view is adopted:

> The strategic alliance is the most basic, simple, and straightforward form of cooperative venture. All variants of the strategic alliance—joint ventures, equity partnerships, and franchise alliances—are built on the operating foundation of the strategic alliance. What is absolutely essential to understand is that the basic and fundamental principles for operating any consortium are the same, regardless of the form or the nature of the legal agreements (Lynch, 1993, p. 24).

Whatever the specifics, the key, overall, is new forms of organization, ones emphasizing flexible structures and allowing for nontraditional management approaches. Moreover, technological developments, especially in computer and communications technologies, serve both to facilitate and support such innovative approaches.

UNDERSTANDING INTERORGANIZATIONAL COOPERATION

Cooperative relationships can be defined as those special affiliations between at least two organizations, aimed at pooling resources, having joint activities, and aspiring strategically to enhance competitive advantage. As Huxham (1996, pp. 14 & 28) explains: "Collaborative advantage is concerned with the creation of synergy between collaborating organizations....Collaboration is defined as exchanging information, altering activities, sharing resources and enhancing the capacity of another for mutual benefit and to achieve a common purpose." Ideally, there should be respect for organizational autonomy and individuality; mutual sharing of information, risks, and rewards; and an emphasis on some sort of long-term or permanent commitment.

A strategic alliance, by definition then, is a relationship between organizations where cooperation produces more value (or a lower cost) than does market transaction. In order for such value to occur, participants must agree on what it is, need each other to achieve it, and share the benefits. Moreover, such a relationship should be characterized by tight operating links, mutual vested concern about each other's future, strategic orientation toward long rather than short term, senior-level support, reciprocal sharing, and coordinative management styles based on collaboration not hierarchical power (Lewis, 1990, 1995).

Partnering—Variations on a Theme

In simple terms, partnering can be between organizations in the same business; between those that traditionally have had master/ servant or buyer/supplier relationships; or outsourcing, in which external organizations take on responsibility for performing necessary but non-core functions (Pollock, 1994).

Furthermore, organizations select from a menu of alliance types according to variables such as their R&D capability, size, capital structure, and so on. Research (Fombrun & Kumarasway, 1991) suggests that organizations with larger commitments to R&D often focus internally, wanting to compete on their own rather than with external allies. Size is also important, in that larger organizations tend to pursue more of all alliance types, whether contractual or equity-based. Profitable organizations incline toward forming non-equity alliances, while those less profitable tend to form joint ventures.

Urban and Vendemini (1992), propose three significant forms of organizational cooperation:

- Adaptation cooperation is based on the need to ensure a competitive position for each of the firm's activities and covers the management of and changes to activities. It focuses on facilitating access to better quantitative positions (better supply capacity, development of market share); and promoting access to better qualitative positions (control, development, and acquisition of key factors of success). Its aim is to accelerate downstream skills of sales and distribution and upstream skills of technology.
- Functional cooperation is justified by the quest for an essential congruity between the various functions within an activity and at company level. It rationalizes the management of functions,

aiming to reduce costs within functions—intra-activity or intra-organization per se.

- Coordinated cooperation is suggested by the congruity of the combination of activities within a company. It harmonizes the management of the portfolio of activities and is aimed at the viability of the company. Major objectives include the bringing together of complementary advantages (e.g., distribution networks) and coordination of similar advantages.

There are many varieties of the basic strategic alliance. Variety relates to rationale—from government regulation, through risk reduction, to the demands of international competitive forces. Relationships can focus on one or all of the following aspects— distribution or marketing alone; distribution or marketing alongside other functions (manufacturing, R&D, product integration); or technology access only (joint R&D, technology transfer, licensing). Variety also relates to issues of competition. As Yoshino and Rangan (1995) suggest, we can have:

- Procompetitive alliances—these are generally interindustry, vertical value-chain relationships (for example, those between manufacturers and their suppliers or distributors).
- Noncompetitive alliances—generally intra-industry links among noncompeting firms.
- Competitive alliances—similar to noncompetitive alliances in terms of the joint activity but contrasted through partners often being direct competitors in the final product market.
- Precompetitive alliances—characterized by the joining of organizations from different, often unrelated industries to work on well-defined activities such as new technology development.

They also emphasize that such types of alliances are capable of being transformed over time.

As we can see, many approaches to defining alliances exist. Of particular use is Yoshino and Rangan's (1995), defining what is necessary and sufficient for strategic alliances as follows: they must retain independence; share benefits and performance control; and maintain ongoing contributions to one or more strategic areas.

The most common and important interorganizational link in business, Lewis (1990) contends, is that of the vital customer-supplier relationship. He argues that, in the past, traditional arm's length supply chains were sufficient. Today, however, competition has been driving supply chains in the majority of industries toward integration. Individual firms are gradually being forced into becoming part of an environment of cooperation and mutual commitment where, through productive relationships, they can better meet the increasing demands on them—value chains founded on innovative, integrated arrangements. Furthermore, for him, maximum value from suppliers is a prerequisite for delivering maximum value to customers, and a supplier base is often narrowed down simultaneously with efforts to upgrade quality (Hunter, Beaumont, & Sinclair, 1996). In such relationships what is required is fundamentally different ways of working between customers and suppliers, radical change, and having agreements that really reflect the longer term goals of both sides (Ralf, Hughes, & Cox, 1995).

Burton (1995) offers five potential options for building collaborative advantage as matching those five competitive forces elaborated by Porter (1990):

- horizontal—with others at the same stage of production process or producing similar products;
- vertical—with component or service suppliers to the organization;
- selective partnering—with special channels or customers (e.g., lead users) involving collaboration beyond the normal transactional relationships (e.g., Motorola);
- related diversification alliances—with producers of both complements and substitutes; and
- "prospecting" diversification alliances—with organizations involved in previously unrelated sectors and offering cross-industry fertilization not apparent before (e.g., multimedia industry).

Choice relates to understanding one's own distinctive competencies, those of potential partners, and deciding what is best to gain the most sustainable collaborative advantage among the network of possibilities. Burton (1995) emphasizes the need to devise "a composite strategy" between competitive and collaborative policies and capabilities of an organization. While all organizations, whether consciously or unconsciously, have a composite strategy, he argues that what often fails to eventuate is a congruence between them. What is critical is achieving appropriate balance between the two in each aspect of an industry environment; and to integrate them in order to avoid potential clashes.

Alliance Evolution

There is continued interest not only in the emergence of organizational alliances but also in the evolution of these and the specific forms they take (Ebers, 1997). Clearly, interorganizational cooperation is dynamically being molded and restructured through actions and understandings of the parties involved. Initial structures and attitudes evolve through interaction, reconstructing, and embodying new governance structures, expectations, and processes in the relationships. Such cooperative relationships develop and evolve in terms of a repetitive sequencing of the following stages, each assessed from the perspective of efficiency and equity (Spekman, Isabella, MacAvoy, & Forbes, 1996):

- formation—developing and extending throughout the organization the vision and a common set of values and expectations for the alliance;
- metamorphosis—moving from vision to definite organizational alliance architectures through (a) establishing coordination in terms of governance structure and (b) investment in terms of contributing financial, human, physical, and intellectual capital to the relationships; and
- stabilization—focusing on staying the course and adapting the relationship to internal and external environmental pressures.

Moreover, these formal and informal processes produce the institutionalization of the relationship through formal role relationships increasingly being supplemented by personal relationships; substitution of formal legal contracts by increasing psychological contracts; and with the extension of time, formal agreements mirror the information commitments and understandings. Not surprisingly, then, constant renegotiation over time is required as ongoing relationships bring with them changed attitudes and expectations and the very process of interaction itself.

The phase immediately before entering the alliance is critical. As Reardon and Spekman (1994) suggest, numerous questions concerning expectations need clarification:

- Do we know the key resource gaps facing the venture?
- Have objectives been realistically linked to resources?
- Have major strategic issues and challenges been identified?
- Have key business risks been uncovered?
- Have we performed an analysis of partner strengths and weaknesses?
- Do they understand our expectations and we theirs?
- Have we protected ourselves as much as possible from breakdowns in communication between us, now and in the future, with regard to shifts in expectations?

Networks of Alliances

Instead of viewing organizational relationships in isolation, Hakansson and Snehota (1995) urge that they be regarded as part of a broader context, namely that of a network of interdependent relationships where each relationship is embedded in or connected to other relationships. Single business relationships are, therefore, generally part of a larger whole in which relationships in one situation can affect other relationships in terms of interdependence. Indeed, it may be argued that network structure can affect performance and constrain or enhance the capacity of specific firms to shape industry development (Madhavan, 1996).

Networks of alliances do provide an alternative structure to that of markets or hierarchies in terms of governance (Powell, 1990). They offer a solution to managing in uncertain environments through interdependence and cooperative practices; provide strategic flexibility; facilitate organizational learning; and have become a central issue in developing organizational innovation. Given the difficulty of building a trusting, durable relationship with one organization, multiple relationships, however, while offering more ways of creating value than individual chains, simultaneously multiply chances for conflict and confusion (Lewis, 1995).

What is developing is a seamless, global, digital network of networks—a most ubiquitous innovation. In addition, at the macro level what is emerging, particularly in high-technology industries, is that the core of competition goes beyond a few interorganizational links to that between actual constellations of organizations. Revealed is a corporate community consisting of an elaborate network of organizational linkages. In competition, now constellations of organizations are pitted against one another (Fombrun & Kumarasway, 1991).

Consequently, it is becoming clear that, with the proliferation of alliances, organizations able to effectively manage networks of alliances will do best in global competition. Managerial competencies, therefore, need enlargement in terms of managing differently not only internal and external networks, but also networks of networks. The change from managing one or even a few strategic alliances to managing major networks of alliances, including those with an international emphasis, is enormous. It may, indeed, be what our age of entrepreneurial globalization comes to regard as the next frontier of management challenge (Yoshino & Rangan, 1995).

Rationale for Alliances

Given that organizations generally wish to retain their autonomy, there must be very good reasons for entering into interorganizational relationships. For, in being part of such relationships, they lose part of their freedom to act independently, to control domain and affairs, and must expend scarce resources and energy in developing and maintaining such relationships in the face of potential returns often remaining unclear or intangible (Van de Ven & Walker, 1984). Such relationships, then, must really make a difference and not be regarded as stopgap strategic measures. Rather, they need consideration from a new perspective, as "part of the 'extended' corporation, neither internal nor external, but intimately connected" (Lynch, 1993, p. 18).

So, a critical issue is to understand why organizations enter into strategic alliances. Certainly, markets affect the structure of industries and organizations (Wells & Cooke, 1991). There are, however, numerous driving forces. Chief among these reflected in the literature are:

- cartelization of industry to reduce competition or some related purpose;
- size and structure—economies of scale (the larger and more diversified an organization, the more likely it is to be involved in multifaceted relationships);

- sharing and reducing risks;
- access to capital;
- access to labor and expertise;
- bringing together complementary resources;
- generating synergy through combining capabilities or operations;
- products (special characteristics required by other organizations);
- entering new markets (especially international);
- overcoming barriers to markets;
- increasing competitive positioning;
- monitoring and neutralizing competitors;
- access to technology and/or technology interrelatedness;
- dispersing new technologies;
- overall cost reduction;
- the cost of R&D;
- improving customer-supplier links;
- outsourcing;
- dealing with government regulation;
- speed—in product development, distribution, and competitive positioning;
- acquiring new organizational knowledge and guiding its migration;
- increasing innovation;
- faster learning;
- prestige/image (enhanced reputation);
- increasing efficiency;
- building flexibility of responses to environmental change; and
- a culture and leadership oriented toward multiple organizational relationships.[1]

More broadly speaking, alliance formation can be opportunity (proactive) or problem (reactive) driven with alliance strategies based on internal or external drivers (Lynch, 1993). Of course, if the initial driving forces of any partner in the alliance diminish then the alliance needs restructuring or renegotiating.

Today, one of the critical issues in alliance motivation is that of knowledge management (discussed in more detail in chapter V). Indeed, as Badaracco (1991) argues, it is knowledge itself, especially its globalization, that is changing the boundaries of organizations, reshaping them and changing our familiar notions of organizations and organizing. Alliances as knowledge links—whether single focused and tactical or multifocused and strategic—thus serve to enhance organizational learning and the joint creation of new knowledge and capabilities. Such knowledge alliances are characterized as follows:

- a central objective is learning and creating knowledge;
- there is more intimacy (through personnel working closely together) than product links;
- they can be formed with a very wide range of partners; and
- they have greater strategic potential than product links in extending or renewing core capabilities or creating new ones.

Others suggest a far less considered approach to relationships. For example, Yoshino and Rangan (1995, p. 71) have found that, "Firms usually enter into alliances in ad hoc fashion, driven by immediate, tactical reasons." Some of the organizations they studied went into alliances basically to remedy current operational problems and had often not considered the strategic issues and risk/benefit implications over the long term. For such organizations this often meant disastrous results.

FINDING THE RIGHT PARTNER

Finding the appropriate partner involves commitment, hard work, and discovery. Or, as Harrigan (1995, p. 14) puts it: "Everybody wants to dance with Prince Charming, but you may have to kiss many frogs before you find him."

The potential for failure is ever present in interorganizational relationships. Indeed some statistics suggest that approximately half of all strategic alliances fail (Sankar, Boulton, Davidson, Snyder, & Ussery, 1995). However, the potential for failure can be decreased by clearly understanding the assets and competencies of partners involved, adequately estimating risks and benefits, grappling with issues such as culture and compatibility, and having well-designed cooperative procedures.

Moreover, falling in love with the ideal and potential of the relationship at the expense of coming to terms with its reality—warts and all, must not blind one. It is critical to deal with the issue of compatibility—one must establish that there is the right chemistry between partners in all its myriad forms. Superficial attractions, like best price, are not the basis for long-term partnering success and such relationships call for special organizational norms and desirable traits not present in all organizations. Productive relationships must be built on combining unique strengths in order to achieve joint missions, on strong and firm business relationships capable of enduring over the longer term and judged against specified deliverables (Harari, 1994; Ralf, Hughes, & Cox, 1995).

So choice is not just about the soundness of a business deal. Choice must be grounded in a compatibility that includes a variety of nonbusiness attributes—management styles, personalities of senior personnel, ethics, security, and the like are critical (Herring, 1994). Culture is also a crucial variable. In customer-supplier alliances, particularly, both parties need the same attributes—the capacity for trusting relationships, an emphasis on continuous improvement, expertise in cross-functional teams, commitment to achieving long-term alignment, and encouraging partners' undertakings (Lewis, 1995).

Furthermore, Herring (1994) suggests the important role of corporate intelligence activities for assessing the real compatibility of a potential partner. This should include some sort of personality assessment, especially of senior personnel, and surveillance of a potential partner's activities in order to ensure the organization is not exploited in the partnership, especially with regard to intellectual property and core competencies.

Strategic alliances should be used when one can answer in the affirmative the four Cs test proposed by Brouthers, Brouthers, and Wilkinson (1995, p. 18):

- complementary skills are offered by the partners;
- cooperative cultures exist between the firms;
- the firms have compatible goals; and
- commensurate levels of risk are involved.

For situations where competitors are considered for partnerships a variety of tests are involved. For example, can those working together be separated from those who must compete with each other in the marketplace; and do the benefits outweigh the risks (Lewis, 1995)?

Miles and Preece (1995) consider the current emphasis on choosing like-minded partners and how, while this might assist the broad ongoing alliance management process, the partners may miss out on the potential benefits of having traditional ideas constructively challenged. Options are to chose to sometimes form alliances with organizations not as similar as prescriptions advise; to seek partnership with an organization whose internal strengths are different; or search for new relationships when the old ones are becoming stale.

MANAGING STRATEGIC ALLIANCES

Clearly, the new organizational forms of cooperation demand innovative mind-sets and management competencies. With changed structural arrangements, as part of the extended organization and operating under a different set of rules and frameworks, alliances cannot be managed, commanded, or controlled in the traditional way. Culpan (1993) goes so far as to state that interorganizational cooperation necessitates changing organizational philosophy, culture, the planning process, structure, and management techniques.

In particular, attention must be paid to managing interdependency, unique information flows, diverse cultures, personalities, learning, knowledge, and styles of operation and organizing (Badaracco, 1991; Lynch, 1993; Yoshino & Rangan, 1995). Traditional organizational dominance must give way to notions and practices of mutual dependency for success.

Hakansson and Snehota (1995) focus alliance management across:

- activity links—those technical, administrative, commercial, and other organizational activities capable of being connected in different ways to those of another organization as a relationship develops;
- resource ties connecting the different resource elements (technological, material knowledge resources, and other intangibles) of the organizations involved; and
- actor bonds connecting actors and influencing how they perceive each other and form identities with respect to one another.

They argue that management competencies must focus not only on the particular alliance dimension—dyad or otherwise—but also how this affects the individual organizations and third parties involved.

Another useful starting point for alliance management is provided by Cowan (as cited in Crowley & Karim, 1995) who recommends that in partnership relations critical implementation steps include: (1) establishing top executive-level relationships between parent organizations of partners; (2) identifying problems that may occur; and (3) building project teams that respond quickly to critical issues.

Effective Partnerships

While there is no one best unique model for organizational partnering, there are a growing number of successful long-term relationships where organizations have worked together for mutual benefits. At the heart of a successful relationship is real collaboration for mutual advantage—a win-win approach. Successful alliances are not just a matter of good luck but rather about the effective integration of corporate strategy, human chemistry, and operational management (Lynch, 1993). The nature of the commitment made by the partners involved in a relationship, it may be argued (Bergquist, Betwee, & Meuel, 1995), is the central ingredient for success. Such commitment is grounded in a covenant more than a contract, involving an organizational structure instilled with trust in competency, intentions, and shared perspectives and values. For, "Alliances, like marriages, do not work just because promises are made" (Lewis, 1995, p. 36).

Rai, Borah, and Ramaprasad (1996) outline the following critical alliance elements:

- partner congruity—whether or not partners are in complete agreement about alliance purpose and process of goal achievement;
- partner evaluation—scrutinizing partners in terms of capabilities, values, commitment, and resources;
- organizational advocacy—ensuring explicit top management support and alliance champions in organizations involved;
- government policies—having supportive government environments to facilitate cooperative arrangements;

- organizational issues—having shared mind-sets concerning business assumptions, operating procedures, and criticality of events;
- cultural concerns—organization culture must be understood as affecting individual and organizational assumptions;
- human resources management practices—acknowledging the criticality of appropriate staffing and selection of key alliance personnel; maintaining their continuity; and having appropriate performance appraisal, reward, and compensation systems in place; and
- partner dominance—complete dominance by one partner over another or others is always problematic.

Some specific success factors for managing alliances, compiled from theory and experience, include the following.[2]

1. Alliance mind-sets:

- approaches that add value to both organization's activities;
- a mutually beneficial relationship with commitment on both sides to some credible, significant nonrecoverable investments;
- commitment to an ongoing relationship, including proper alliance development;
- clearly defined and unambiguously formulated aims;
- a clear, shared sense of direction;
- expectations discussed at the outset;
- shared objectives and understandings about tasks to be done;
- commitment of all parties at all levels to the shared vision and goals;
- long-term views;
- explicit motives;
- joint interest;
- interdependency;
- open collaboration;
- flexible problem-solving approach;
- managerial competence to optimize along the dimensions of cooperation and conflict;
- mechanisms by which learning from each partner can occur;
- capacity to maintain strategic flexibility;
- protection of core competencies;
- budgeting the time necessary for making the alliance work;

- importance to the bottom line; and
- exit options considered.

2. Structure and cooperation mechanisms:

- methodical organization of cooperation arrangements (including coordination);
- effective coordination processes;
- alliance management assigned to a specific individual or group;
- weekly monitoring process initially;
- determining early on what the mechanisms for the following activities will be—developing strategy, making key organizational decisions, and assigning financial accountability;
- continuing alignment between organizations;
- continuous (real-time) measurements and evaluation of the relationship and projects (milestones and goals);
- mutually constructive decisions;
- egalitarian and information-dependent systems.

3. People issues:

- effective relationships between people;
- equity in developing the relationship and projects with all stakeholders' interests considered;
- strong team processes;
- substantial delegation and empowerment;
- clear conflict resolution and decision mechanisms;
- open and honest communication at all levels, grounded in mutual respect;
- communicating the strategic vision from the beginning;
- trust in terms of sharing information without fear or hidden agendas;
- a functional issue resolution system that resolves issues rapidly, starting at the lowest levels, and in a fair manner without fault finding or exploitation;
- a reward structure reflecting partnership rather than individual success;
- understanding and support from all organizational levels, including the vital visible support from executive levels;

- building relationships at every value interface;
- personnel continuity; and
- demonstrated leadership at all organizational levels in order to provide the requisite strategic, tactical, operational, interpersonal, and cultural integration.

4. Culture concerns:

- understanding the importance of cultural factors;
- methods for bridging cultural gaps;
- a culture that encourages rapid and effective problem resolution, grounded in long-term personal relationships;
- a supportive and mutually caring organizational culture to allay the inevitable anxiety of boundary-defying partnerships;
- real openness toward outsiders;
- an undertaking to ongoing extension and development by all participants;
- a commitment to learning, to using critical thinking and clear personal and organizational aspirations, values, and associated competencies.

Structural Arrangements

Common sense dictates that structure is important in providing the backdrop for ongoing interaction between alliance partners, and partners' strategic and operational objectives, whether overt or covert. Furthermore, it plays a central role in keeping strategic and operational flexibility and offering a productive environment in which to nourish interorganizational relationships. Indeed, Parkhe's (1995) research supports the link between alliance performance and structure and that such linkage varies according to partner type, partner nationality, organization culture, strategic direction, and management practices.

Discussing strategic technology partnering, Hagedoorn (1993) emphasizes that different interorganizational structures and modes of governance for partnering relationships affect how technology is shared, the organizational context, and the potential economic outcomes for participating organizations. For him there are two distinct structuring approaches:

- contractual arrangements that incorporate technology exchange agreements, customer-supplier relationships, joint R&D agreements, one-directional technology flow approaches; and
- cooperation with strong modes of interorganizational governance that incorporate forms such as joint ventures, research corporations, and minority investment.

The first he characterizes as generally more oriented toward cost-economizing and the second much more strategically motivated.

Others define structure types in terms of the following:

- a team structure with members reporting to separate functions and cooperating as needed to meet their organization's commitments to the client; or
- a program structure where members, working in separate organizations, report to the same executive, are controlled in so far as supporting the interface required, and are given sufficient authority to coordinate all relevant activities within their organization to meet its commitments to the customer (Lewis, 1995).

For Bergquist, Betwee, and Meuel (1995) the structures of partnerships follow one of the following three:

- partnership of agreement motivated primarily by legal compliance and usually intended to maintain traditional ways of operating a business (e.g., professional partnerships by lawyers);
- partnerships of function consisting of two or more organizations working together for a variety of pragmatic reasons and characterized by complementarity, compensatory relationships less than legal compliance (cross-licensing agreements, strategic alliances, and joint-power agreements popular in the public sector); and
- partnerships of commitment centered on collaboration and joint development (e.g., the virtual organization).

Partnerships of function tend to typify the early stages of relationships while those of commitment emerge later and tend to generate other partnerships.

Whatever the particular model followed, there are a range of structural issues that need consideration. For example:

- Whether or not to locate a partner organization's personnel in the partner's facilities: such location can aid understanding and decrease the response time for the joint resolution of problems (Lewis, 1995).
- Should there be joint boards with membership from partner organizations?

In customer-supplier alliances we recognize the first step in building a powerful network that reaches far up the value chain to deliver the best possible value to the final customers. In such relationships what is required is integration of separate organizational processes into seamless operations that emphasize combined goals and continuous improvement over the long term. Cooperation in design and development, for better timing and costs is desirable. Now, while such relationships should be close, these alliance structures should also allow for suppliers' independence through limiting volume, facilitating learning, respecting suppliers' cost structures, and accepting separate decision making. This independence provides customers with the strongest and most committed suppliers. Both, however, should share appropriate risks and understand that, while in the short term exclusivity may be beneficial, non-exclusivity is better in the longer term (Lewis, 1995).

For relationships with competitors a variety of approaches can be adopted. For example (Carlin et al., 1994):

- divide and conquer—transactions by departments or divisions are separated; or
- centralize intelligence—centralize management of the relationships with (a) those involved in the relationship informing others of what is happening; and (b) creating a high level task force or committee collecting information about the relationship and informing collaborative decisions.

Legal Arrangements

There are multiple ways of establishing and consolidating interfirm cooperation agreements, including the heads of agreement, a letter of intent, the outline agreement, and formalities involving contracts and other documents. Clearly contracts can help alliances get started by providing a certain level of assurance and through clarifying roles, responsibilities, and consequences in terms of conflict management. Understandably, organizations entering into cooperative alliances need to choose a suitable legal basis on which to secure the best out of their agreements and provide appropriate guarantees across a wide range of areas for the individual organizations concerned. Legal contracts paint the broad brush picture of the collaboration but it is up to management to put in the fine details in practice.

So contracts themselves are inadequate and an overreliance on legal arrangements, of whatever type of base, is anathema to any serious strategic partnership. Given that alliance partners' activities are joined across an interface and that the broad range of tasks and issues involved cannot be well embraced in contracts alone, alternatives are required (Lewis, 1995).

One alternative is the covenant, rather than contracts, based relationship, grounded in information sharing, goal clarification, and commitment to constructive problem solving. Better than just relying on legal arrangements, such ingredients reinforce and build mutual trust in terms of intentions, competence, and perspective (Bergquist, Betwee, & Meuel, 1995).

Interpersonal Relationships

Consequently, the quality of interpersonal relationships is, not surprisingly, critical to interorganizational relationships. Alliances are essentially between people and personal relationships shape and modify their evolving structures (Ring & Van de Ven, 1994). Therefore, in alliances close and regular personal contact is required, covering all levels of an organization, both policy and operating ones. Such interpersonal relationships protect the alliance from opportunism on the part of partners involved, strengthen partnership, and safeguard the relationship when problems appear.

The following items all contribute to relational competence and need serious consideration and effort for alliance success. Fundamental also is development and nurturing of a cooperation mind-set. Using teamwork, allowing for participation, performance measures and rewards for cooperation, encouraging individual and organization learning, and knowledge management throughout the relationship may assist this.

Coordination and Control

While the essence of alliance management may lie in harnessing interdependence, in interpersonal relations and connections, some more overt and tangible means of coordination are also important. Urban and Vendemini (1992) suggest that there are three types of coordination available:

- coordination is achieved within each partner's existing organizational framework;
- the partners decide to form an ad hoc task force to be responsible for the administration of the cooperative agreement; or
- where the stakes are particularly high and complex, leading to a long-term cooperation, a special legal structure is created: a "program management company," consortium, or something similar.

Moss Kanter (1994) indicates the types of leadership required for a variety of functions, emphasizing the central risk of change at the heart of them:

- strategic integrative function served by organizational leaders keeping in touch with one another, sharing information, and solving mutual problems;
- tactical integration provided usually by middle management, developing plans for specific projects and the like;
- operational integration by staff in training and organization development providing adequate resources;
- interpersonal integration by leaders throughout the organization functioning at the informal and social levels; and
- cultural integration by the administrators of the partnership sharing values and understanding differences.

More specific coordination strategies include planning, monitoring, feedback, and control mechanisms. Cooperative strategies include voluntary interaction; information strategies focus on influence and persuasion; and control strategies include financial incentives or sanctions, mandates, structural approaches, and the like. Informal coordination focuses on interpersonal relations and informal communication, while more formal approaches include structural mechanisms, a variety of linkage types, or approaches such as co-location or contracts (Alexander, 1995). Using multifunction teams from each partner, as a means of managing the new entity, is a popular approach (More & McGrath, 1996).

The importance of a liaison person or alliance manager is a critical concern. Such an individual is a vital ingredient, the one to carry forward the alliance at each of its life-cycle stages. This individual must be flexible in playing numerous roles—from strategic sponsor (visionary and emissary); through advocate (carring the vision and rallying organizational personnel); networker and facilitator (linking functions, areas, people, and partners); mediator (dealing with alliance problems); and manager per se (shouldering alliance responsibility for achieving goals and objectives and maintaining course). As Spekman, Isabella, MacAvoy, and Forbes (1996) point out, such individuals have alliance mind-sets enabling them to see the world as a series of connections.

Objective measuring of performance and contribution to the alliances is also an important control and coordination mechanism for all involved in alliances. This is especially useful in making relationships more predictable as a basis for mutual trust. Such measurement can include, for instance, desired results, organizational interface, organization and management, and output (Lewis, 1995).

Issues of Commitment and Trust

While there are many studies on strategic alliances in a wide variety of industry sectors, one factor that emerges clearly is that trust and commitment provide the basis for effective interfirm alliances and the nature of ongoing relationships. Furthermore, trust is a most efficient approach to alliance governance; it expands the range of possible alliances, permits organizations to enter into partnerships otherwise impossible, and avoids the stifling nature of contracts in better enabling partnership adaptability to changing environments (Gulati, 1995).

There are several dimensions of trust (Bergquist, Betwee, & Meuel, 1995):

- trust in intentions, based on how each partner views the others' honor and commitment;
- trust in competency, relating to specialization of functions in the partnerships and centered on capacity, accessibility, and dependability; and
- trust based on a shared perspective forged through complementary attitudes regarding the business of the relationship.

One, then, can differentiate between a risk-based view of trust where contractual means offer some way of hedging organizational bets against uncertainty; and a more restrictive mode of trust based on moral integrity or confidence in the goodwill of others. The latter is a type of trust essentially developed through interpersonal interaction, leading to social-psychological bonds that provide a basis for dealing with uncertainty through mutual norms, sentiments, and friendships (Ring & Van de Ven, 1994). Here, personal relationships, as indicated in the previous section, are pivotal in shaping and modifying the structure and process of alliances.

To ensure an effective climate of trust, it has been suggested that the following are required (Wolff, 1994):

- a well-defined alliance scope;
- the alliance is considered important by all parties involved;
- a long-term view;
- absence of excessive doubt;
- a basis in complementary strengths;
- equal contributions among partners;
- equal benefits to parties involved;
- no significant strategic conflicts;
- no domination;
- management autonomy;
- flexibility in approach;
- anticipation and respect for differences in corporate cultures;
- contribution of top-quality people;
- a joint steering committee meeting periodically to review progress against goals; and
- personal links between key individuals in the relationship.

Of course, commitment and trust relate to levels of cooperation versus any competition endemic in the relationships. Where there is little competition, alliances are much easier to enter into and manage because there is less risk and suspicion in the relationship. With competition, the situation becomes more complex. The solution for making trust possible in such situations can reside in separating conflict from cooperation; having the benefits of cooperation obviously outweighing any risks; and allowing the time necessary for people to create the requisite comfort levels (Lewis, 1995).

Conflict and Power

While in more equal relationships it is easier to control harmful power struggles, in many relationships there is, if not overt, then at least covert, inequality of power. The power dynamics of one partner being more powerful than the other(s) is often the case, for example, in customer-supplier relationships where commercial leverage is a potent driver (Hunter, Beaumont, & Sinclair, 1996). In such relationships there are many pressures, including that of pricing. One cannot deny this nor should one accept a simplistic view of cooperation as easily acceptable and straightforward in every case of collaboration.

Where power relationships occur unaddressed, with one organization using its position of leverage in extracting harmful concessions from its partner(s), any basis in trust and commitment and respect for partner interests is destroyed. The use of destructive techniques such as coercion, confrontation, and domination are viewed as counterproductive and are very likely to strain the fabric of the partnership. These techniques, as well as smoothing over or avoiding the issue, do not fit with the more proactive tone of a partnership in which problems of one party become problems affecting both parties (Mohr & Spekman, 1996). Such power relationships are anathema to alliances and can be managed better, or even largely avoided, by considering how prospective partners deal with other firms during a partner selection process (Lewis, 1995).

Problems of power emerge in alliances from the following issues (Reardon & Spekman, 1994):

- inequity and asymmetry;
- a mind-set of competing for the largest share of the pie;
- failure to ensure cooperative decision making;
- little mutual commitment and participation;

- a "calling the shots" management style; and
- power-oriented and overly rigid and suspicious negotiators.

Instead of these traits, culminating in manipulation or coercion, what is required, they argue, is emphasizing consensus and persuasion and understanding that power is really related to mutual dependency. Power in alliances, therefore, is more readily shared the more partners depend on one another. This includes the power wrought by information—in terms of technical and relationship knowledge (knowledge of one's partner), the latter providing the basis for successful negotiation.

As an alternative to power and political games, these authors recommend persuasive tactics in alliances based on motivation, participation, and reward, with the latter targeting joint problem-solving, communication, and relationship-building activities rather than profits alone. What should be targeted is motivation for ensuring alliance success; employee involvement in alliance success; training for participative management; adequate time and program type for such participative management; effective internal communication about policy information and practice; and reward systems focused on employees contributing to alliance success.

Communication Processes

Communication is very often ranked by management as one of the most critical ingredients in any organizational venture (Cauley de la Sierra, 1995). Many researchers and practitioners (for example, Urban & Vendemini, 1992; Bergquist, Betwee, & Meuel, 1995), however, regard vibrant communication as central to coordination with key members in a dynamic alliance—at the heart of a partnership's vitality (Mohr & Spekman, 1996).

Clearly, relationships need communication structures that accommodate the requisite of mutual and constant exchange of information and communication processes—both formal and informal. They are critical to building and maintaining the relationships and communication does much in allaying any mistrust among partners. In particular, communication strategies that deal specifically with present and potential mismatches between partner expectations are important in alliance relationships (Reardon & Spekman, 1994).

This emphasis on communication is hardly surprising given the many real and potential problems that can occur in conflict situations or in relation to appropriate flows of information and its degree of openness. So additional investment in communication, particularly face-to-face, is pivotal in alliance relationships where the nonroutine and risks from misunderstandings are more pervasive. Partners must be informed on all matters and issues need to be surfaced when they become evident (Lewis, 1995).

Reardon and Spekman (1994, p. 75) suggest the following critical questions about communication in alliances:

- How frequently should we communicate?
- Who will communicate with whom?
- What modalities (telephone, face-to-face, memos) are appropriate?
- What types of information will be shared?
- What types of information are proprietary?
- How will we deal with communication problems?
- What aspects of our respective company cultures might hinder communication?

Culture

Important as organizational culture is to individual organizations, as indicated in chapter II, it is a critical foundation for embedding effective partnerships. Flexibility, dealing with uncertainty, a supportive environment, and a collaboration rather than competition mind-set are essential. Reward structures should also reflect the emphasis on cooperation and group achievement instead of the more traditional approaches. Ideally what is required is:

- moving away from confrontation and competition toward acceptance and collaboration;
- developing and sustaining respect for individual rights and collective responsibility in cooperation; and
- moving to a partnership of commitment through a culture and community of shared commitment and interdependency (Bergquist, Betwee, & Meuel, 1995).

Understanding of partner cultures, then, is critical to building a compatible partnership culture. This includes relational management of subcultures, including the difficult area of professional and management cultures. Moreover, alliance performance critically reflects a distinctive alliance culture of its own, based on the internal cultures of organizational partners and developed as a separate entity through interpersonal and group communication, and joint activities of a formal and informal kind that can enhance the development of like mind-sets and facilitate partner relations.

Senior Management Involvement

Alliances succeed by what goes on "in the trenches" and in organizational leadership. However, without the success of the latter, without executive drive and support, the former is impotent. So senior management commitment and frequent—preferably face-to-face—personal involvement is vital. While the daily routine of alliance management can be undertaken by some sort of alliance manager, senior executives must do more.

As both research (for example, Urban & Vendemini, 1992; Yoshino & Rangan, 1995; Spekman, Isabella, MacAvoy, & Forbes, 1996) and practice make clear, senior executives must also:

- emphasize the link between alliances and corporate strategy, clarifying the real place of alliances in the organization's strategy and ensuring a particular alliance is bound to the organization's strategic intent;
- foster throughout the organization a belief in organizational cooperation as a tool for competitive advantage;
- drive the alliance vision throughout the organization, ensuring that the commitment to, and belief in, alliances and what is negotiated at executive levels actually gets to lower level managers who have to deal with the relationship on a day-to-day basis (this is really where alliances are made or broken);
- ensure all comprehend why the alliance is justified and its place in the organization's overall goals and objectives;
- promote organizational commitment and reciprocity;
- play a critical role in negotiation and shape shared strategic intent;
- guide and manage overall, including clarifying risks and benefits, and seizing new strategic opportunities;

- assure widespread acceptance and understanding of the objectives and processes involved in the alliances throughout the member organizations, thus avoiding unnecessary duplication or undercutting of efforts;
- appoint the most appropriate people as alliance managers;
- make proper resource allocation;
- design reward systems to contribute to alliance success;
- understand the time frames of alliances;
- engage in ongoing critical review;
- comprehend alliance evolution, including that of forming into a network of alliances;
- ensure a corporate culture that accommodates cooperative relationships—one that erases an us-versus-them attitude, that encourages organizational learning, and that balances cooperation and competition;
- foster the kinds of environments conducive to forming effective alliances;
- maintain alternative options and fall-back positions to deal with potential failure; and
- end alliances when necessary in the least dysfunctional way.

Unquestionably, top management must shape and communicate shared strategic intent as, perhaps, its most potent role (Yoshino & Rangan, 1995). Yet it is also crucial to understand possible differences between senior management decisions and actions and how these are translated into operational decisions and activities at lower organizational levels—the impact of complex internal organizational structures and processes on alliance management per se (Bresnen, 1996).

BENEFITING FROM COOPERATIVE RELATIONSHIPS

While it is true that there are some short-term benefits emerging from cooperative organizational relationships, it is really only in the long term that major benefits are realized, with several years usually required for developing deeper changes and solid, meaningful relationships.

International research (for example, Urban & Vendemini, 1992; Lynch, 1993; Yoshino & Rangan, 1995) features the following benefits accruing to alliance participants:

- strategic flexibility, especially in adapting to change;
- synergies through combined strengths;
- increased global competitiveness;
- a faster path to meeting complex demands of the environment (especially when large and small organizations combine);
- cost reduction and/or infusion of capital;
- risk sharing;
- extended opportunities for learning;
- enhanced credibility;
- entry to markets and better market intelligence;
- closeness to new customers;
- access to functions (e.g., distribution);
- sharing of research costs;
- improved technology transfer and faster adjustment to new technology changes;
- better export opportunities and management; and
- reaching critical size (especially for small and medium-sized firms: strategic alliances can offer a more cost-benefit solution than creation of subsidiaries or acquisitions).

If well managed, perhaps one of the most important advantages of organizational alliances is in the area of learning and knowledge management. An organization's know-how is partly that accruing and developing from its relationships with other organizations, customers, and a range of critical stakeholders—acquired through both informal and formal links. Furthermore, existing knowledge is confronted in such relationships through interaction with the knowledge of other participants, leading to the creation of new knowledge (Hakansson & Snehota, 1995).

Finally, Miles and Preece (1995) argue that strategic alliances can help an organization to serve its current needs. But, importantly, they can assist organizations to confront their dominant logic by offering alternative views that may challenge partner ideas and therefore facilitate the evolving pattern of "unlearning" and "relearning" in the strategic formulation and implementation process. They do warn, however, that (p. 4):

> For management...this increased use of alliances brings mixed messages. While it is clear that alliances can aid the firm in efficiently carrying out their strategic plans, the increased use suggests that simply having an alliance is

no longer likely to provide a firm with a competitive advantage. If all firms have alliances, advantages will arise only to those firms who maximize the value added from these arrangements. In most strategic alliance arrangements, it is not clear that this is being done.

REAL PROBLEMS IN
COOPERATIVE RELATIONSHIPS

In spite of many advantages, we must not disregard the potential drawbacks of such cooperative relationships including their management difficulty and riskiness. For example, there is potential for unequal gains; problems with cultural clash (individual and organizational); difficulties with role ambiguity; partners possibly allying with competitors; and the chance of antitrust charges. Moreover, while there are growing efforts at alliance formation, paradoxically, current efforts at downsizing, reengineering, delayering, and outsourcing act in destroying the very stability required to develop successful partnering. Indeed, even the best practices in partnering, such as open communication, may backfire in terms of increasing an organization's vulnerability (Culpan, 1993; Zemke & Zemke, 1994; Badaracco, 1991).

Paramount among areas of concern that have emerged in the literature (for example, Urban & Vendemini, 1992; Lynch, 1993; Zemke & Zemke, 1994; Bureau of Industry Economics, 1995; Yoshino & Rangan, 1995; Mitchell & Singh, 1996) are:

- finding the proper partner;
- levels of risk;
- levels of commitment;
- relationship ambiguities;
- lack of shared vision;
- time obligations;
- time lags between input and results;
- disclosure of confidential information;
- intellectual property;
- legal considerations;
- cooperation perceived as a threat to autonomy;
- control issues;
- personalities involved;
- personal interests outweighing corporate responsibilities;

- trust in individuals and the relationship;
- levels of confidence;
- failure to structure for genuine collaboration;
- existence of ulterior motives in partnering;
- managerial and administrative competence;
- operational effectiveness and equity in problem solving;
- restrictive managerial mind-sets;
- a short-term business focus;
- communication difficulties;
- dysfunctional cultures;
- mixed messages about priorities;
- differing managerial cultures among partners;
- managing complexity per se (activities, environment, and partner competencies);
- maintaining an appropriate balance between competition and cooperation;
- strategic shifts over time;
- adequate monitoring and measurement of effort to benefits;
- loss of critical proprietary information;
- organizational disruption;
- adaptation difficulties in terms of costs and routines;
- the cost of establishing and renewing cooperative agreements;
- interdependence making independent action difficult;
- rigid organizational attitudes, culture, practices, and policies; and
- time constraints for appropriate decision making.

One set of "deadly sins" can provide a pattern in alliance failure:

- planting the seeds of destruction before the legal agreements are signed;
- focusing on peripheral versus core issues;
- too-hasty negotiations and closing of deals—agreements without adequate strategic planning;
- failing to get both senior and middle level commitment and support;
- closing a deal without operational planning; and
- failure to maintain a win/win environment (Lynch, 1993).

Harrigan (1995) also importantly suggests that some alliances fail for reasons outside the control or influence of relationship partners.

These include government policies, industry reform, competitor tactics, or revised sponsorship attitudes.

Another major area of concern is that of partnership transformation or change of some sort. Certainly changes in personnel can cause difficulties, especially if they concern leaders or critical boundary spanners in the system. For example, Spekman and colleagues (1996) argue that perhaps the most serious problem that can disrupt an alliance is a break in relationship between alliance managers (often initiated by new managers not skilled or committed to partnering). So too can success or problems in the partnership. Critical here is the acceptance of change processes, ongoing commitment, and desire and capacity to learn. Finally, in any partnership it is important to retain enough independence to allow the relationship to be terminated before it becomes destructive or dysfunctional (Bergquist, Betwee, & Meuel, 1995).

THE ANSWER?

In one sense, partnering is an option to decaying hierarchy as a preferred organizational form. But, despite its growing popularity, strategic partnering may not be the ideal solution for every organization. Furthermore, one cannot deny the real difficulties involved, including the high rate of failure. No wonder then, while "Trust is good...for many companies, hostility may still be more profitable" (Anonymous, 1995, p. 65).

While there are few formal measurement systems to assess alliance success (Rai, Borah, & Ramaprasad, 1996), a recent study (Bergquist, Betwee, & Meuel, 1995) showed that one out of three partnerships examined failed; other overseas studies by McKinsey & Co, Coopers and Lybrand, among others, show that five out of 10 alliances fail (Ernst & Thomas, 1996); seven out of 10 joint ventures do not meet expectations or disband; and that international alliances are even more prone to failure (Stafford, 1994). Bain and Co. found that only 2 percent of all alliance negotiations actually produced lasting performance improvements for those involved. Further, even if they succeeded, strategic alliances were expensive exercises (Rigby & Buchanan, 1994). Aside from the failure rate, some writers warn against alliances because of the risks and costs involved—lost proprietary information, disruption of organizational life, and difficulties with adjustment—and the management complexities (for example, Porter, 1990; Mitchell & Singh, 1996).

While understanding these concerns, the view proposed by Yoshino and Rangan (1995) seems more sensible—that management must learn to deal with the difficulties of alliance management and that such relationships, founded on interdependencies, are the essential way that firms can grow into formidable global competitors. Critical also is the concern that, while assisting innovation, in one sense, "...the resulting web of interrelationships between firms within specific industries can be viewed as an impediment to innovation and long-term economic efficiency" (James & Weidenbaum, 1993, p. 101). Freezing industry structures in terms of rigid frameworks of cooperation, therefore, could be the death knell of industry innovation and growth.

So we have paradox. On the one hand, research shows that strategic interorganizational relationships clearly help organizations adapt to the uncertainties of the market economy by introducing some stability, reducing risks, and expediting acquisition of technical or commercial expertise (Urban & Vendemini, 1992). It is argued that they are pivotal to competitive success (Yoshino & Rangan, 1995). Furthermore, such relationships, as evident in the computer and entertainment industries, are capable of transforming the industry per se. On the other hand, there are high failure rates and many concerns about alliances as indicated above.

Put simply, then, strategic alliances are not the magic bullets that many advocates have envisaged and argued for as the solution to industry ills. They are not a panacea per se, and alliances involve risks and costs, and altered mind-sets. Much depends on how well they are managed, from initial assessments and planning, throughout. Importantly also, the alliances that confer optimum benefits are part of long-term strategic plans rather than regarded as short-term palliatives. Furthermore, the real organizational challenge lies in transforming basic collaborative agreements into productive and strategically effective relationships (Yoshino & Rangan, 1995).

In spite of such difficulties, however, it is imperative that organizations consider alliances systematically, understanding their benefits and problems, having a valid rationale for entering such partnerships, and then pursuing them where the sum of the whole is more fruitful and where individual players, ideally, are not subordinate, either financially or legally, to others in the game. Given this, cooperative agreements can provide another weapon in the organizational armory of better achieving management policy, change, and competitive advantage.

NOTES

1.   Literature consulted here inclues the following: Badaracco (1991); Urban and Vendemini (1992); Lorange and Roos (1993); Carlin, Dowling, Roering, Wyman, Kalinoglou, and Clyburn (1994); Cauley De La Sierra (1995); Howarth, Gillin, and Bailey (1995); Cantwell and Barrera (1995); Pollard (1995); Sankar, Boulton, Davidson, Snyder, and Ussery (1995).

2.   Literature consulted here includes the following: Urban and Vendemini (1992); Parkhe (1993); Harari (1994); Bergquist, Betwee, and Meuel (1995); Lewis (1995); Yoshino and Rangan (1995); Miles (1996); Mallam and Huang (1996); Ernst and Thomas (1996); Rai, Borah, and Ramaprasad (1996); and More and McGrath (1996).

Chapter IV

Managing Mind-sets

We will only ever see what it is that our theories enable us to focus upon. All ways of seeing are simultaneously ways of not seeing (Clegg, 1990, p. 20).

Extraordinary management involves questioning and shattering paradigms, and then creating new ones. It is a process which depends critically upon contradiction and tension...frame-breaking extraordinary management is a process of persuasion and conversion....It is not about consistency or harmony, rather it is destabilising and irregular....[it] is the use of intuitive, political, group learning modes of decision-making and self-organizing forms of control in open-ended change situations. It is the form of management that managers must use if they are to change strategic direction and innovate (Stacey, 1993, pp. 301-302).

NEW MENTAL MODELS

As indicated in chapter II, increasingly, today, we are finding chaos out of order and vice-versa, requiring organizations to develop strategic thinking founded on unpredictability, open-ended futures and turbulent change, weak cause and effect links, irregular patterns, ill-structured problems and opportunities, and continuing contention. Indeed, current critical theory challenges many of the very bases of traditional management thinking and research in the face of such an environment, questioning the generally accepted view of the neutrality or virtue of management as self-evident, straightforward, and unproblematic (Alvesson & Willmott, 1992). Moreover, the very nature of organizational studies itself has had to change mind-sets, moving through romantic, modern, and postmodern eras, and undergoing much self-reflection and transformation of both content and process (Clegg, 1990; Reed & Hughes, 1992).

In order to cope with environmental change we must constantly question and change our submerged mental models and assumptions that determine our perceptions of reality, how we think and learn, moving beyond skilled incompetence and recognizing that each new situation may require something different. In many situations we simply must let go of our baggage, we must unlearn. Only when we learn and think in fresh ways can we create new and more appropriate modes of organizing and managing.

Moreover, we need to be clear about the difference between our espoused models—those articulated and used to explain how we behave—compared to the models actually in use—mental models driving our behavior. Strategic thinking, then, requires (Stacey, 1992, p. 104):

- continually developing new mental models for each new situation rather than applying the same general prescriptions to many situations;
- reasoning by analogy and intuition around qualitative, irregular patterns rather than analysis and quantification;
- understanding the whole, interconnected system rather than its separate parts;
- being anchored to the here and now, not the future;
- focusing on process rather than outcome, on the mental models governing the process itself.

Indeed Manz and Neck (1991) argue that what we require currently is to better develop thought self-leadership in others and ourselves. By this they mean analyzing and managing one's assumptions, using improved self-talk (what we say to ourselves covertly), and using constructive mental imagery (imagining results of behavior before it is actually performed).

Morgan (1993, pp. 58-59), building on his earlier work concerning organizational metaphors, also emphasizes the need for changed mind-sets in contemporary and future management:

> Effective managers have to learn to cope with the flux. They have to find creative ways of going with the flow. They have to help coherent, relevant initiatives emerge from the dynamic and unpredictable events that surround them. They have to be skilled in managing disorder and in helping their organizations self-organize and evolve in a relevant, open-ended way. This new context challenges much of the old rhetoric of rational planning and control.

He calls for creative management in terms of the competency of what he labels "imaginization," defined in terms of:

- improving our abilities to see and understand situations in new ways;
- finding new images for new ways of organizing;
- creating shared understandings;
- having personal empowerment; and
- developing capacities for continuous self-organization.

Managers in changing environments are called upon to adopt a variety of new images. First he asks them to become strategic termites in terms of management and leadership styles—not dysfunctional termites who attract exterminators, but functional ones who build and adapt as circumstances demand: termites build successful homes in a coherent way but one that is piecemeal and unrestrained by predetermined plans. It suggests management driven by a broad sense of vision but not trapped by it; of managing as emergent, self-organizing, open-ended, and evolutionary, allowing for order to arise from chaos.

Second, he asks them to rethink organization design and managerial styles, promoting more flexible, decentralized ways of operating, by adopting the image of a spider plant. Here we break constraints set by the usually large central bodies; develop good "umbilical cords" for successful decentralization; grow different "cords" (as in hybrid plants) for managing different situations; and encourage bumblebees providing cross-pollination and coordinators in the service of the offshoots.

Work by Bolman and Deal (1997) suggests we need to be flexible in using multiple approaches. They offer four frames and appropriate combinations of these from which we can view and manage organizational processes:

- The structural frame aims to develop organization structures consistent with an organization's mission, its strategy, and environmental constraints. Emphasis is placed on organizational goals, roles, technology, and economic factors.
- The human resource frame aims to create a better fit between the individual and organization in terms of needs, skills, and values.

- The political frame aims to develop political skill and acumen, focusing on power, conflict, and the distribution of scarce resources as the central issues.
- The symbolic frame aims to improve organizational functioning by moving outside the assumed rationality of the other frames, highlighting the cultural, theatrical, and nonrational dimensions of organizational life.

Also recently, Chia (1996, p. 426) suggests that university business schools have a critical contribution to make to the business community:

> ...through adopting a deliberate educational strategy which privileges the "weakening" of thought processes so as to encourage and stimulate the entrepreneurial imagination. This requires a radical shift in intellectual priorities from teaching analytical problem-solving skills to teaching aspiring managers and entrepreneurs the art of "paradigm-shifting" through a negative pedagogy. The experience of ambiguity, confusion and chaos are central to the relaxing (or weakening) of our boundaries of thought and the nurturing of the entrepreneurial imagination.

Others have encouraged continuing links between organization and management studies and the humanities in order for us to better comprehend processes and phenomena that traditional modes do not explore as well. It is suggested we pursue more extensively several of the insightful offerings (while noting all their difficulties) that some organizational scholars have been pursuing through literary theory—using deconstructive, rhetorical, and narrative analysis; historical analysis; and the use of a philosophical perspective (Zald, 1996). Indeed, the grand master of management thinking himself, Drucker (1989, p. 223) has said that:

> Management is...a liberal art: "liberal" because it deals with the fundamentals of knowledge, self-knowledge, wisdom, and leadership; "art" because it is practice and application. Managers draw on all the knowledge and insights of the humanities and the social sciences....But they have to focus this knowledge on effectiveness and results...management will increasingly be the discipline and the practice through and in which the "humanities" will again acquire recognition, impact, and relevance.

ORGANIZATION LEARNING

The notion of organizational learning has actually been around since the 1950s, especially relating to organizations learning about and adapting to their environment (Daft & Huber, 1987). Some even argue for an earlier emergence of the concept in the 1920s (Marquardt & Reynolds, 1994). Coopey (1995), however, differentiates between a long-time interest in learning as a concept in organization theory and the more recent interest in the idea of the learning organization. The former is concerned with enhancing processes of learning in order to improve individual and collective organizational actions via better knowledge and understanding. The latter focuses on the design of organizations to deliberately facilitate the learning of members and therefore improve collective adaptation.

Whatever its real historical standing, it is clear that the theoretical foundation for understanding the current growing interest in knowledge management processes, as discussed in the next chapter, lies firmly in that of organizational learning as a multilevel concept, encompassing at least those cyclical processes that include skill learning, personal awareness, and transformational change (Hawkins, 1994). Further, while there is no specific consensus on the what and how of organizational learning, there is some overall agreement (Lundberg & Brownell, 1993, p. 34):

(1) that organizational learning is more than the sum of members' learning, (2) that environmental alignment is vital, and (3) that the probability of learning is affected by the degree of environmental turbulence, the rigidity of organizational structure, the adequacy of the organization's strategy, and the strength of its culture.

In order for an organization to learn there must be systemic health aligned around a combination of the following four factors (Schein, 1996, p. 2):

- a sense of identity, purpose, or mission;
- a capacity on the part of the system to adapt and maintain itself in the face of internal and external changes;
- a capacity to perceive and test reality; and
- some degree of internal integration or alignment of the subsystems that make up the total system.

If such systemic health exists, then Daft and Huber (1987) point to two paths an organization must travel in order to learn:

- the systems-structural path concentrates on information acquisition and distribution, emphasizing structure for allowing tangible data and message transmission and storage; and
- the interpretive path, emphasizing the information sharing and interpretation of human participants.

Types of Learning

While not a wholly new concept, as mentioned earlier, recent interest in the topic of organization learning has burgeoned. Earlier on, Shrivastava (cited in Daft & Huber, 1987) offered four major approaches to thinking about it:

- adaptive learning where the organization adapts to problems, opportunities, and changes in the environment through adjusting goals, decisions, and behaviors;
- assumption sharing where shared assumptions and values lead to organizational theories-in-use;
- development knowledge where acquiring knowledge of the relationship between organizational actions and environmental outcomes defines learning; and
- institutionalised experience where learning is accumulating efficiencies through experience and tradition and where it is affected through size and bureaucracy.

Later, McGill, Slocum, and Deli (1992) and, especially, Argyris (1991, 1993) differentiated between two types of learning that have come to dominate current thought on the issue:

1. Single-loop or adaptive learning is incremental and adaptive and focuses on changing organizational routines. It centers on present problem solving without exploring the appropriateness of current learning behaviors. It is pertinent for conditions of predictability, closed and contained change situations where cause and effect links are fairly well clear—where learning feedback moves from actions to outcomes and consequences and returns to some responding action again.

2. Double-loop or generative learning emphasizes practices leading to both a new framework for learning and new routines. Its core is ongoing experimentation and feedback in a continuing examination of the way organizations define and solve problems, their basic "programming" for information processing and evaluation, in other words. Such learning reveals what alternative ways of seeing a situation could lead to more effective action. It is appropriate for open-ended situations where consequences are largely unknowable and cause and effect links very unclear—where there is reflection on implications of action outcomes for the way in which we interpret such outcomes, for the mind-sets that determine our perceptions and guide how we discern problems and opportunities.

It is considered that the latter type of learning really differentiates the learning from the non-learning organization.

Isaacs (1993), Director of The Dialogue Project at MIT's Organizational Learning Center, offers a third type of learning:

3. Triple-loop learning as dialogue—learning about learning through revealing and altering the tacit infrastructure of thought. Such learning is collective, a sustained inquiry into the processes, certainties, and assumptions underlying everyday organizational experience. It concentrates on exploring fundamental habits of attention and assumptions behind traditional problems of thinking. This is especially useful for inquiry and collective learning in teams. Such learning reveals why individuals have certain goals and what leads them to being predisposed to learning in certain ways.

Here dialogue is differentiated from debate (win-lose) or discussion (consensus). It explores or alters underlying patterns of meaning and surfaces the fundamental patterns leading to disagreement at the outset. This provides an environment in which people can consciously participate in creating shared meaning and discern their part in a larger pattern of collective experience. Insights gained from such dialogue can change people's ways of thinking and acting in organizations.

Furthermore, it is argued that the centrality of dialogue to organizational learning resides in its ability to promote collective thinking and communication. It helps deal with the need for intelligence beyond the individual; the failure of current efforts at fostering collective thinking based on procedures that block information and communication channels; and the behavioral rigidity that results from the popular superficial ideologies of "vision" and "values."

Finally, we need to move beyond learning as mere acquisition of new knowledge and insights, into what Isaacs is, perhaps, pointing to. This is the issue of "unlearning"—the need to uncover assumptions and to unlearn outdated knowledge, practices, and methods for processing experiences. McGill, Slocum, and Deli (1992) stress that it is the vital precursor to learning, to having new experiences, and of finding new ways of experiencing.

They also explore four different kinds of organization emerging from use of the learning perspective:

1. The Knowing Organization: By The Book—This organization is based on a one-best-way approach to management, with a philosophy grounded in rationality and valuing efficiency above all else. It does things by the book and has standard policies, procedures, rules, and regulations. Managers control employees by enforcing the rules, enforcing conformity, routine behaviors, and risk-avoidance. The organization's emphasis on the need to know and its focus on single-loop learning block real learning from experience.
2. The Understanding Organization: Virtue in Values—This organization has a focus on the core values and beliefs of the organization, on the organization culture. This is a new "one-best-way," still offering predictability and control through culture but not such regimentation per se. Strong culture organizations can also constrain real learning, not able to escape their own myths and core values.
3. The Thinking Organization: From Analysis to Action—This organization is geared to quick-fix problem solving without adequate understanding of causes, of fundamental problems, inadequate experimentation, and proactive perspectives. Reactive reliance on programs to solve business problems constrains management thinking and frustrates learning. Programs per se are not the difficulty; it is rather the use of them as simple solutions to complex problems that is at fault.

4. The Learning Organization: Enhancing Experience—This organization is committed to learning from every aspect of organizational experience and about the process of experience per se. What sets it apart is its capacity to learn. Its management creates and fosters a climate promoting learning, encouraging experimentation, open communication, promoting construc- tive dialogue, and facilitating the processing of experience. In particular the organization has a teaching-learning orientation to its customers and revels in change as an input that leads to learning.

Levels of Learning

The basis of organizational learning resides initially in the individual as a necessary but not sufficient cause of organizational learning. Collective organizational learning is much more complex and is more than the sum of the individual parts as such. Consequently, consideration must be given to the different levels of organizational learning.

One useful levels approach is outlined as follows (Tiemessen, Lane, Crossan, & Inkpen, 1996):

- The individual—learning is achieved by individuals and organizational learning is the sum of its individuals; learning activities involve intuiting (the subconscious process of creating tacit knowledge) and interpreting (the conscious process of assigning meaning to data, behavior, and events).
- The group—learning is more than the sum of individuals and communication and integration of individual learning is required for organizational learning; learning activity here is integrating (sharing, comparing, and resolving individual views into a shared understanding).
- The organization—learning is founded in knowledge structures, systems, and procedures, so embedded as to be apart from the individual; learning activity here is institutionalizing, the way of incorporating new knowledge and skills into the organization's systems, structures, and procedures.

There is, of course, considerable interaction between the levels and activities mentioned.

Furthermore, much of the basis of productive learning resides in unlearning as mentioned earlier. Here a critical issue is that of organization memory. Memory is essentially stored information from past organizational history, useful for present decision making. It plays three critical roles in the organization—information, control, and political—and affects performance in terms of the existence of mental and structural artifacts (Walsh & Ungson, 1991). It is critical to organizational learning and knowledge because these are affected by the very distribution of memory, its accuracy, and how it might be treated as a constraint (Weick, 1979).

The reason that organizations preserve knowledge of the past is in order to have that knowledge serve current decision making through lessons learned. In this sense memory can be functional in terms of learning from mistakes. But it can also be dysfunctional if it serves as an obstructive constraint.

Here we can leave aside the debates concerning the anthropomorphism of claiming that organizations have memories. Of course memory initially resides in individuals but can occur in systems and structures and many dimensions of an organization's culture (Walsh & Ungson, 1991).

The solution is not the free-for-all expression of feelings and emotions that can immobilize decision making and learning but rather double-loop learning and a disciplined effort to reveal and test those undiscussable matters blocking organizational learning. This must be achieved at individual and group levels, where we continually grapple with the process of interaction. Here we have openness, active listening and a disposition to changing one's mind. We can advocate our individual positions but simultaneously have others test those very positions. We can reveal attributions about the motives of others with evidence for such attributions. We move from the traditional to the new:

- away from a concern with the individual expert or visionary to a concern with the effect of personality, group dynamics, and learning behaviors of managers in groups;
- from the stability of continuing consensus based on "rational" reasoning to the creative instability of contention and dialogue with the periodic consensus it produces around particular issues;
- away from condemning the messiness of real life business decision making as dysfunctional politics and then ignoring

it, to examining, understanding, and dealing with organizational defense mechanisms and game playing;

- away from a perception of organizational learning as a simple process relating to outcomes to an understanding of organizational learning as a complex process of continually questioning how we are learning;
- away from the closure of problem solving to the opening up of contentious and ambiguous issues;
- away from trying to apply general prescriptive models to many specific situations, to developing new mental models to design actions for each new strategic situation (Stacey, 1992, p. 126).

MEANING CREATION, INTERPRETATION, AND DEFENSIVE ROUTINES

As mentioned in chapters I and II, there are diverse approaches to understanding organizational reality, from the more objective end of the spectrum to the subjective. In the latter:

> Organizations can be conceived as socially constructed phenomena, understood as systems of shared meaning and maintained by social, political and symbolic processes. Meaning creation, as the basis of human organizing, shapes actions, events and organizational environments—internal and external, and fosters personal identities via a complex mix of socialization processes and interpersonal relationships (Brown, 1995, p. 951).

While many still adhere to a traditional machine metaphor of organizations, others are reconceptualizing organizations as information-processing entities in terms of receiving, processing, storing, and retrieving information. However, they are also meaning creating and interpretation systems, focused on shared meanings conjured up from social interaction (Burrell & Morgan, 1979), and herein lies both their pleasure and pain, just as it does with the human being per se. Consequently, while the literature is fairly replete with methods by which firms gather knowledge, including competitive intelligence—from facts to organized information sets, the major organizational challenge remains in the process of building procedural knowledge, cognitive strategies, and attitudes (Dodgson, 1993).

Human beings, as meaning creators and interpreters, often develop rigid mind-sets preventing recognition of problems, unlearning,

learning, and effective knowledge creation and management. So while organizations are exhorted to embrace learning and transform themselves into learning entities, this is no easy matter. Learning how to learn and turning such learning into value-added knowledge is a difficult task in our turbulent organizational environments.

Even the very learning approach we tend to use unconsciously can create problems for coping in our current environment. As well as differentiating between simple and complex thinking and learning we must recognize the organizational defensive routines we have that limit the new perspective taking we must adopt. We can have useful learning inhibited by defensive systems such as (Tiemessen, Crossan, Lane, & Inkpen, 1996):

- abstraction wars—lobbing abstract arguments to and fro at each other;
- dilemma paralysis—no corrective action occurs because the problem is regarded as too great; and
- fragmentation of thought—self-created categorization that prevents seeing the whole picture (Isaacs, 1993).

Some time ago Argyris (1990) and later Argyris and Schon (1996) suggested learning inhibitors resided at the individual level where errors often provoked individuals to engage in actions that reinforced such errors; and in group and intergroup dynamics enforcing conditions for error. A defensive routine makes matters undiscussable and goes further by making the mere fact that this is so undiscussable—truth is the enemy in an environment of bypasses, cover-ups, and games used to avoid embarrassment and anxiety.

Argyris (1993) has gone on to develop this notion of learning in terms of error detection and correction. For him, errors are mismatches between intentions and actual consequences; and correction involves two approaches—changing behavior as single-loop learning or changing the underlying master program as double-loop learning. The latter type of change and learning is required for correction that perseveres.

He argues that this richer double-loop learning is required for improved organizational effectiveness, but is often undermined or, indeed, prevented from actually occurring because managers try to avoid being negative and censor the truth from emerging. In other words, management prevents both themselves and employees from taking responsibility for their own behavior through learning to understand it. Such strategy, he claims, is really anti-learning. It defeats the purpose of knowledge management.

Moreover, what appears to be the case is that it is our psychological mental models, our individual defensive reasoning, allied with organizational defensive routines that prevent the opening up of individuals to real learning. Organizations parcel out roles and responsibilities that create a bias against personal learning and commitment and continuously emphasize extrinsic rather than intrinsic motivation, thereby opening the door to defensive reasoning. So, by encouraging employees not to consider their own attitudes and behavior and by focusing on management to fix problems, any chance of empowerment, intrinsic motivation, responsibility, and useful organizational learning is eliminated.

More specifically, defensive routines for Argyris (1993, p. 15) are:

> ...any policy or action that inhibits individuals, groups, intergroups, and organizations from experiencing embarrassment or threat and, at the same time, prevents the actors from identifying and reducing the causes of the embarrassment or threat. Organizational defensive routines are anti-learning and over-protective.

They exist in the difference between what is said and what is actually done, in the communication of inconsistent messages, acting as if such messages are not inconsistent, and making previous actions, as mentioned above, undiscussable, and the undiscussability undiscussable. Collusion thus occurs at all levels, from the individual upwards, and organizational cultures reinforce, bypass, and cover-up. Such routines impact negatively on organizational performance, largely because of inhibiting the detection and correction of error and inhibiting problem solving and decision making. Consequently, it is inadequate to overcome symptoms of such defensive routines: one must address their causes at both individual and organizational levels. The solution offered is to explore behavioral patterns through understanding pattern designs embedded in individual and organizational mind-sets. One can't realistically, however, eliminate all problems as new ones will always emerge. So the challenge is to develop a learning culture which allows new problems to be dealt with effectively. It is also about confronting our own mental models and psychological rigidity affecting the very core of individual and organizational reality.

As if this were not difficult enough, there is another side to organizational learning and intelligence that is clear when we think of organizations as emotional cauldrons—that of individual and collective emotional intelligence. Such intelligence is the capacity to move beyond a simple image of the rational organization—to read and manage the emotional dimension of organizational life. This is especially necessary given the emphasis on teamwork where emotional and social intelligence is a vital competency for helping interpersonal and group harmony (Goleman, 1995).

THINKING EMOTION

While we yearn to uphold a view of organizations as rational, orderly entities, we acknowledge that people are not entirely rational and objective but can also be subjective, irrational, and nonrational and difficult to manage. This provides a paradox and current thinking is breaking down the traditional mind-sets and challenging the myth or organizational rationality, to allow new perspectives that include concerns about "the managed heart" (Hochschild, 1983); and that encourage reflection on emotion, intuition, and imagination and the part they play in our daily organizational lives. Moreover, it is argued (Alvesson & Willmott, 1992, p. 1) that "management is too potent in its effects upon the lives of employees, consumers and citizens to be guided by a narrow, instrumental form of rationality." Or, more broadly, as Fineman (1993, p. 1) reasons:

> Emotions are within the texture of organizing. They are intrinsic to social order and disorder, working structures, conflict, influence, conformity, posturing, gender, sexuality and politics. They are products of socialization and manipulation. They work mistily within the human psyche, as well as obviously in the daily ephemera of organizational life.

In spite of ongoing debate on emotion in organizational life (see Ashworth & Humphrey, 1995), clearly feelings are not left outside organizational gates but play a vital part in every dimension of our messy organizational worlds. Albrow (1992, p. 323) even goes so far as to call organizations "emotional cauldrons"! This has always been true of organizational life but, other than some work on stress and an emphasis on work satisfaction and job enthusiasm, the organizational literature has largely turned a blind eye. This is surprising given the recent structural and performance emphasis on downsizing, rightsizing, reengineering, and the like, much of which clearly evokes fear of change, of job loss, and trauma on the part of many in the organization. It is clearly evident in the work Jackall (1988) has done that reveals the real need for constant acting on the part of managers driven by anxiety in an organizational world that is capricious and unfeeling overall.

Consequently, if considering the centrality of emotional organizational life, we need to understand both the positive emotions and norms designed to ensure a level of desired work performance and a range of negative, "controlling" ones, including fear, embarrassment, shame, and guilt (Flam, 1993). Or, as Ostell (1996, p. 529) puts it:

> It takes only a moment of reflection to realize how regularly emotional reactions, both pleasant and unpleasant ones, occur at work. Employees can be *elated* by the success of gaining a promotion, *anxious* at having to make a public presentation, *angered* by what they see as unreasonable managerial behavior, *fearful* of being made redundant, *happy* with the outcome of an appraisal interview, *ashamed* of some aspect of their performance, *admiring* of the knowledge and skills of their manager, *jealous* of the success of colleagues, or *excited* by the prospect of a new work project. If these emotional reactions, particularly the unpleasant ones, are intense and persistent, however, they can interfere with ongoing behavior thus becoming disruptive and having maladaptive consequences.

Emotions, forming an often unconscious subtext for organizational behavior, are physiologically, psychologically, and socially created. Psychodynamics is a useful tool in this area as is social constructionist work. The latter, emphasized here and focused on emotion as fundamental to the negotiation of a shared organizational reality, is revealed in organization theory most recently in three particular areas:

- culture which underlines the meaning structure in organizations in the sense of both overall organizational culture and the many subcultures that constitute it, and provides a basis for individual meaning creation, emotion management, and organizational negotiated order;
- politics as the lifeblood of negotiated order and meaning creation in revealing social actors mobilizing support or

opposition to organizational policies, rules, goals, or means in
which they individually or in groups have some stake; and
• dramaturgy as reflecting the way in which the self is socially
constructed by self and others through means such as roles, self-
presentation, and impression management—performance on
the organizational "stage" (Fineman, 1993).

Some studies, such as Wouters (1989) and Hosking and Fineman
(1990), have highlighted emotional labor as in face-to-face service
work such as airline and hotel industries, and in professional areas
like medicine and social work. Here we don a "face" to meet the
"faces" that we work with, often resulting in emotional dissonance,
in strict confines of what is agreed-upon emotional display, such as
a forced nicety, in different contexts. We find feelings as a commodity
for achieving instrumental goals, manipulated by recruitment,
selection, socialization, and performance evaluation practices within
the context of an organization's social reality. We also discover that
rationality is associated with positive masculinity whereas
emotionality is often equated with negative femininity (Mumby &
Putnam, 1992).

Emotional balance has recently been discussed in the previously
mentioned popular work of Goleman (1995), largely in terms of
emotional intelligence. He regards such intelligence as crucial for
organizational life—being skilled in emotional competencies, being
attuned to the feelings of others in the workplace, and consequently
being better able to lead and manage throughout the organization.
Critical for contemporary and future organizations are the emotional
skills associated with the capacity to air grievances as helpful
critiques; creating an organization that values diversity; and being
able to work in groups and teams, to collaborate, and to network
effectively.

Kets de Vries (1991) speaks of the growing awareness of the
inadequacy of the classic management theory of rational
organizational action. He suggests that it is timely that a growing
number of organizational practitioners and scholars are accepting the
real limitations to logical organizational decision making and
admitting that extrarational and even irrational forces can affect
leadership, strategy, structure, culture, and the like. Through many
examples he illustrates the usefulness of putting organizations "on
the couch" in order to unravel different rationales for organizational

thought and action, and arguing for the real need to clarify the psychodynamics of organizational life. Furthermore, it becomes clear how necessary it is to ask questions concerning the emotional environment of organizations—how the feelings of employees are managed, what effects emotional management has on individuals and groups, and to explore the emotional aspects of creativity and innovation.

So we have the construction of reality based in unconscious concerns and emotional personae, with such reality designed to protect the way we work and reflecting the social defenses that may undercut organizational success (Fineman, 1993). While defenses may help us function and work in the face of anxiety, they are also the bases of the defensive routines discussed previously as subverting organizational effectiveness.

Rather than using emotional labor to serve the needs of bureaucratic rationality, one can advocate acknowledging feelings, arising from human interaction, as central to participation in organizational life. This enhances collaboration, a sense of community, promotes mutual understanding, and gives employees alternatives for covert organizational control (Putnam & Mumby, 1993, p. 55):

> Organizations do not need to abandon instrumental goals, productivity, or rationality to develop alternative modes of discourse. Emphasizing work feelings calls for including what is currently ignored or marginalized in organizational life. Rationality is not an objective, immutable state. Rather, it is socially constructed and cast as the dominant mode of organizing. Rationality and technical efficiency, however, should be embedded in a larger system of community and interrelatedness. Perhaps organizations of the future could offer society a new alternative, one shaped by emotionally-connected creativity and mutual understanding as necessary elements for human growth.

THINKING INTUITION

We can turn from emotion to intuition as another face of nonanalytical thinking—the two are closely linked in the sense that the latter is really the emotion of knowing although it does not come from emotion per se. Increasingly we find that our conventional, analytical, logical patterns of thinking are inadequate for understanding or coping with the current and emerging scenarios.

Instead, we search for other ways of coping with accelerating change, increasing complexity, uncertainty, and conflict as discussed in chapter II. What we find is the need for a sense of inner stability, an anchor of simplicity, a deeper level of internal support system, a special ability of synthesis, and a deeper level of perception. In order to cultivate such qualities we turn to intuition for facilitation (Parikh, Neubauer, & Lank, 1994).

In terms of the practical application of intuition in major decision making in organization environments, we can contrast the thinking executive who emphasizes deduction, objectivity, facts, and problem solving by breaking down into parts, with the intuitive executive who is more inductive, subjective, feeling, and who looks at the whole in problem solving. The latter recognizes that intuition plays a key role (Agor, 1989, p. 11):

- where there is a high level of uncertainty
- where there is little previous precedent
- where reliable "facts" are limited or totally unavailable
- where time is limited and there is pressure to be right
- where there are several plausible options to choose from, all of which can be plausibly supported by "factual" arguments.

While there are numerous definitions of and debates about the concept, some may help illuminate the complex issue:

- Intuition is the brain evoking past memories and experiences for dealing with current problems.
- Intuition, as a consequential experience, is part of rational thinking but the experience itself is inexplicable by the individual involved other than to reason retroactively.
- Intuition is knowledge gained without rational thought as a sort of "Eureka factor"—awareness of an answer which you have been seeking for some time.
- Intuition, for which some have a genetic predisposition, guides decision making through being a rational and logical brain skill developed from the input of factual and feeling cues.
- Intuition acts on four main levels: physical intuition in which we have a strong bodily response to someone or something without knowing why; emotional intuition in which we experience intuitive signals as feelings; mental intuition in

which we see a pattern or order apparently unrelated to facts; and spiritual intuition in which we see the future impact of present actions, emphasizing the transpersonal and oneness of life.

- Intuition is often impeded by projection mechanisms (attachment/dishonesty); stress factors; time constraints; or lack of confidence. It may be activated through using relaxation techniques; mental and analytical exercises (Agor, 1989).

Of course there exists much scepticism about such an intangible as intuition, especially if popular advocates of intuition suggest management should place more emphasis on it than traditionally approved systematic, rational analysis. Behling and Eckel (1991) suggest that part of the problem with accepting the call for intuition resides in the fact that the term is understood in a diversity of ways: as a sixth sense of paranormal power; a personality trait; an unconscious process; a set of actions; as distilled experience; or as a residual category—what is left over from analytical decision making. For them these differing perceptions create problems in advocating intuition as a managerial tool and they urge that, until the confusion created by such differing conceptualizations is eliminated, we cannot test and evaluate the reality, worth, and potential of intuition for contemporary organizational life. So, while the concept and process of intuition for managing in a changing environment is still unclear and many remain sceptical about its use, it is certainly an ingredient that warrants some ongoing attention.

THINKING EXISTENTIALLY

Alongside the growing interest in the nonrational dimensions of organizational life have come some efforts at understanding such life in existential terms. For example: "These existential arguments capture emotions which underpin organizations at their most fundamental level. Our ingenious efforts to organize will create purpose out of rootlessness—but chaos, the void, is always just round the corner" (Fineman, 1993, p. 24).

Existential thinking concerns questions about the basis of human life and the human experience of the human condition—themes around life, death, responsibility, loneliness, despair, tragedy, anxiety, meaning, joy, love, transcendence, and spirituality. The existential approach involves fully and courageously embracing life in its entirety, including its tragic and magical aspects, and being able to confront both life and death. In the terms of this book, using such a perspective provides an alternative understanding for the purpose of work activities and can aid sense-making of our organizational complexity and turbulence (Pauchant & Associates, 1995).

More particularly, existentialism focuses on (Giddens, 1991, p. 55):

- Existence and being: the nature of existence, the identity of objects and events.
- Finitude and human life: the existential contradiction by means of which human beings are of nature yet set apart from it as sentient and reflexive creatures.
- The experience of others: how individuals interpret the traits and actions of other individuals.
- The continuity of self-identity: the persistence of feelings of personhood in a continuous self and body.

In organizations these questions translate, for example, into seeing the organization as real and permanent, an effort to allay our unconscious concerns about the fleeting, fragile, and apparently rather meaningless existence we live—they offer answers for our existential anxiety and so we invest in them. Efforts at resisting change, as discussed in chapter II, are an outgrowth of this underlying need for stability and permanence (Fineman, 1993).

Moreover, we find concerns about finding meaning in work; how we resist the myth of organizational perfection; rediscovering courage and responsibility in organizations; and the various journeys that occur in the search for meaning in organizations. Organizations themselves have been painted as places of existential construction where human energy is harnessed for their benefit by providing for people meaning fulfilling the need for existential commitment and self-transcendence. Thus, for many, career is the central organizing element and source of meaning in their lives, pursued throughout the history of management under Taylorism's management of the body; Mayo's management of the heart; and current efforts to manage fantasies and desires. Furthermore, we find advocacy within the existential frame for:

- notions of organizational effectiveness, excellence, and performance evaluation needing to incorporate not only economic values but also social, moral, ecological, and spiritual ones;
- work being seen in terms of individual and social development as well as production;
- addictive work patterns in an unbalanced life that deaden sensitivity and alienate the individual from the self and others being avoided;
- finding alternatives for living a superficial and inauthentic life by encouraging reflection and self-nurturing at all levels of the organization;
- creating environments, a true community, management styles, and organizational relationships within which humans can find meaning and develop, can become the beings they chose to be, to determine choices and accept responsibility for them;
- having the organization become a collective adventure rather than journeys led by solo heroic leadership; and
- adopting a dialectical view that sees both the constructive and destructive dimensions of organizational life (Pauchant & Associates, 1995).

THINKING FUNNY

With such an existential canvas providing a novel perspective on managing changes, that of humor also seeks to nurture organizational life, remembering that "They who laugh, last" (quoted in Goodman, 1991, p. 95). Besides, existentialism's need to come to terms with reality is also at the heart of the comic: "perhaps the crucial task for those of us in search of truth is to create a way of communicating which will enable us to make people laugh at truth, to make truth laugh" (Mulkay, 1988, p. 223).

Organizations are arenas for both work and play, with emotions suppressed or disguised theoretically in the former and more "permitted" in the latter. Indeed, the broader interest in pleasure per se is on the agenda for management theory in the 1990s and beyond, although it needs to be broader than a current interest in pleasure as a commodity to be exploited (Burrell, 1992).

In addition, increasing work on organizational humor confirms that it should be regarded as an important resource rather than a subversive force. Importantly, humor is vital to managing change. As Katzenbach and the RCL Team (1997) point out, one of the common characteristics of successful change leaders is a sense of humor, not only about themselves but of their situations.

We can take as a serviceable definition here the view that, "Humour is any type of communication that intentionally creates incongruent meanings and thereby causes laughter" (Duncan & Feisal, 1989, p. 19). Given this base in incongruity, it is not surprising that the contemporary organization, guided by rules of rationality, is a place where humor thrives.

Humor in organizations is used to achieve specific purposes relating to self-preservation, getting one's way, or getting things done. As such it is not usually neutral, trivial, or random. For management humor is a sword, brandished in influencing and persuading, motivating, and uniting, and used for facilitating change and speaking the unspeakable. Further, its management uses encompass shielding—deflecting criticism, coping with failure, defusing tension, and making organizational life more bearable. Not surprisingly, then, organization theorists, researchers, and practitioners are increasingly becoming aware of how an understanding of the uses of humor is crucial to managerial effectiveness (Barsoux, 1993).

There seems to be general agreement that humor, play, laughter, and the like are beneficial in our everyday lives. Certainly, workplace humor exists in all organizations and can be a distinguishing feature of an organization's culture. Clearly, many messages and much organizational meaning are conveyed and created through the exchange of various dimensions of humor and laughter, possibly with joking as a pivotal focus for much interest.

Perhaps in our era, humor's great use is to provide perspective—to see that there is more to life than the corporate world and that the image of the logical, rational, and sane progress of organizational life is, indeed, flawed. At its best, humor provides the alternative vision and practice, a different tool for a productivity that is based on happiness, growth, and healing (Holden, 1993).

Yet, surprisingly, there is generally little serious concern with the value of humor as either a communication, training, or management tool. Indeed one can side with the view that "...the study of humour in management has never really gotten started" (Duncan, Smeltzer, & Leap, 1990, p. 255). And, up until fairly recently, there seems to have been a dearth of interest in the educational research literature on the laughing-learning connection (Powell & Andresen, 1985; Coleman, 1992).

However, there is a glimmer of hope on a few fronts. First, the ongoing interest in corporate culture has renewed interest in organizational humor. Second, from a pragmatic perspective, workplace humor seems to have become part of the issue of workplace stress management—humor workshops for large organizations such as IBM are now not so uncommon. And third, there seems to be a growing number of training films both using humor and espousing the value of humor in organization life.

The majority of studies on workplace humor have been concerned with superiority theories of humor and particularly with that of joking behavior. Yet, other theoretical perspectives have been involved, such as incongruity theories focused on disjointed or ill-suited pairings of ideas; disposition theories focused on audience likes/dislikes; and culture theories exploring social norms, identity, and so on (Duncan, 1985). Mulkay (1988) explores the broad social dimensions of humor, emphasizing the linkage of humor to social structure (that is, growing out of it and having positive or negative consequences on the structure within which it occurs). He also differentiates between "pure humor" that, as perceived by those involved, has no implications other than the realm of humorous discourse; and that of "applied humor," one that makes an obvious contribution to serious interaction and is regarded by some as having serious consequences.

Other writers, such as Duncan and Feisal (1989), believe that the dichotomy many researchers have drawn between work and play is a false one, and they highlight the important role of humor in the workplace. Kahn (1989, p. 46) supports this approach, emphasizing the diversity of humor in organizations: "Organizational life contains its share of the outrageous, the wickedly funny, and the ironic and perverse, expressed in the course of conducting ostensibly serious affairs."

Moreover, Fine (1984, pp. 85 and 98) guides us to the fundamental significance of humor in human interaction:

> These components characterize humour as communication and imply a relationship between speaker and audience. First, humour typically requires an immediate audience response. Second, the implications of a humorous

remark generally can be denied by its maker with little loss of face. Third, humour contains dense layers of meaning for its participants beyond the overt meanings of its language. Together these features help distinguish humorous interaction from other interactions considered "serious."...Humour is obviously not the only technique by which identities and situations are negotiated in interaction, but the realization that this does occur in situational humour suggests that humour is of more than evanescent interest to students of social interaction.

Kets de Vries (1990) makes the point that using humorous communication allows for greater risks in getting difficult messages across than employing alternative communication modes. This is supported by Kahn (1989) who suggests that other forms of communication cannot allow for such effective delivery and reception of messages. The key to humor's usefulness lies in its ambiguity, allowing things to be said without defensiveness or threat, and offering the option of taking communication seriously or not or both. Various issues are acknowledged without being raised specifically and we come to understand that they can be simultaneously considered funny and not funny.

This is clear in the examples drawn from professional organizational settings such as the early seminal, now classic, study in the field—Cosier's (1960) study of hospital humor. A more recent paper of interest also explores humor in the medical domain. Locke's (1992) study examined what she called "the comedic microperformance" as a way in which professionals in a paediatric hospital were able to use comedy to influence the emotions displayed and experienced by their clients. Such performances were able to help replace negative emotions by more positive feelings in the professional relationships concerned.

By way of demonstration, she conjures up an example of what she has named "Mastery Play," the skillful use of humor to replace negatives with pleasure, ease, and confidence on the part of patients and parents (Locke, 1992, p. 23):

To illustrate, a physician is examining a little girl. As he listens to her chest with the stethoscope, she begins to get fidgety and a little cranky.

His eyes grow large and his mouth opens wide as he asks, "Is your breakfast in there?"—his right hand is making contact with her tummy. The little girl laughs. He continues, his right hand now tickling her, "I'll find your breakfast!" (the pace of his words and his hand quickens). He now pokes her bellybutton and asks, "Shall we take it out?" The little girl wriggles on the examining table—her small hands trying to intercept that of the physician—and amidst her giggles squeals, "Nooo!" (wide smiles from mom and dad). The physician continues to poke her belly, thwarting her defensive attempts, "If I take it out, will your breakfast fall out?" Still squirming—her hands shielding her bellybutton—she calls out insistently, "Yes!" By now her parents are laughing too. Here is no further contact with the abdomen.

In a matter of moments, the child's abdomen and internal organs have been palpated without her realizing it. The above example is indicative of a mastery performance because play is enacted during the physical exam of the patient. In any other setting, an observer of the proceedings would conclude that man and child were just having fun.

So laughter and medicine are now serious partners and, in recognition of this, in 1991 the first free National Health Service Laughter Clinic was actually set up in Great Britain (Holden, 1993).

In another professional setting, that of police work, Pogrebin and Poole (1988) discovered the following strategic uses for a diverse array of types of humor:

- jocular aggression attacking supervisory or management personnel provides a means through which subordinates expressed dissatisfaction with their superiors or the overall organization itself;
- audience degradation where the butt of humor is the general public, or police customers per se, allows for the sort of putdowns that serve to promote a sense of moral superiority and help maintain the dichotomy between police and policed;
- diffusion of danger/tragedy where humor allows police to deal with the uncomfortable topic of fear, to enable empathy with colleagues' feelings of fear and vulnerability, and to temper the tragic events occurring in the work situation; and
- normative neutralization relating to the bending of formal rules and procedures in order to effect "street-justice," helping reinforce the work perspectives and organizational status.

Their investigation clearly revealed how a serious message may be dramatized by its humorous presentation; and, importantly, that humor allows for the presentation of organizational concerns without directly threatening the very system that fosters them.

Decker's (1987) study of 290 workers' job satisfaction and the role of humor in rating of supervisors, revealed that subjects rating their supervisors high in sense of humor reported higher job satisfaction.

Another study (Vinton, 1989) of an American midwestern corporation, QRS Inc., demonstrated that humor shared among its employees revealed much of the organization's cultural characteristics and provided insight into other organizational issues, such as socialization. In the same period, Feigelson (1989) asserted that, unlike dysfunctional laughter at another's expense, self-deprecating humor can be useful, especially in the workplace where managers need to find ways of breaking down real or perceived barriers between themselves and their subordinates. In his analysis (pp. 154-155) based on observed humor, he developed a taxonomy of humor among employees as follows:

1. puns
2. goofing off (slapstick)
3. jokes/anecdotes
   a. humorous self-ridicule
   b. bawdy jokes (sexual or racial basis)
   c. industry jokes
4. teasing
   a. teasing to get things done
   b. bantering—the great leveller.

Vinton (1989, p. 164) found that, aside from humor helping to create a more pleasant work atmosphere, there were particular functions evident in three specific forms of humor:

- telling self-ridiculing jokes signaled to other organization members that one was willing to participate in a teasing relationship.
- teasing was used as a pleasant way of getting work done in such close quarters.
- bantering, another form of teasing, helped lessen the status differentials that existed among the employees.

He also found that humor increased organizational understanding of socialization and succession as part of the overall culture.

Such studies, and the more recent work of Barsoux (1996), demonstrate that the benefits of workplace humor are many. For example, research has so far uncovered the following advantages. Workplace humor, when used judiciously, may:

- have a liberating effect
- reduce or eliminate tension
- reduce anxiety
- make organizational confusion more bearable
- assist in breaking down prejudice
- be a coping mechanism
- facilitate relationships by breaking down interpersonal barriers
- aid persuasion
- relieve frustrations relating to perceived organizational impotence
- relieve boredom and monotony
- break a negative spiral
- be a significant source of job satisfaction
- provide an alternative information source
- suggest approachability
- aid more effective and efficient organizational communication
- improve customer service and understanding of consumer behavior
- improve problem solving and increase creative thinking
- reveal areas needing management attention
- facilitate change and assist change management through lowering resistance and tension
- promote stability during organizational change
- help employees deal with novel situations
- make for better training retention
- create rapport
- enhance trust and motivation
- help participation and responsiveness
- increase alertness physiologically
- be attention-grabbing
- aid memory
- encourage plurality of vision
- reinforce shared values at all levels
- shape and perpetuate corporate cultures
- underpin national management styles

- affect role-sending
- promote a sense of belonging
- affect group performance in facilitating group cohesiveness
- allow for reframing familiar situations, challenging the norm; and
- facilitate organizational learning and renewal.

Nevertheless, there are many potential problem areas as well, some of them being:

- distinctions between male and female responses to aggressive humor
- the insensitive dimensions of ethnic humor
- sexism in humor
- abrasive humor can be an irritant
- humor may be disguised rebellion/resistance
- humor can express hostility.

More recently, the interest in organizational culture, has spawned an exploration of humor for corporate analysis. For example, Kahn (1989) suggests that it is useful as a diagnostic tool precisely because it is through humor that organization members, consciously and unconsciously, communicate about themselves, their relationships, their groups, and their organizations—using jokes, ironies, laughter and pranks, and the like. Given that each statement contains its own truths, we can put together a rich tapestry of various truths, thus tapping into a rich source of information, understanding, and interpreting used to clarify the dynamics of individual and group life in organizations.

Other uses of humor are those in presentations, joking on the job, team building, encouraging creativity and innovation, aiding leadership, conflict management, change management, stress management as mentioned earlier, corporate documentation, and, of course, the whole arena of advertising and marketing.

Joking on the Job

Duncan and Feisal (1989) assert that humor most often assumes the form of joking in work groups. The authors argue that (p. 22) "joking is not altogether funny. On the contrary, it is serious business from a management standpoint." They found that their study of workplace humor demonstrated how joking among managers and employees affected their relationships and performance. It was vital, therefore, they concluded, that managers understand the role of joking because such knowledge improved employee cooperation and productivity.

Certainly, while it is clear that humor and work group joking behavior is situation, organization, and culture specific, there are universal dimensions to the phenomenon. For example, its occurrence is closely tied to the inherent need of most human beings to be part of a group. Other universal features may be encompassed by the following thumbnail sketch (Duncan, 1985, p. 556):

> Sometimes humour is disguised in such a way that only those familiar with the group's culture understand it. At other times the joke is obvious and easily comprehended by everyone. Sometimes the joke puts down another group member, and sometimes the humour actually makes the "victim" feel more a part of the group. Because of the pervasiveness of work group humour, we must assume a priori that it performs some social and/or task-oriented function.

Workplace joking has been explained in terms of the following:

- opposition to authority (those against superiors and those against the rules (Frisch-Gauthier, 1961);
- intra-group humor used to construct and defend group identity (Duncan, 1984);
- a means for social integration in a disintegrated world (Linstead, 1988); and
- command-level joking serving as a management tool (Cosier, 1960) creating divisions among subordinates, approximating superiors and subordinates, and masking authoritarian relations (Dwyer, 1991).

Studies on joking behavior have often focused on two key dimensions—on the functions and meanings of joking behavior in organizational life; and on the actual techniques, processes, and mechanics involved in joking behavior (Ulian, 1976). Other work has emphasized issues such as racism, ethnicity, or sexual harassment. For example, Smeltzer and Leap (1988) considered the appropriateness of joking behavior in work settings and compared how different groups rated the propriety of neutral, sexist, and racist jokes in such settings. In their study 165 subjects were asked to evaluate the appropriateness of three types of jokes in work settings. The researchers found that racist and sexist jokes were considered more inappropriate by whites and females than blacks and males; and that all joking behavior at work was considered by inexperienced employees to be less appropriate than experienced employees.

Individual and group characteristics, coupled with organizational values and culture (micro and macro) determine both how a joke will be "taken" and its ultimate effects on human organizational performance; other determinants relate to historical dimensions and demographics—the ethnic, racial, and sexual composition of organizational personnel (Duncan & Feisal, 1989). Vice-versa, finding what an individual or group considers funny, is revealing of individual and group values. Significantly, these authors also emphasize that joking occurs within friendship cliques, and relates to emergent leadership and followership preferences, and peer perceptions of the performance level of individual group members.

In their research, Duncan and Feisal (1989) focused on social network choices and joking patterns in a variety of 25 work groups. This revealed four stereotypical group members: the "arrogant executive" and the "benign bureaucrat" at the managerial level; and the "solid citizen" and "novice" in the nonmanagerial ranks. Their work also clearly demonstrated that understanding joking behavior was informative of group interaction such as friendship and leadership patterns and provided a vital lens for exploring the very structure of humor behavior more generally. Unlike some earlier theorists who suggested that management has a monopoly on joking, Duncan and Feisal (1989, pp. 28-29) found that one's role in the larger social network, rather than group status, was more predictive of one's position in the joking pattern:

> We found no evidence at all to suggest that managers should remove themselves from the joking pattern...to improve their status or gain respect. In fact, a well-placed, self-disparaging joke can sometimes help the manager by letting the group know that he or she is a real person. Being the butt of a joke is not always negative....Trust, respect, and friendship determine a group member's position in the pattern of joking behavior far more than official status does. In short, joking plays a greater role in reflecting and illustrating an individual's status than it does in determining it.

Another feature of work-related joking is that patterns of joking will be regular through time when power and work relations remain stable. Moreover, it appears that work relations, the modes by which the workers' relationships to their work are managed, are reflected in the very content of jokes (Dwyer, 1991).

Emphasizing the power dimensions of humor in organization life, Dwyer (1991, pp. 7-8) uses a triad theory of analyzing organizational humor. In terms of joking, he suggests that:

> In humour, three social actors have been located, the initiator of the joke (I), the target (T), and the audience (A). A joke is defined as successful when the audience responds to the initiator through laughter: A and I form a coalition against T....The joke can be made in one of three types of coalition: improper, conservative, or revolutionary. Such coalitions either win or they do not in the organization. A coalition is said to win when it dominates the other member of the triad.

His work demonstrates the rational calculation of the likely success of a joke being based in the perceptions of power distributions and estimated capacities to form winning organizational alliances. It is, therefore, no surprise that we may interpret alterations in joking content and form as indicators of changes in work relations and power shifts.

Importantly, as Zijderveld (1983) suggested, we can learn much about organizational communication from jokes and joking behavior. Having touched on joking behavior earlier, it is important to again look at it from the communication perspective. Given the meaning-centered approach to communication it is also clear that, in joking, people are playing with meanings. This can be done for a variety of reasons—for fun, or more complex psychological and sociological needs.

Finally, it is important to ground consideration of organizational joking within the context of the organizational culture within which joking occurs. Its efficacy also relates to historical contexts and different types of society (Palmer, 1994). Used discerningly, however, Duncan and Feisal (1989, p. 29) indicate that: "It is always wise to think of work group humour as more than idle behaviour; managers who pay attention to the employees' joking relationships can learn much about what is really happening in the workplace."

Humor in Training

While many still believe that humor and work are mutually exclusive activities, today major corporations like AT&T, Kodak, Du Pont, and IBM are using the constructive aspects of humor through having humor consultants advising on company-wide humor training and programs.

It seems, therefore, that the workplace is beginning to formally acknowledge the seriousness of humor in organizational life. Certainly this is the case in the training arena. Warnock (1989), reporting in *Lifelong Learning*, clearly espouses the view that humor used appropriately is a powerful tool. He outlines how it can help adult educators positively affect changes in people's knowledge, attitudes, skills, and aspirations, and the didactic process. This is done through the benefits of tension release, increasing creativity, elevating bonding, enhancing enjoyment, and relieving boredom.

Another study reported in *Training* (Zemke, 1991) suggests the real importance of humor in training, but sees success only resulting from adhering to the following guidelines: using a modicum of apt, relevant humor in an informative presentation; using self-disparaging humor to enhance a presenter's image; understanding that humor is only one of many factors that enhance interest; realizing that apt, relevant humor does not affect persuasiveness; and grasping that satire has rather unpredictable results.

The classic of humor in training videos is the work of the English comic actor, John Cleese, who has for many years starred in humorous videotapes aimed at making training an enjoyable, unstressful experience. These, according to James Ross (personal communication, May 21, 1993) of First Training, are still highly successful, particularly with staff to supervisory levels. They are essentially based on using negative humorous antics to reinforce lessons about appropriate behavior in organizational life. He emphasizes the benefits of humor in training films for breaking down inhibitions.

So humor has become a saleable commodity in a novel way in recent years. As one writer puts it:

> Humour, it seems, now is being taken more seriously in business. And for good reason, say a new breed of "humour consultants." Their message to business: Lighten up. Take your job seriously but don't take yourself so

seriously that you can't laugh at yourself. All the changes and uncertainties in companies today are creating enormous stress, and one of the best ways to relieve that, to remain healthy, is through humour. Laughter is being hailed as medicine that can help cure a corporation as well as an individual (Braham, 1988, pp. 51-52).

Such consultants are not necessarily joke tellers or stereotypical stand-up comedians. Their motive is to provide us with alternative perspectives on organizational reality, to replace rigidity with flexibility, and currently, on providing ways of dealing with the complexities and stresses of daily life. C.W. Metcalf, for example, as a corporate comedian with an international program (workshops, audio, and videotapes), focuses on humor as a coping mechanism, helping individuals enhance their mental and physical health; to survive and thrive in our current stressful environment; to improve morale, team-building, and communication; and to enhance creativity and change management. Corporate comedian, Rodney Marks (personal communication, December 4, 1996) believes his art enables organization personnel to better reflect on their entrenched mind-sets, often traditional and outdated attitudes to organizational life in the 1990s and beyond, and to confront the need to change such mind-sets in a less threatening environment. He sees the purpose of his work as "making people more aware of what they were doing, including revealing how they were acting themselves."

As has been suggested earlier, humor, when used appropriately, can maximize learning and creativity. In the learning process, by reducing tension and capturing attention it can increase retention and develop mental flexibility in training sessions (Goodman, 1991). The use of humor in educational media focuses on its chief advantage of gaining and maintaining audience attention.

Problems here again relate to some of the key variables—those of culture, ethnicity, age, sex, role, status, and the like that affect both the creation and reception of humor in terms of form, substance, and functions. However, further difficulties do emerge. While humor seems successful in attracting and sustaining organizational audiences, it is not so clear that the educational message is easily acquired—debates in the education and media fields have not proved conclusive. We need also to be mindful of some of the cross-cultural insensitivity occurring in training video humor. Humor is, after all, an essentially social phenomenon.

Consequently, we need to deal with the issue that, while there are many similarities in terms of universal dimensions of humor, there are, indeed, cross-cultural differences as well. This is true of institutionalized and patterned humor in particular (Apte, 1985). Such concerns are supported by the work of Hofstede (1991) on cultural differences and identities.

We need, then, to understand the universal and the peculiar in our own national brand of humor and what our own people actually require in terms of humor in training. There is uniqueness of national humor and that provides grist for the mill of workplace educators, researchers, and all those involved with creating and using educational technology software and hardware. We must comprehend this tool, however, with both eyes open. Understanding humor in the workplace means adopting a perspective that acknowledges both the playfulness and profundity of workplace humor.

So it is, indeed, opportune to heed the plea of Barsoux (1991, p. 68) to recognize that "humour is the sharpest arrow in the manager's quiver." It is about time that management writers recognize that fact, and start to acknowledge the scope for humor in management. Kahn (1989, p. 69) is optimistic about the future of exploring the humor dimension in organizational life, suggesting that:

> Organizations are often very funny places. They contain their share of the ironic, the perverse, and the ludicrous. I suggest that we can supplement our sober understanding of serious issues in organizations by attending to such humour, or more precisely, by listening for the various messages humour can deliver if we are attuned to its wavelengths. This argument assumes that humour contains various truths about people and their relationships, groups and organizations. It does not, however, assume that humour consists only of those truths. Humour is also simply playful.

These dimensions of humor play a significant, fundamental role in responding to the need for creating and adapting changing mindsets in the closing years of our decade and into the next. They help us cope and manage in a changing environment, prepare us for the learning required, and make it more possible to bear our existential human burdens—organizational and otherwise.

Chapter V

Managing Knowledge

Where is the wisdom we have lost in knowledge? Where is the knowledge we have lost in information? (Eliot, 1965, p. 147).

What has the accountants' mental knickers in a twist is the difficulty of measuring and managing the chief ingredient of the new economy: intellectual capital, the intangible assets of skill, knowledge, and information (Stewart, 1994, p. 68).

To be truly effective, knowledge management must be accompanied by organizational change (Marshall, Prusak, & Spilberg, 1996, p. 99).

THE INTELLIGENT ORGANIZATION

The pressure for transforming traditional organizational paradigms and reinventing organizations into the twenty-first century, necessitates better management and leveraging of an organization's intellectual capital:

...the management of knowledge goes far beyond the storage and manipulation of data, or even of information. It is the attempt to recognize what is essentially a human asset buried in the minds of individuals, and leverage it into an organizational asset that can be accessed and used by a broader set of individuals on whose decisions the firm depends (Marshall, Prusak, & Spilberg, 1996, p. 79).

Organizational knowledge consists of objective assets such as documents, contracts, databases, and the like, and the more subjective ones relating to skills or competencies, culture, and so on. It is the latter type that is the most complex and difficult to manage and requires a real understanding of the human side of knowledge management. In a globally dispersed and increasingly fragmented workplace environment, where the only certainty is uncertainty and chaos, management today is gradually recognizing organizational knowledge as a key asset, and the leverage of such knowledge as one of the few sustainable tools for competitive advantage in the global knowledge economy.

The ability to manage human intellect and its conversion into useful "product" is, perhaps, the most critical management skill in our age, providing the ultimate in competitive edge. Unfortunately, in most organizations managing intellectual capital is still unexplored territory. Moreover, knowledge bases and how an organization acquires, articulates, and enhances the knowledge that it controls actually define an organization's uniqueness (Dodgson, 1993). Such recognition is the first step on the rocky path of knowledge management.

Why such a rocky path? Underlying the growing enthusiasm for knowledge management are an array of difficulties. For example:

- Knowledge is, per se, an abstract concept that is difficult for a results-oriented concrete approach to management and might be easily dismissed as unrealistic academic theorizing.
- Management, used to working with tangible assets, confronts knowledge as an invisible, soft, diffuse, slippery, intangible asset—one not only hard to find but difficult to retain.
- Currently it is difficult to actually measure, grade, count, or even cost-justify the value of knowledge.
- Debate continues on where to acquire knowledge and when one gets it, where the supposed high value of knowledge resides; who in the organization should be charged with its responsibility; and how it might be budgeted, valued, or depreciated.
- Few organizations have appropriate cultures for valuing the creation and sharing of knowledge (Clippinger, 1995, p. 46).

In short, the rocky path generally entails deep and wrenching rethinking of the very basis of organization, organizing, and managing. It will require abandonment of many traditional assumptions, organizational structures, and management processes—changing the very patterns of thought. It necessitates understanding not only intellectual resources or capital but also emotional ones.

That it is a path we must tread is clear. Two examples suffice. The crises of Barings, Kidder Peabody, and Metallgesellschaft demonstrate, alongside problems of culture and control, the clear mismanagement of organizational knowledge (Marshall, Prusak, & Spilberg, 1996). By contrast, Japanese management continues to set the standard for the successful intelligent organization into the twenty-first century—appreciating and managing interrelationships and skillfully managing and mobilizing knowledge (Senge, 1993).

Such an intelligent organization today tends to be linked to best-in-world intellectual capabilities through the most efficient means possible, focusing on understanding, maintaining and developing core competency strategies, and outsourcing the rest (Quinn, Anderson, & Finkelstein, 1996). Its intellectual capital involves three elements (Saint-Onge, 1996, p. 10):

- human capital—the capabilities of the individuals required to provide solutions to customers;
- customer capital—the depth (penetration), width (coverage), attachment (loyalty), and profitability of customers; and
- structural capital—the capabilities of the organization to meet market needs.

Tiemessen, Lane, Crossan, & Inkpen (1996, p. 4) posit knowledge management as "the *consciously embedded* structures, systems and interactions designed to permit the management of the firm's pool of knowledge and skills." The concept of knowledge management, however, seems to include a wider variety of perspectives—knowledge creation, knowledge capture, knowledge usage and dissemination, and knowledge measurement. Even current practice of such management suggests different emphases. For example, Hughes Corporation wants a knowledge highway to avoid reinventing the wheel; BP in order to have the right source of expertise to quickly deal with problems in its globalized business; and Bechtel to make full use of project team knowledge (Marshall, Prusak, & Spilberg, 1996).

Understanding organizational knowledge, learning, and intelligence, and managing them, is always complex and problematic. The current burgeoning literature in the field does not always accept this with its often simplistic notions relating to managerial control and productivity. Yet there are some central notions that, while acknowledging difficulties in the field, nevertheless, offer some useful guidance to the minefield.

ORGANIZATIONAL KNOWLEDGE

Organizational learning and unlearning, as discussed in chapter IV, are a basis for organizational knowledge. Yet learning is just one aspect alongside others such as access to knowledge; the transfer and housing of expressed knowledge through technical and nontechnical means; and gathering and transforming critical information about customers, competitors, and the like. Indeed, learning is but one dimension in the creation of organizational knowledge (Hiebeler, 1996; Nonaka, 1994). So more is required in terms of value added— the organization must become intelligent and based on strategic knowledge management (Edvinsson cited in EIU/IBM, 1996).

Some perceive of knowledge as a useful, actionable, and meaningful resource retained by an organization despite individuals' comings and goings (Arthur Andersen cited in Hiebeler, 1996). Others understand real knowledge, as consisting of mostly deep and strategic insights, moving beyond being mere data or information (Kurtzman, 1996). Moreover, we need to differentiate among key concepts employed: data as the basis for information; information as the meaningful patterns arranged out of data; and knowledge, as the application and productive use of information, enabling and being enabled by learning (Davis & Botkin, 1994).

In today's organization relevant capability differentials, based on intangible resources, provide for sustainable competitive advantage in knowledge management. Such resources may be broken down into assets—items such as intellectual property rights, trade secrets, contracts, databases, and reputation; and then the more subjective resources relating to skills or competencies or know-how (employees, suppliers, advisers, etc.) and, collectively, the organization's culture (Hall, 1992). The latter include the many methodologies that, for example, mark out earlier attempts at knowledge management by major consulting companies.

Badaracco (1991) argues that the changing shape of contemporary organizations is grounded in the globalization of knowledge which he summarizes in the following four propositions:

- the large, potentially commercializable knowledge pool in the world is expanding rapidly;
- this pool of knowledge has contributions from a growing number of countries, organizations, and universities;

- part of this knowledge is migratory in that it moves quickly and easily, encapsulated in formulas, designs, manuals, books, or machinery; and
- some of this knowledge is embedded and moves slowly because it resides in intangibles, in complex social relationships.

Different Types of Knowledge

Knowledge at the organizational level can be manipulated in several different ways: internal operations or R&D groups can generate knowledge; sources inside or external to the organization can access it as required; it can be formally transferred before being used, through training, or, informally, via on-the-job socialization; a variety of forms such as reports and graphs can represent knowledge in forms that provide easier access; and it can be embedded in processes, systems, and control after its validity is tested. The steady development of a culture, grounded in incentives and appropriate leadership that values, shares, and uses knowledge, facilitates these varied knowledge processes (Marshall, Prusak, & Spilberg, 1996).

Leif Edvinsson, Director of Intellectual Capital at Skandia, a Scandinavia-based insurance firm, focuses on organizational intellect, explaining that:

- intellectual assets are the richest for the organization;
- financial results are determined by intellectual capital; and
- two kinds of intellectual capital exist—the human as the source of innovation and renewal; and the structural as the basis for exploitation (e.g., information systems, knowledge of market channels and customer relationships, and management focus), for turning individual know-how into collective property (cited in Stewart, 1994).

The concept of intellectual capital or the intelligent organization is also important for others. For example, Brooking (1996) spends time defining intellectual capital as the organization's intangible assets that enable it to function and splits such capital into four categories. The first two are the same as Edvinsson—human-centered assets and infrastructure assets; to this she adds market assets and intellectual property assets. Such capital, she argues, is increasingly important as organizations become more and more dependent on intangible assets.

Arthur, Claman, and DeFillipp (1995, p. 9), in considering how the intelligent enterprise affects individuals' careers, argue that "each arena of firm competency mirrors a distinct arena of personal competency, and a different form of knowledge...and intelligent careers reflect the application of these forms of knowing." They distinguish three different types of knowledge:

- "Knowing why," which is competency related to motivation and identification with the organization's culture;
- "Knowing how" concerns the skills and knowledge individuals bring into an organization's total know-how; and
- "Knowing whom" is competency relating to the individual's set of interpersonal relationships that can enhance the organization's networking activities.

Another useful categorization of knowledge types emerges from the literature on organizational learning (Collins as outlined in Blackler, 1995):

- embrained—knowledge located in brains that depends on conceptual skills and cognitive abilities as in knowledge of;
- embodied—knowledge located in bodies that is action oriented and probably only partly explicit as in knowledge how;
- encultured—knowledge located in dialogue and acquired through achieving shared understandings;
- embedded—knowledge residing in systemic routines; and
- encoded—knowledge as information provided through signs and symbols.

This results in four different knowledge-based organizations:

- the knowledge-routinized organization where knowledge embedded in technologies, rules, and procedures is emphasized;
- the expert-dependent organization where the embodied competencies of key members is emphasized;
- the communication-intensive organization where encultured knowledge and collective understanding is emphasized; and
- the symbolic-analyst-dependent organization where the embrained skills of key members is emphasized (Blackler, 1995).

Perhaps the best known outline of knowledge types emerges from the work of Polanyi (1958, 1966) and Nonaka (1991, 1994):

- explicit knowledge—knowledge that is more easily shared, methodical, and formal; articulated, formal, systematic, easily shared, and communicable (e.g., in product specs, formulae, computer programs, reports);
- tacit knowledge—knowledge we have but cannot express easily; unarticulated, highly personal, difficult to formalize, hard to communicate to others; including both a "know-how" component that is an informal difficult-to-pin-down skills basis and a cognitive aspect comprising mental models, beliefs, and perspectives deeply ingrained, taken for granted, and hard to articulate (e.g., intuition, perspectives, beliefs, and values based in experience and determining mind-sets and behavioral patterns).

Nonaka looks at the ways that learning occurs, based on the ways in which tacit and explicit knowledge interact:

- tacit to tacit where personal knowledge is passed from one individual to another, as in an apprenticeship or mentoring relationship, but where knowledge is not made explicit and available to the entire organization (not easily leveraged by the organization as an entirety);
- explicit to explicit where existing explicit knowledge is combined and synthesized but is limited to what is already available (not really extending the organization's knowledge base);
- tacit to explicit where existing knowledge is melded with an individual's tacit knowledge to create new knowledge that may be shared by the organization as a whole (a powerful process allowing for benefit to the entire organization); and
- explicit to tacit where new explicit knowledge creates new tacit knowledge through internalization by organizational members (internalized explicit knowledge benefiting individuals and organizations).

So, for him, the process of knowledge creation, especially as it affects organizational innovation, is critical. Here the central core is making personal knowledge available to others—the way in which individuals create knowledge out of a dialogue between their tacit and explicit knowledge, individually and in relationships. This results in reinvention of individuals, the organization, and perhaps even broader systems.

The key for converting tacit knowledge into explicit knowledge, he argues, lies in using figurative language and symbolism to articulate intuitions and insights—the use of metaphors to link contradictory things and ideas; analogy to resolve such contradictions; and modeling to crystalize the created concepts and embody them in a way that makes the knowledge available to the rest of the organization.

Of course, for many organizations the problem is not the creation of organizational knowledge but rather how to capture and share that knowledge already existing within the organization but that is held within an individual's mind, a department, a division, or the like (Hiebeler, 1996).

Knowledge Workers

People as organizational human resources both accumulate and create invisible assets of knowledge. Knowledge workers today are the owners of a knowledge-based or knowledge intensive means of production (Drucker, 1993). As such, they have to be attracted, motivated, rewarded, renewed, and must be served by management who provides the appropriate structure and environment in which their benefits may be reaped (Marquardt & Reynolds, 1994).

Especially challenging is the capacity to manage an organization's professional intellect as a maintainable commodity through support and leverage. This is an intellect based on knowledge in disciplines that requires continuous updating and which operates on four levels, moving from the least to the most important:

- Cognitive knowledge represents the basic mastery of a professional discipline, the know-what;
- Advanced skills are turning discipline knowledge into effective execution, the know-how;
- Systems understanding emerges as the knowledge of a discipline's underlying cause-and-effect relationships, the know-why; and

- Self-motivated creativity as composed of will, motivation, and adaptability for success, the care-why.

While intellect resides in the brains of professionals, the organization's systems, databases, or operating technologies, can also house the first three levels. The most valuable intellect at the fourth level is often found in its culture (Quinn, 1993; Quinn, Anderson, & Finkelstein, 1996).

Nonaka (1991), however, stresses that in the knowledge-creating company, rather than considering invention of new knowledge as a specialized activity, it should be at the core of an organization's human resources strategy. All personnel should be perceived as knowledge workers and knowledge creation regarded as a way of behaving and a way of being. Moreover, knowledge work should not be a separate category but part of changing the organization of work in the direction of knowledge intensification (Knights, Murray, & Willmott, 1993).

CONTEXTS FOR KNOWLEDGE MANAGEMENT

While many conceive of organizations in hard, tangible terms of structures, machines, and the like, knowledge management is embedded in much more fluid, intangible domains—the social, political, and symbolic processes of shared meaning and relationships shaping actions, events, and internal and external organizational environments (Brown, 1995).

Knowledge and Structure

It comes as little surprise that organizational structure is basic for effective knowledge management. Yet this is easier said than done, given that "knowledge is reshaping firms' boundaries, altering the work of managers, and undermining many of our familiar, deeply rooted ways of thinking about companies" (Badaracco, 1991, p. xii).

Traditionally structure is about formal arrangements accommodating organization and environmental needs, and the delineation of formal roles and relationships depicting desirable patterns of activities, expectations, and exchanges among management, employees, customers, and other important stakeholders (1997).

Many have suggested that it is bureaucracy and rigid hierarchies, lumbering elephants in terms of size and agility that are to blame for ineffectual knowledge management. The result has been restructuring of some sort, in an attempt to increase flexibility and responsiveness to environmental changes.

Furthermore, part of the drive behind many organizations downsizing and reengineering or restructuring during the 1980s and 1990s, was the view that middle managers were merely paper pushers and could, therefore, be largely eliminated through flattening traditional organizational hierarchies. However, in hindsight, many are recognizing that such management actually played a vital role in the transfer, access, and generation of knowledge. Besides, while new knowledge mechanisms are now being devised and instituted, much knowledge itself has, thereby, been lost and new processes do not spring up in the same natural way as did their predecessors (Marshall, Prusak, & Spilberg, 1996).

In a larger sense, the memory evident in structures, including in networks, can also be lost through, for example, restructuring, downsizing, outsourcing, transferring key personnel, overreliance on contract staff, or inappropriate information systems not geared to nonroutine learning. This is a major problem insofar as, for organizational learning and effective knowledge management, individual learning must become embedded in organizational memory (Field & Ford, 1995).

The issue of structure and control is also a vexing one, given the revolution in human relationships required for effective knowledge management. Traditional structures and boundaries, with mechanisms in place for a high degree of control, have given way to more pliable structures and an emphasis on creativity, innovation, and learning. Concomitantly, as discussed in chapter I, there is growing rhetoric about, if not effort, toward more self-monitoring and empowerment, in influencing rather than directly controlling people.

Today, however, as we saw in chapter III, there is a concern to move to the concept of organizational architecture—meeting the organization's needs and desires through shaping behavioral space in terms of:

- purpose—learning and managing knowledge in a global environment;

- structural materials—sophisticated information and communications technology is the structural backbone for the organization, allowing for different ways of organizing and managing work, and facilitating collaboration, teamwork, learning, and knowledge management;
- style—traditional hierarchy is losing out to more decentralized organizations with more autonomous and responsible self-managed teams and a major focus on customers and suppliers; and
- collateral technologies—new approaches to selecting, training, assessing, and rewarding people (Nadler, Gerstein, Shaw, & Associates, 1992).

For a global learning organization a diverse array of architectures is required, including:

- a social architecture that supports integrated relationships and fosters teams, self-management, empowerment, and sharing;
- a knowledge architecture that provides for storing shared knowledge and collective intelligence and easy access by any one, at any time, from any place; and
- a technological architecture that contributes the environment for integrated technological networks and information tools in order for all to have access to and exchange of information and learning (Por cited in Marquardt & Reynolds, 1994, p. 43).

A hypertext approach of three layers, involving both hierarchy and nonhierarchy, may also be considered:

- a knowledge base one relating to culture and procedures;
- a business system one relating to the operations of normal routine kinds involving hierarchy and bureaucracy; and
- the project system layer where many self-organizing teams create knowledge (Nonaka, 1994).

The other key aspect of knowledge management is effective use of computing and telecommunications technologies. Moreover, given that new technologies affect all knowledge types and processes in the organization, they provide the appropriate medium for organizing itself (Blackler, 1995). They offer assistance through intranets, networks, groupware, teleconferencing, and the like. Yet, in as much as new knowledge creates new technology, so too does new technology create new knowledge (Badaracco, 1991). Unfortunately, many organizations are still not very good at ensuring efficient, productive use of knowledge-sharing technologies (Hiebeler, 1996).

Knowledge and Culture

The production of knowledge is, however, no easy matter. As Badaracco (1991, p. 18) explains: "Knowledge is a social product, the result of interactions among people, and is not stamped out by presses or put together on assembly lines."

New organizational structures, controls, and knowledge tools are invaluable in assisting the process of knowledge creation and management but an effective organizational culture provides motivation beyond knowledge and skills (Marshall, Prusak, & Spilberg, 1996). Indeed, Lundberg and Brownell (1993) argue that the symbolic/cultural perspective, founded in communication as the sense-making process by which individuals make organizational life meaningful, is what best explains how organizational members can share certain views of the world and align their activities. Argyris and Schon (1996) also point to the critical nexus of organizational learning and culture, with culture being simultaneously the consequence of an organization's prior experience and learning and its basis for a continuing capacity to learn. They argue that we have spent too little time on understanding the deeper aspects of this dimension of knowledge management and too much on individual and group learning.

Culture—the chemistry of the organization, its invisible structure determining values, norms, rules, and the common perspective (Itami & Roehl, 1987)—is one way of storing up an organization's memories, in both verbal and nonverbal formats that range from language and structure, to documents, myths, stories, rituals, symbols, systems, routines, know-how, procedures, and the like. It is culture in which an organization's tacit knowledge is embedded, providing entry points through which information can be transmitted and processed into knowledge (Saint-Onge, 1996).

While the basic learning unit may be the individual, learning occurs within the social context, the community, of the formal organization. This is particularly so in terms of group learning, where the combination of individual knowledge and beliefs form into shared cognitive structures and coordinated action (Crossan, Tiemessen, Lane, & White, 1995). These processes both affect and are affected by the organization's cultural ambience, providing the framework for individual and collective knowledge development and management.

Schein (1996), mindful of the growing evidence of learning being a social process occurring in a community of practice, outlines three critical types of organizational communities or subcultures that must be considered in order to better manage learning and organizational knowledge as a whole:

- The operator culture, the "line"—the subculture developed around subsystems delivering the products or services arising from the organization's primary task or mission; it is oriented toward making the systems work and recognizing people as the organization's best asset; here operators can defeat or subvert management through use of their teamwork skills.
- The engineering culture, the technocrats and designers—the subculture developed around those responsible for designing the processes required for delivery of an organization's products and services and for its own maintenance; such groups tend to have an allegiance to the professional groups outside the organization in which they are employed; this culture is oriented toward the technical elegance of design, and abstract, efficient, and simple solutions; people are considered to be noise and the most common source of errors.
- The CEO culture—the subculture developed around CEOs focused on financial viability and their own accountability; such a powerful global community focuses on financial control, growth, and organizational survival; it regards people as a cost to be minimized and uses impersonal management through systems and routines; it tends to side with the engineering rather than operator culture.

The critical task for knowledge management is to better comprehend the valid assumptions of each of these cultures, and to get each subculture to better understand themselves and the others. Each subsystem or community, and each individual within these, must do so in order that the organization as a whole has a real chance to learn, change, and be transformed as appropriate.

Culture, as a social product, is created and maintained by organizational communication, even more so than national or other cultural domains within which such culture is embedded. Its symbolic base provides meaning for its inhabitants, legitimates certain types of activities, and can justify particular patterns of social relations (Phillips & Brown, 1993). Communication's role is central also. Lively internal communication, collective dialogue related to collaboration, which underpins learning as socially constructed understanding and empowers collective wisdom, is critical to all organizations (Blackler, 1995).

Communication and culture are also inextricably linked in the vital process of merging individual and collective learning (Dodgson, 1993). Sharing dialogue, creating new perspectives, allowing for conflict and discussion in order for individuals to question existing knowledge premises and so generate new knowledge, allows for the conversion of individual tacit knowledge into collective explicit knowledge—an inherently social process (Marshall, Prusak, & Spilberg, 1996).

Ideally, such communication occurs in what has become known as "the learning culture," one in which the development of individuals and the transformation of the organization is encouraged. This is achieved by fostering a questioning spirit, experimentation, differences, openness, and tolerating disequilibrium. Here the processes and structures combine to inform shared mental models of how the organization might best function within its environment (Coopey, 1995).

What is required, then, is to move from a culture of competition versus cooperation. It is almost a truism that in order to facilitate organizational knowledge the value of cooperation is critical. Individual ambition and achievement are commendable in their own right, but few today possess the depth and breadth of knowledge to act individually or, if they do, can sustain this for any real period of time (due to individuals exiting or industries changing, for example) (Marshall, Prusak, & Spilberg, 1996).

While, however, many may mouth platitudes of cooperation, in reality they continue to see cooperation as wimpish and competition as the real driving force, both at the individual and organizational levels. A climate of competition, unfortunately, leads to the hoarding of information or filtering of accuracy of information, and individual and interdepartmental rivalry. This is accelerated where job insecurity leads to a fear of sharing knowledge because this may jeopardize individual jobs and careers (Field & Ford, 1995).

A further problem arena in the organization's culture is the reward system, a visible reminder of what the organization believes in practice. Knowledge management is likely to fail if the sharing of knowledge is not a real basis for advancement and effectiveness in organizations. In addition, whatever the level, in a learning organization, what individuals know ought to take second place to what they can learn, and simplistic answers should always be regarded as less important than penetrating questions (Kofman & Senge, 1993).

The other vital component of cultural difficulties relates to the question of leadership. For example, if senior executives do not really commit to sharing or developing organizational knowledge, or if there are inadequate numbers of role models exhibiting the desired behaviors, successful knowledge management is impossible (Hiebeler, 1996). Appropriate leadership for knowledge management is undercut through, for instance:

- management being incapable of collaborating for knowledge management because of their interpersonal incompetence and rigid mind-sets (Saint-Onge, 1996);
- leaders limiting tasks according to the current resource base, thus retarding future development by not stretching an organizations invisible assets (Itami & Roehl, 1987);
- communication problems at all levels being ignored; or
- assuming uniformity in learning capabilities within an organization and, therefore, failing to provide adequate coordinating mechanisms for learning and knowledge management overall (Dodgson, 1993).

One other key concern in knowledge management is with professional culture. One of the problems in many organizations is that experts and professionals tend to have an allegiance to their own disciplines, their own professional cultures before that to their colleagues and organization. It is their peers and extra-organizational associations that play a role in ongoing knowledge enhancement and help in shaping their cultures and codes of conduct primarily. These, accordingly, can have a major impact in sustaining professional subcultures within organizations and influencing the direction, processes, and shaping of organizational knowledge (Bloor & Dawson, 1994). Another complexity in knowledge management of the professional, as Argyris (1991) points out, is that those not used to failure find it very difficult to learn how to learn from failure.

Knowledge and Power

While culture provides the pivotal basis for knowledge management, unfortunately, not all in the organization participate equally in its creation and maintenance. Here we find the links between culture, power, and knowledge management—carefully managing communication and cultural production, as a way of legitimizing the position of powerful individuals and groups. The management of the organization's social fabric, by such people, produces taken-for-granted social categories and practices and causes particular social arrangements to be experienced as natural and unavoidable. This type of covert social control thus becomes a central aspect of organizational power relations and removes the need for exercising more direct, overt control (Phillips & Brown, 1993).

This is hardly surprising given the central nature of information as a contemporary organization resource and consequent source of power (Pfeffer, 1992). Technological expertise in current organizations also involves power issues. So, looking at the changing systems of knowing, that is, looking not only at content but also at the processes of knowing, alerts us to the fact that knowing is contested, is a political activity involved with conflict and power (Blackler, 1995). At the macro level the focus is on sources and bases of power; at the micro on bargaining techniques and political tactics. For a more comprehensive understanding of power in organizations, macro and micro perspectives need integration (Brass & Burkhardt, 1993).

Consequently, to effectively manage organizational knowledge, the political dimensions must be considered. In practice this is often ignored. For example one consultant (cited in Hiebeler, 1996) states that 80 percent of the biggest spenders on information technology are really not politically prepared for knowledge-sharing technologies.

Even current literature often omits discussion of a power and political perspective on knowledge management. Coopey (1995) claims that the literature touches on differences of interest, value, and the like, but fails to examine the most suitable form of government for a learning organization, the legitimization of political processes within the learning organization as facilitating learning arising from difference, challenge, and conflict.

Some do briefly and grudgingly admit the existence of power and politics but fail to deal with it effectively. In the general view of the learning organization, for instance, conflict is often viewed as constructive rather than destructive, collaboration in teams is critical, and control is not considered in political terms. For example, Field and Ford (1995) urge the value of differences and toleration of conflict. Senge (1993), on the other hand, downright rejects the reality of organizational politics as other than totally dysfunctional and to be obliterated. Such a view is unrealistic as the political dimension of organizational life is an ever present one, particularly during times of change. It is a vital context for knowledge management.

Changing traditional cultures to learning ones, oriented toward intellectual capital and knowledge management, as discussed above, unfortunately often includes altering the distribution of power and of rewards. This is likely to increase political action given perceived threats to power bases and make political skills at a premium (Moss Kanter, 1989). Even before any effort to change cultures, it is clear that, whether formal or informal, the very structure of an organization is itself political in helping or hindering the ability of individuals and groups to influence decision making (Ryan, 1995). Moreover, Coopey (1995, pp. 201-202) suggests that:

> ...the "learning organization," like the notion of "organizational culture"...might well be destined to be transformed from a root metaphor within the organizational learning literature—helping to explain the nature of organizational activities and performance—into a prescription to help managers retain control under dramatically changed external circumstances.

This is likely, he argues, because the changed structure of learning organizations, while having fewer managerial levels and positions, will likely still maintain for such positions better access to important information, capacity to accumulate more organizational knowledge, formal authority, personal influence, and the like to give them a stronger power base than their colleagues. These and others at different organization levels may also refuse to allow their tacit knowledge to be translated into explicit knowledge for the collective, in order to protect themselves (Senge, 1990).

Such views are upheld by a recent EIU/IBM report (1996) where survey respondents emphasized problems relating to access to supposedly privileged information and difficulties with organizational politics. That the political role of organizational memory can be easily abused is also clear (Walsh & Ungson, 1991, p. 77):

> ...individuals and groups can manage information to acquire power; once in power, they can selectively retain and retrieve information to consolidate it. By actively managing what information is acquired, retained, and retrieved, people in power can maintain, if not enhance, their standing in ways that correspond to their beliefs and ideology. Moreover...retrieved information can be distorted and manipulated to serve self-aggrandizing ends.

KNOWLEDGE MANAGEMENT IN ORGANIZATIONAL RELATIONSHIPS

Organizational knowledge resides not only in individual organizations but also derives from their relationships with other organizations at the interorganizational level, through association with customers, suppliers, and a whole range of critical stakeholders. Such alliances, as discussed in chapter III, therefore, are a crucial dimension to knowledge management (Badaracco, 1991, pp. 10 and 12):

> Knowledge links are defined by the learning and creation of knowledge. Many of these alliances reflect the special character of embedded knowledge: it is sticky—it moves only slowly and awkwardly among organizations. For one organization to acquire knowledge embedded in the routines of another, it must form a complex, intimate relationship with it. The knowledge cannot be put in a formula or a book and then exchanged for cash.

Much of what has previously existed as informal organizational interaction is now increasingly being formalized in a variety of strategic alliances and modes of outsourcing. Such relationships are a foundation for the development of organizational know-how and competence, the place where existing knowledge can be confronted with that of other parties, leading to the creation of new knowledge (Hakansson & Snehota, 1995).

Tiemessen, Lane, Crossan, and Inkpen (1996) outline the differences between two dimensions of knowledge particularly important in the interorganizational context. First, the application of knowledge—firm-specific knowledge, market-specific knowledge, partnering knowledge, plus resource integration knowledge; second, the prominence of knowledge—explicit (more prominent) and tacit (less prominent knowledge). Moreover, organizational boundaries containing such dimensions will continue to blur as the knowledge revolution gathers pace. Knowledge intensive competition is an effect of and is caused by alliances, with collaboration helping organizations learn from each other and accelerating the movement of knowledge on a global scale. Alliances as knowledge links thus serve to enhance organizational learning and the joint creation of new knowledge and capabilities.

While there are a variety of reasons for alliance formation, Badaracco (1991) argues a central one is that of capitalizing on knowledge that can range from simple product links to the more intangible knowledge links. For him, it is only by enhancing an organization's unique advantages or core capabilities that long-term success can be achieved. Such capabilities exist in an organization's repository of embedded knowledge, personified in particular individual and group relationships, attitudes, norms, and communication patterns distinctive to each institution. Knowledge links among organizations, wrought by the revolutionary globalization of knowledge, are vital because it is difficult to replicate embedded knowledge. Such knowledge alliances, however, provide for learning specialized capabilities from each other, for combining such capabilities in order to shape new embedded knowledge, and help grow each organization in a way that is beneficial to both.

He describes the characteristics of knowledge links as:

- having a central objective of learning and creating knowledge;
- sharing more intimacy (through personnel working closely together) than product links;
- being able to be formed with a very wide range of partners; and
- having greater strategic potential than product links in extending or renewing core capabilities or creating new ones.

Some interorganizational knowledge, he suggests, can migrate quickly but in order to do so:

- knowledge must be packaged (e.g., contained in a formula, manual, design, in a piece of machinery) and clearly articulated;
- such a package requires an individual or group capable of opening it and grasping the contained knowledge;
- sufficient incentives must exist for the individual or the group to do so; and
- no barriers must exist to stop them.

This is contrasted, in the discussion, with some knowledge that is embedded rather than migratory, moving slowly even if it is of high commercial value. This embedded knowledge exists basically in specialized relationships among individuals and groups and in those special norms, attitudes, information flows, and methods of decision making that shape their dealings with each other. Yet it is such knowledge, strategically crucial, that is accessible through alliances based on knowledge links, providing opportunities for those involved to learn and create such knowledge from and with each other. Such embedded or tacit knowledge resides in partnerships, in relationships at interpersonal, group, department, organization-wide levels, whole industries (e.g., multimedia), and geographic regions (e.g., Silicon Valley).

Key problems outlined are the still predominantly competitive rather than cooperative mind-set about organizational relationships in a global environment; and that few organizations are able to create an environment within which embedded or tacit knowledge can be shared with another. They lack the competencies and trust necessary to enable personnel to have the requisite direct, intimate, and extensive exposure to the social relationships across organizations involved in relationships. Trusting staff, equipment, ideas, and, perhaps, even cultural traits to flow across organizational boundaries, is often just too tall an order.

Furthermore, the management of interorganizational relationships, including those for knowledge management purposes, is often not well done and even the literature acknowledges the general lack in collaboration management skills (for example, Moss Kanter, 1989; Gomes-Casseres, 1994). Moreover, very little research has occurred that explores how collaborative learning occurs or how the competencies required develop (Tiemessen, Lane, Crossan, & Inkpen, 1996).

There are, additionally, dangers in knowledge collaboration (Badaracco, 1991; Tiemessen, Lane, Crossan, & Inkpen, 1996). One critical problem is that of asymmetrical learning where one partner learns more than the other(s). Another is that, with the genuinely open communication required in such relationships, vulnerability increases, with today's ally easily becoming tomorrow's enemy and exploiting what was learned from the past relationship.

A multiple array of other barriers to interorganizational knowledge collaboration also exist, often mirroring those discussed earlier as residing within organizations per se. These include intercultural difficulties, the influence of parent organizations, and legal and government frameworks.

SOME POSSIBLE ANSWERS

The problem areas we have covered above are complex indeed and there are certainly no simplistic answers to many of the issues raised. There are, however, some guidelines emerging from the literature and research work in the area that may assist. For example, we can make intellectual asset management an explicit task by following a process (Petrash cited in Stewart, 1994):

1. define the role that knowledge plays in your organization;
2. assess the knowledge and strategic assets of your competitors;
3. classify your portfolio by detailing what you have, what you use, and where it belongs;
4. evaluate the worth of your assets, their cost, how to maximize their value, and whether you should keep, sell, or abandon them;
5. invest in plugging the knowledge gaps or exploiting knowledge bases for competitive advantage through R&D or alternatives; and
6. assemble the new knowledge portfolio and continue the process indefinitely.

Others stress the importance of ensuring, through knowledge management, that (Marshall, Prusak, & Spilberg, 1996, p. 100):

- the firm understands what knowledge it has and seeks out the knowledge it needs;

- organizational knowledge is transferred to those who need it in their daily work;
- organizational knowledge is accessible to those who may need it as events warrant;
- new knowledge is rapidly generated and made accessible throughout the organization;
- controls are developed to embed the most reliable and robust knowledge;
- organizational knowledge is tested and validated periodically; and
- the firm facilitates knowledge management through its culture and incentives.

The following action steps to increase an organization's capacity to learn are also proposed (Marquardt & Reynolds, 1994, p. 110):

1. Transform the individual and organizational image of learning.
2. Create knowledge-based partnerships.
3. Develop and expand team learning activities.
4. Change the role of managers.
5. Encourage experiments and risk-taking.
6. Create structures, systems, and time to extract learning.
7. Build opportunities and mechanisms to disseminate learning.
8. Empower people.
9. Push information throughout the organization and to external associates (customers, vendors, suppliers, and so forth).
10. Develop the discipline of systems thinking.
11. Create a culture of continuous improvement.
12. Develop a powerful vision for organizational excellence and individual fulfillment.
13. Root out bureaucracy.

Yet, while these broad guidelines help to some extent, it is clear that the cornerstone for knowledge management resides in individual and team learning, grounded in developing individual and collective skills and capabilities, particularly:

- the capacity to consider and articulate personal vision;
- a systems orientation—understanding external systems perspectives and interrelatedness, but also understanding one's internal systems, one's mental models;
- balancing inquiry and advocacy through understanding our assumptions;
- developing shared mental models; and
- focusing on dialogue rather than discussion (Senge, 1993).

Saint-Onge (1996) argues that the tacit knowledge in each of the three segments of the organization's intellectual capital—human, customer, and structural—must be congruent in those aspects affecting the organization's activities. This enables more productive pathways for effective meaning exchange and communication that enhances mutual understanding and helps unravel the myriad of mind-sets that interact in organizations. Communication is itself inherently about meaning creation and re-creation and therefore is central to the issue of organizational knowledge management. Little wonder, then, that increasingly the need to engage in dialogue, not just debate and discussion, is seen as fundamental for growing organizational knowledge (Isaacs, 1996).

Such tacit knowledge must also be systematically renewed—by finding ways of making meaning from knowledge—for organizational sustainability. This type of renewal requires understanding of how knowledge is formed and how individuals and organizations learn to use knowledge wisely. That is the process from random data, through data compiled into a meaningful pattern that eventuates in information; to knowledge as information converted into a valid basis for action; and finally into wisdom, in which we know implicitly how to generate, access, and integrate our knowledge as a guide for action. This process is one that moves from explicit to entirely tacit knowledge. It is about managing the knowledge process rather than knowledge embedded in the individual or teams (Hiebeler, 1996).

Managing the process effectively involves choosing and use of the most effective medium. Media are different in their capacity to convey meaning among organizational members, ranging from the richest medium—face-to-face—to the poorest as in formal, unaddressed documents. Moreover, as Daft and Huber put it (1987, p. 20), in order to ensure organizational learning, "Organizations...need to design two systems—a logistical system to handle the processing of data and an interpretive system to enable the appropriate perception and understanding of data." So, by using rich media we are facilitating interpretive learning, and media of lower richness may be used when the basis of learning is characterized by the logistical processing of objective data. Therefore, media choice influences what and how organizations learn and how well knowledge is managed.

The Issue of Structure

We must ensure appropriate structures for knowledge management that assist learning. It is likely that in order to do so we must discard rigidity and red tape and emphasize teamwork and holistic thinking (Marquardt & Reynolds, 1996).

Overall, however, in trying to achieve the aim of developing the intelligent organization and having optimum knowledge management, appropriate conditions must be established. These should allow for free individual and team decisions, leading to interconnection and coordination toward a collective good instead of pure chaos. The ideal structural architecture for the intelligent organization is flexible and responsive, driven by the free choices of personnel in the middle and bottom of the organization, making appropriate connections and synergies, rather than by brilliant designers at the top. There should be a heavy emphasis on teams and networks (internal and external) as the key structural weapons. The role of the center is in providing the conditions to empower those working for effective systems management and supplying the vision or focus in order that organizational parts have positive synergy with each other (Stein & Pinchot, 1995).

Managing knowledge that is intangible, invisible, situational, and ephemeral, is made much more possible in contemporary organizations through modern information and communications technology such as, hypermedia tools, decision support systems, and expert systems. Clippinger (1995) argues that it will become increasingly possible to capture and leverage much of the natural, formal, and incidental knowledge and expertise of a company through digital media (e.g., e-mail, multimedia, groupware). He also points to the ways in which interactive media permit simulation as a critical basis for organizational learning and developing tacit knowledge. Given such advantages it is likely that we will see an increase of more tools for authoring, valuing, visualizing, and sharing knowledge.

Structure for Quinn, Anderson, and Finkelstein (1996) should also be geared toward professional intellect, with the authors advocating a move away from hierarchy toward an inverted organization, with the center providing support services that leverage the professional in the field. A spider's web self-organizing network is also recommended in order to rapidly bring individuals together, when knowledge is dispersed among professionals, to solve a particular problem and then disbanded after the project concludes. In such groups the processes of communication, interpersonal and technology mediated, are as critical as the knowledge each specialist area brings to the project. They also stress the need for more radical organizational structures, supported by specifically designed software systems, designed to capture, focus, and leverage capabilities to the fullest. These are the glue joining highly dispersed service-delivery centers and leveraging the critical knowledge bases, intellectual skills, and accumulated experience in professional organizations. Such systems can also serve to bond professionals to the organization, giving them databases, analytical models, and communication power that they cannot find elsewhere and which enable them to extend their performance beyond their personal limits, allowing them to achieve more inside the organization than as individuals.

Many also argue that the structural basis for the intelligent organization is teams. This should be supported by an appropriate environment that helps team choice, reward and measurement of the whole team, training in teamwork per se, coordination by the team itself, and integration of the team purposes with those of the organization as a whole, with clear definitions of accountability throughout (Stein & Pinchot, 1995).

Accountability is one part of organizational control and if traditional approaches are no longer valid for current knowledge management that requires flexibility, creativity, and innovation, then it must be made clear what takes the place of traditional organizational authority and control. Simons's (1995) alternative of a system of four levels of control was briefly outlined in chapter I.

Hirschhorn and Gilmore (1992) suggest traditional boundaries of hierarchy, function, and the like have been replaced by an array of psychological boundaries, invisible to management, but needing to be recognized and used productively for the effective flexible organization of the 1990s and beyond. These they call:

- Authority boundary—"Who is in charge of what?"
- Task boundary—"Who does what?"
- Political boundary—"What's in it for us?"
- Identity boundary—"Who is—and isn't—us?"

For them, the boundaryless organization has an authority that is not about control but more about containment of those variables that disrupt productive work. Moreover, their solution to managing these more ambiguous relationships and boundaries is to become much more aware of one's own and others' feelings. This enables management to understand the boundaries people require in relationships in order to do their best.

We are, then, talking about a fundamental change in order to allow for the process and benefits of knowledge management. Yet, as Ghoshal and Bartlett (1996, p. 23) emphasize, in successful organizational transformation, structure is not the sole solution but "is as much a function of individuals' behaviors as it is of the strategies, structures, and systems that top management introduces."

They underline four elements of the transformational behavioral context—discipline, support, stretching individuals through enhancing expectations, and trust. These are most effectively developed sequentially by supporting the three key stages of organizational renewal: simplification (building front-line initiative), integration (realigning cross-unit relationships), and regeneration (ensuring continuous learning).

The Issue of Culture

Such an overall context and the foundation for organizational knowledge management must reside in organization culture—one that facilitates learning, knowledge creation, and management. Innovation and fostering a variety of learning strategies, allowing mistakes in terms of appropriate learning experiences, and providing adequate financial support are critical. So too is empowerment, achieved through reducing dependency, encouraging responsibility and self-reliance along with adequate skills and information bases, and treating ail as adults. Moreover, the organization must understand everyone as creating and working with knowledge, and provide the capacity to share information and knowledge in a variety of ways that focus on community and include such sharing, on a real-time basis, through appropriate technology. Management must also target learning space and time. This is about providing the adequate physical, social, and mental space to be creative and innovative, and appropriate time frames within which to learn (Marquardt & Reynolds, 1994).

Another useful start to thinking about productive cultures for knowledge management is provided by McGill, Slocum, and Deli's (1992) outline of the managerial practices found in generative (double-loop) learning organizations:

- openness—a willingness to suspend the need for control; cultural-functional humility with managers recognizing their background, values, and experiences are neither necessarily better or worse than those of others;
- systemic thinking—being able to see the whole not just its parts; recognizing connections between issues, events, and data points; emphasizing collective learning; structural relationships centered on networks instead of traditional hierarchies;
- creativity—centered in personal flexibility and a willingness to take risks unfettered by fear of punishment for failure;
- a sense of personal efficacy—based on self-awareness (through self-reflection and feedback from others) and being a proactive problem solver; and
- empathy—having a sensitivity and concern for human nature and being interested in (and capable of) repairing strained relationships.

Two other features of a productive culture are revealed in a move away from hoarding information and outmoded rivalries: first, that organizational information is freely available and organizational intelligence is shared throughout, including financial, productivity, strategic, customer, and resource information. The other is that rewards (not always remuneration based) must relate to all levels of learning—individual, team, and organization wide (Field & Ford, 1995).

Leadership is also critical and it is top management who creates the appropriate culture and environment for knowledge management, reducing obstacles and providing the ambience for teams and networks as the basis for the learning organization. Such management must have a deliberate strategy and be committed to the learning organization and knowledge management. Middle managers, however, Nonaka (1991) argues, are, the "knowledge engineers" in the knowledge creating company, in that they synthesize and make explicit the tacit knowledge of both front-line employees and senior executives, and incorporate it into new technologies and products.

Consequently, management and organizational leaders must develop skills in setting up environments where learning can occur. These are environments that are "safely dangerous" in allowing individuals to risk in a climate of safety and no recriminations, and where dialogue is enabled and emphasized (Isaacs, 1996). Moreover, senior management commitment could be made tangible by appointing a knowledge executive charged with being responsible overall for knowledge management in the organization (EIU/IBM, 1996) such as is the case with McKinsey & Co.'s director of knowledge management.

Quinn, Anderson, and Finkelstein's (1996) solutions to effective management of professional intellect for the intelligent enterprise include recruiting the best; forcing intensive early development; ensuring increasing professional challenges; evaluating and weeding. To leverage professional intellect, they emphasize the need to boost professionals' problem-solving abilities by capturing knowledge in systems and software; to overcome their reluctance to share information; and to organize around intellect rather than physical assets.

Schein (1996, p. 12), however, remains sceptical of simplistic solutions to the complexity of culture, learning, and knowledge management:

> ...the Learning organization is a complex beast consisting of many systems whose separate learning and change efforts must be coordinated and integrated. It is time to accept the reality of this complexity and stop oversimplifying systemic learning processes by touting particular remedies like leadership, vision, re-engineering, total quality, customer focus, systems thinking, and the like. Ultimately what is new in this field is the recognition that transformational learning, however necessary it may be, will require patient and careful research before we can advocate any particular learning mechanisms of how to do it.

The Issue of Power

The innovative energy of individuals and groups in organizations is released in the intelligent organization through preventing monopolies of power from squashing them. Hoarding of information as sources of personal power and monopolies of power revealed by organizational cliques who destroy whatever disagrees with their own thinking are not countenanced in such organizations (Stein & Pinchot, 1995). Furthermore, education is required for those managers who fear losing power through changing management roles and a move away from traditional managerial control (EIU/IBM, 1996).

The Issue of Collaboration

Wathne, Roos, and Von Krogh (1995) emphasize the most important factors for knowledge transfer between two or more cooperative partners are—openness (frankness and willingness to share knowledge); channels of interaction (rich versus poor communication media); trust; and prior experience (and the current existing knowledge structure, determining the ability to internalize knowledge).

Other critical features required for successful knowledge collaboration are realistic aims and expectations of relationships; a shared interest and value-adding potential; clear cooperative arrangements; effective coordination; clear mechanisms for learning; structural flexibility; clear alliance management; balancing cooperation and competition; visible real commitment; and senior management support and involvement.

Knowledge Measurement

While some organizations, though recognizing the value of organizational knowledge or intellectual capital, are finding it difficult to extract, even more are finding it perplexing to measure. This is largely because knowledge valuation and measurement requires more than the traditional quantitative economic approach. Moreover, one needs not only to assess outcomes but also process.

Edvinsson of Skandia, mentioned previously, emphasizes the link between human and structural capital as equaling intellectual capital. He outlines some of the nonfinancial measures of intellectual capital as follows: number of customers; how many ideas customers give the company and how they are developed; the ratio of software packages to employee numbers; how many use the Internet; the amount of networking between customers and employees; how many innovative ideas are produced; the employees' level of education or training; the flow of ideas and information between departments; retention and turnover figures; and how many articles are published or patents granted (cited in Thornburg, 1994).

Today many organizations, such as Dow Chemical, Skandia, and Hughes Aircraft, are proving that we can identify knowledge assets of an organization, that we can devise management processes to enhance them, that we can show how managing intellectual capital aids financial performance, and we can measure how knowledge actually adds value to the organization. There is an increasing range of robust tools being devised to do just these tasks (Stewart, 1994).

For instance, Sweden's Skandia insurance company, mentioned earlier, is using a knowledge accounting tool that tries to identify and organize measurement of knowledge-based intangibles such as creativity (EIU/IBM, 1996). Another example is that of Arthur Andersen (cited in Hiebeler, 1996) who, together with the American Productivity & Quality Center, has developed and launched, in 1995, a diagnostic tool, the Knowledge Management Assessment Tool (KMAT) to help organizations analyze the effectiveness of their knowledge management process and compare it with the efforts of other organizations. Consisting of 24 items relating to knowledge management practices, within a knowledge management model focused on four enablers—leadership, technology, culture, and measuremen—the KMAT assists participants in evaluating their ability to manage organizational knowledge. Such scorecards include both financial and nonfinancial measures of performance and tend to focus on process rather than outcome.

There is, of course, much room left for improving the link between knowledge management and financial results, but at least a promising start has been made (Hiebeler, 1996). Furthermore, theoretical work in the area is also gathering pace as is demonstrated in the recent work of Strassman (1996) who offers a portfolio of metrics useful for valuing computers, information, and knowledge.

DILEMMAS

Clearly, however, the field of organizational learning and knowledge management is still in its infancy and subject to the same sort of "hype" that are many other new concepts and heralded managerial magic bullets. The fact that organizational change is required for really effective knowledge management is not easy to accept for many organizations (Marshall, Prusak, & Spilberg, 1996).

Few people or institutions overall are essentially very comfortable with the way in which knowledge management demands that we reshape an organization's boundaries, that we change the work of managers, and that we move away from the comfortable familiarity of traditional and deeply rooted ways of conceiving organizations and organizing (Badaracco, 1991). Nor are they easy about perhaps having to change at the individual level as well. It is also the case that organizational learning and knowledge creation per se are only part of the problem. The translation of such learning and knowledge into action is often difficult and the end to which such activity aspires is often unclear and troublesome in its own right.

Moreover, as Levinthal and March (1993) warn, it is important to be aware of some important limitations to organizational learning and knowledge management per se. First, organizations have to balance the competing goals of developing new knowledge and exploiting current knowledge and competencies. Second, organizations tend to approach learning from experience by simplification and specialization, both of which contribute to three forms of learning myopia—the tendency to ignore the long run, the tendency to disregard the big picture, and the tendency to overlook failures. The consequence is not to throw out efforts after organizational learning and knowledge management but rather to do so in terms of realistic evaluations and expectations.

Finally, Blackler (1995, p. 1035) takes issue with much current thinking about knowledge, arguing that the traditional abstract, disembodied, individualistic, and formalized conceptions of knowledge are unrealistic:

> First, rather than talking of *knowledge*...it is more helpful to talk about the process of *knowing*. Second, to avoid segregating the forms of knowing..., old concepts...need to be abandoned and *new approaches to conceptualizing the multi-dimensional processes of knowing and doing need to be created.*

Given this, idealism must be tempered by reality and a commitment to confront and change ourselves, our conceptions, and our organizations. Such arduous tasks underline the truth that quick fixes and magic bullets will not suffice for knowledge management of any real or lasting value into the twenty-first century.

Chapter VI

Managing Responsibly

In fact, ethics has *everything* to do with management. Rarely do the character flaws of a lone actor fully explain corporate misconduct. More typically, unethical business practice involves the tacit, if not explicit, cooperation of others and reflects the values, attitudes, beliefs, language, and behavioral patterns that define an organization's operating culture. Ethics, then, is as much an organizational as a personal issue (Paine, 1994, p. 106).

Modern management theory is constricted by a fractured epistemology, which separates humanity from nature and truth from morality. Reintegration is necessary if organizational science is to support ecologically and socially sustainable development (Gladwin, Kennelly, & Krause, 1995, p. 874).

...unless organizations have both a soul and a conscience they will not deserve their place in modern society and will not long survive (Handy, 1997, p. 157).

THE ORGANIZATION IN SOCIETY

Maynard and Mehrtens (1993) argue that business is moving along a set of waves of change. The first was the agricultural revolution but, for us, it is the later three that are critical:

- the second wave—rising with industrialization and focused on materialism (competition, self-preservation, and consumption) and the supremacy of human kind—the worldview is that we are separate and must compete;
- the third wave—postindustrial and suggesting a developing interest in balance and sustainability (sensitivity to conservation, cooperation, and the sanctity of life)—the worldview is that we are connected and must cooperate; and
- the fourth wave—the future with emphasis on integration of all aspects of life and responsibility for the whole (the need to

relate and interact in a way that nourishes human and nonhuman kind)—the worldview is that we are one and choose to co-create.

This evolution suggests a move away from a narrow bottom-line approach to success that has often ended only in alienation—from nature, our work, each other, and ourselves; to one based in wholeness and connectedness (Ray & Rinzler, 1993). It is one that regards organizations as creators of value, serving various stakeholders, understanding the moral effects of business, and adopting a global stewardship role.

So, today, many recognize that business and society are not distinct entities but rather are inextricably linked, including in mutual responsibility (Wood, 1991). More and more organizations are being evaluated on their social performance and the notion of corporate social responsibility is growing in importance. Accelerating, too, is the belief in, and perhaps the demand that, business is the institution in our contemporary world that is powerful enough to implement the changes required for social and ecological sustainability (Hawken, 1993).

The major facets of such consideration include corporate social responsibility focusing on the products of corporate action; corporate social responsiveness emphasizing individual and organizational processes; and business ethics, pointing to value-based reflection and choice relating to the moral significance of actions taken by individuals and the organization as a whole. The former two focus on action, while the latter much more on thought. Organizations behave here along a dimension that goes from proscriptive (within regulation and law) to anticipatory and preventative (moving beyond mere compliance to accepting broader criteria for action) (Luthans, Hodgetts, & Thompson, 1990). We can also outline the range in terms of the reactive—denying responsibility and doing less than is required; the defensive—admitting responsibility but fighting it and doing the least required; the accommodative—accepting responsibility and doing all that is required; and the proactive—anticipating responsibility and doing more than required (Clarkson, 1995).

Much depends on how the demands of, and accountabilities to, different organizational constituents is balanced with both the good of organizations and society in mind and with a long-term, as well as a short-term, perspective considered. Such a need for balancing and a holistic and long-term perspective occurs increasingly in a climate where business is regarded as having a social responsibility and needing to be responsive to society in a way that transcends a purely economic perspective (Manley with Shrode, 1990).

Wood (1991, p. 693) defines such responsibility as "a business organization's configuration of principles of social responsibility, processes of social responsiveness, and policies, programs, and observable outcomes as they relate to the firm's societal relationships." Key points of her model include the following:

- Principles of corporate social responsibility encompass institutional principle—legitimacy; organizational principle—public responsibility; and individual principle—managerial discretion.
- Processes of corporate social responsiveness include environmental assessment; stakeholder management; and issues management.
- Outcomes of corporate behavior embrace social impacts; social programs; and social policies.

Here three pivotal concerns are emphasized. First, what is operative at the institutional level—legitimacy—involving what is expected of any individual business in the business-society relationship, because of its institutional membership; second, the outcomes of an organization's activity as another aspect of such a relationship in terms of public responsibility; and, third, the issue of managerial discretion involving how, within an organization's structural constraints, individual managers emphasize their responsibility in behaving as moral actors and promoting socially responsible results.

Importantly, socially responsible organizations must today meet growing expectations from various arenas through stakeholder groups. These include customers, employees, suppliers, shareholders, the political arena, the broader community, and the environment. Such diverse communities of interest must be understood, addressed through appropriate organization policies and action, and constantly reviewed in light of ongoing change. The responsibilities for these groups include the following:

- Responsibilities toward customers—customer responsiveness, provision of information, product safety, and ethical marketing.

- Responsibilities toward employees—equal opportunities, developing talent, health and safety, employee welfare.
- Responsibilities toward suppliers—practical help and advice to smaller suppliers, purchasing policies ensuring that small and local companies have a fair share of the business; monitoring suppliers' social responsibility performance; payment policies that help small businesses; and closer arrangements with suppliers through partnership agreements.
- Responsibilities toward investors—performance, ease of purchase, information (through annual reports, etc.).
- Responsibilities in the political arena—lobbying, third world issues, and human rights.
- Responsibilities toward the broader community—corporate and staff giving; secondment; education and schools liaison; small business development.
- Responsibilities toward the environment—reducing noise pollution; having suppliers use environmentally friendly products; energy efficiency; actively working to improve the environment (e.g., inner-city development); and encouraging environmental initiatives (audits and programs) (Clutterbuck with Dearlove & Snow, 1992).

A social responsibility model encompassing the economic, legal, ethical, and discretionary expectations of business by society is advocated by Carroll (1989). This encompasses:

- required economic responsibilities such as being profitable and minimizing costs;
- required legal responsibilities such as adhering to regulations, obeying laws, and fulfilling contractual obligations;
- expected ethical responsibilities such as avoiding questionable practices, operating above the minimum required by law, and asserting ethical leadership; and
- desired discretionary responsibilities such as corporate contributions, community involvement, and support.

Advocates of social responsibility approaches to modern organizational practice must, however, face a barrage of opposing views. These include the perspective that the term is too broad to encompass any real pragmatics; that the market system doesn't work in accord with such views; that taxes already provide for public good; that business doesn't have the experience to deal with social issues; and that the democratic process would be subverted by business moving into the political rather than the purely economic realm. One can rebuff these arguments in a variety of ways, including the fact that, with regard to the last mentioned, business does already act politically as well as economically in terms of its own pressure groups (Manley & Shrode, 1990). However, there is another counter in the growing concern with responsibility and ethics in organizational life from the government, the general public, and the business community itself.

In other words, the time has come for us to deal more fully with how management theory and practice affect our human community, natural environment, and what they contribute toward a sustainable future. Some adopt this approach by having social and environmental audits of organizational performance. More broadly, however, it is suggested that we must all appropriate a new mind-set—away from the extremes of competing views of technocentric or ecocentric paradigms. The technocentric paradigm emphasizes the rational and scientific, human reign, the good of people, and an inert and passive earth that we legitimately exploit; and the ecocentric paradigm stresses wholeness, the nurturing nature of mother earth, rejects our domination over nature, and advocates the good of nature and the simplicity of the good life. Instead, we need to go toward a more viable and integrated perspective, the sustain-centric paradigm, based on the universalism of life, ecological economics and conservation, the good of both people and nature, and the notion of stewardship of the earth as our home (Gladwin, Kennelly, & Krause, 1995).

THE QUESTION OF ETHICS

Two basic approaches support the argument for social responsibility—the ethical and the instrumental. These may be summarized as follows (Jones, 1996):

- Ethical arguments are based on current social norms or religious principles; they suggest organizations and their employees must behave socially responsibly because it is the morally right thing to do; they focus on the way in which the business sector controls the majority of society's resources; and argue for ethical behavior even where it is not cost-effective for the organization.

● Instrumental arguments regard organization-level economic performance as having a positive relationship with socially responsible behavior—organizations can be both profitable and virtuous; socially responsible organizational behavior allows the organization to anticipate and deter problematic government regulation, better differentiate products from competitors, and exploit opportunities from a broader portfolio.

The first may be considered unrealistic by many in today's capitalist society, perceived as neither viable nor sustainable. The second, however, also is problematic in implying that good business practice makes the idea of social responsibility redundant in the light of rational economic behavior based on organizational self-interest. But the relationship is clarified if one adopts Solomon's (1992) view of business as an inherently social practice or ongoing human activity, based on more than a simplistic profit-making orientation and as broad as the concept of a community of people working to achieve shared goals. Indeed, he maintains the stress on organizations as communities displays the centrality of ethics. It reveals that the organization is successful in terms of a sense of mission and direction around a set of core ideas—a set of virtues (honesty, fairness, trust, toughness) and parameters (community, excellence, membership, integrity, judgment, holism)—none of which are purely moral or purely business (Wicks, 1996).

So, internal and external communities are key concepts in terms of social responsibility and ethics. It is clear to all stakeholders involved in such communities that an organization's ethical behavior defines its true nature and beliefs. Such behavior in organizations has recently become a subject of critical concern, both for academics and practitioners. Increasingly, organizations are seeing that an ethical culture can be a strategic advantage, even if it does no more than avoid adverse societal or governmental reactions impacting the bottom line. Unethical behavior can be very costly: for example, financial loss from legal proceedings, destroyed organization image and reputation, and a major impact on relationships with organizational stakeholders. Consequently, ethics training is increasing, focusing on developing employee awareness of ethics and drawing attention to potential ethical issues employees may confront (Harrington, 1991).

Furthermore, at an individual level, in spite of much of the current cynicism in organizational life, it is clear that we act not only in following self-interest or pleasure but also from the basis of moral commitments—rational economic self-interest and ethical and emotional considerations. At the organizational level there is concern for ethics, set as an agenda by mass media, affecting the organization's image and reputation, attracting investors, enticing the best staff, and helping the institution reach out to the broader community involved in the social and political arena. Common ethical problems such as those involving discrimination, conflict of interest, abuse of corporate resources, and the more covert ones that lead to disasters such as Challenger, Three Mile Island, the Pinto car, and the like, mean that we must all be versed in how to handle the ethical dilemmas of institutional life. Moreover, we must understand that individual behavior in the organizational context, including reward systems, examples set, behavioral norms, expectations, and so on, are very influential (Trevino & Nelson, 1995).

Some critics of the emerging concern with ethical business behavior suggest that, instead, the only concern for business is to maximize profits within legal guidelines. However, arguments for ethical and socially responsible behavior suggest that so doing actually works in an organization's best rational self-interest. Others view the need to act ethically in terms of external constraints on the organization's behavior—market forces, legal and political intervention acting for ethical values, and forcing ethical behavior in a free market system. An ethics as an end in itself approach, while not so evident at large, also exists, going beyond the invisible-hand constraint imposed by the marketplace and the visible hand ones wrought by government, media, and labor. Here organizations go beyond minimal compliance in ethical thinking and practice. Indeed, they must, if they wish for more than endorsing moral mediocrity (Manley & Shrode, 1990). Moreover, as Clarkson (1995, p. 112) argues: "the moment that corporations and their managers define and accept responsibilities and obligations to primary stakeholders, and recognise their claims and legitimacy, they have entered the domain of moral principles and ethical performance, whether they know it or not."

Philosophy, culture, leadership, and organizational strategy have a major impact on ethical behavior in the organization. In these it is clear that organizations must move beyond a belief that ethical practice is about avoiding illegal practice. While organizations need well-articulated strategies for legal compliance, what is required is a concern for law, accompanied by managerial responsibility for ethical behavior—combined into an integrity-based approach to ethics management that rests on an ethical framework that is the governing ethos of the organization. For practical ethics performance an organization must have a culture that is sensitive and focused on responsibility, with effective organizational systems to support practice. The basis in integrity lies in management defining and giving life to guiding values, creating an environment supportive of ethically sound behavior, and instilling a sense of shared accountability among employees. Such a broad context can then support the behavior of organizational personnel at group and individual levels (Paine, 1994).

Gatewood and Carroll (1991) offer the following questions to capture standards that may be operationally applied:

1. Does the behavior or result achieved comply with all applicable laws, regulations, or government codes?
2. Does the behavior or result achieved comply with organizational standards of ethical behavior?
3. Does the behavior or result achieved comply with professional standards of ethical behavior?

They argue that these should be supported by normative judgment going beyond organizational or professional cultures in terms of combining the following;

- rights—entitlements of individuals;
- justice—being guided by fairness, equity, and impartiality; and
- utilitarianism—those actions/decisions considered right that produce or tend to produce, the greatest good for the greatest number affected by the action.

The critical hallmarks of an effective integrity strategy may be outlined as follows (Paine, 1994, p. 112):

- The guiding values and commitments make sense and are clearly communicated.

- Company leaders are personally committed, credible, and willing to take action on the values they espouse.
- The espoused values are integrated into the normal channels of management decision making and are reflected in the organization's critical activities.
- The company's systems and structures support and reinforce its values.
- Managers throughout the company have the decision-making skills, knowledge, and competencies needed to make ethically sound decisions on a day-to-day basis.

Messick and Bazerman (1996) argue that poor ethical decisions can often be the result of poor decision making generally, rather than stemming from tradeoffs between ethics and profits, or from failing to consider others' welfare or interests. They point to difficulties surrounding the inaccuracies of our theories of the world, other people, or about ourselves, and suggest that we can improve ethical decision making by focusing on:

- quality—considering all the consequences of actions; basing decisions on high-quality data; being well briefed on the risks associated with potential strategies; and tuning in to the pitfalls of egocentric biases;
- breadth—having stakeholder input; and considering the outcomes for all stakeholders, including as appropriate the outcome not only for present but future generations (as in environmental issues); and
- honesty—having a policy of openness; and being honest with others but also with oneself in avoiding self-deception.

In order to maintain an ethical organizational climate, a variety of guidelines are available, including this set (Clutterbuck with Dearlove & Snow, 1992):

- set a clear example and communicate;
- publish a code of ethics;
- monitor performance;
- use the reward and punishment mechanisms to reinforce correct behavior;
- recruit ethical people;

- train;
- create a framework for registering concern; and
- build openness into the workplace.

Trevino and Nelson (1995) provide a basis for ethical behavior in suggesting that at the individual level we:

- gather the facts;
- define the ethical issues;
- identify the affected parties;
- recognize the consequences;
- distinguish the obligations;
- consider our character and integrity;
- think creatively about potential actions; and
- check our intuition.

At the organizational level they emphasize that, having in place more structural settings such as ethics committees, ethics officers and, most importantly, a range of both formal and informal ways of communicating ethics—from brochures, to mission statements, to codes of conduct, and even a formal whistle-blowing system—are critical to developing and maintaining an ethics culture. The ideal is a commitment and compliance package that provides the best basis for ethical conduct at all levels.

While not the total answer, developing a code of ethics, involving representatives of those affected by it, can be a basis for real acceptance by organization personnel. Such codes should be clear, simple, internally consistent, revised regularly to take organizational changes into account, given to all, and ought to include ways in which violations will be handled. The advantages of such codes include:

- clarifying policy;
- helping individuals resist unreasonable requests;
- providing guidelines on termination;
- boosting the atmosphere of work within an ethical environment;
- clarifying unwanted practices;
- providing avenues for discipline and prosecution;
- reducing the need for coercive means (such as polygraph testing) for detecting unethical acts;

- fostering public confidence in the organization; and
- lessening the need for formal government regulation (Molander, 1987).

Alongside such codes and acknowledging the pivotal role of senior management philosophy and behavior, it is important to:

- clarify the internal approach to ethics, treating it as a matter of business practice;
- explore ethical questions arising from issues emerging as important for the organization to consider;
- examine the organization's practices over the last five years and evaluate outcomes;
- develop appropriate education and training opportunities;
- define the range of ethical issues for the organization to consider;
- understand the appropriate regulatory and legal frameworks;
- explore alternatives that circumvent unethical behavior; and
- reward those who speak up and save the organization embarrassment or worse (Coates, Jarratt, & Mahaffie, 1990).

Ideally, then, the organization can move along a range of stages of corporate moral development, rather than remaining static in one of the lower stages (Starke, 1993, pp. 203-204):

- Stage One: The Amoral Corporation—Pursues winning at any cost; views employees merely as economic units of production.
- Stage Two: The Legalistic Corporation—Concerned with the letter of the law, but not its spirit.
- Stage Three: The Responsive Corporation—Interested in being a responsible corporate citizen, but primarily because it is expedient, not because it's right; has codes of conduct that begin to look more like codes of ethics.
- Stage Four: The Emergent Ethical Corporation—Recognizes the existence of a social contract between business and society, and seeks to instil that attitude throughout the corporation.
- Stage Five: The Ethical Corporation—Balances profits and ethics so completely that employees are rewarded for walking away from a compromising action.

Perhaps now we are in a better position to try for a new synthesis of the various approaches to ethics and responsibility. Frederick (1995) suggests this is possible, using the following theorems as a starting point:

- Business is an inherently normative activity, calling for moral evaluation and judgment of its operations, motives, decisions, policies, and goals.
- Business and society are unavoidably linked together in functional ways, so that what one of them does directly affects the other, posing the possibility that each will suffer harms and/or experience benefits stemming from the other's activities.
- Business's societal impacts are divisible and variable among identifiable groups (called "stakeholders"), whose interests cannot and should not be disregarded or discounted by those who direct and carry out business operations.
- The workplace is an arena saturated with values and ethics that are a function of several factors; a company's history of dealing with ethical issues, the organizational structure relating managers and employees to one another, prevailing ethical attitudes expressed by the company's organizational leaders, the particular personal values brought into the workplace by employees and managers, and the actual (observable) response of organizational authority figures (i.e., managers and professionals) to ethical issues that arise during the workday.
- Moral measures, standards, principles, and criteria are required to judge and evaluate business performance that impinges upon the moral interests and needs of stakeholders and society generally.
- The moral interests of business, corporate stakeholders, and society at large are a function of acquired experience within an array of evolving human communities, where normative meanings may vary in time and place but where they converge toward the sustenance and expansion of life's potentialities.
- Business acquires moral standing in society by carrying out a socially vital economizing function, but reliance upon that function alone provides an incomplete justification of business values, behavior, and operations.

Hand in hand with such an emphasis on ethics is the newly emerging issue of organization justice or fair process. Here justice is perceived as both a substantive matter and as procedural (Ewing, 1993). Concerns over justice tend to arise organizationally when differential harm or benefit occurs to individuals or groups and when actions and processes violate what is the expected organizational norm. Unfortunately, making, applying, and interpreting organizational policies and rules tend to have such effects (Sheppard, Lewicki, & Minton, 1992).

Yet, despite difficulties, as one recent article suggests (Chan Kim & Mauborgne, 1997), such fair process is vital for contemporary managers, a powerful tool for organizations really interested in learning and knowledge management. Because it so deeply affects attitudes and behaviors related to high performance, fair process can enhance creativity and innovation, centered in a climate of trust and credible, just organization processes.

THE NATURAL ENVIRONMENT

Today we can no longer afford to regard the natural environment as something to be conquered as did the climbers of Everest, for example, nor something that can supply our every demand endlessly. Thoughtless exploitation of nature and the failure to see both the big picture and long term have generally led us away from any functional and sustainable relationship between organizations and the environment. We have for too long disassociated human organization both from the biosphere and the full human community, and in so doing, we have possibly fuelled the processes that are destroying our natural, social, and cultural life systems of support (Gladwin, Kennelly, & Krause, 1995; Jagtenberg & McKie, 1997). We have simply not considered nature as a stakeholder in the changing organizational environment. As Shrivastava (1994, p. 707) puts it:

> Only through a fundamental re-theorization of organizations will we be able to pay genuine attention to organization-nature relationships. We need new ways of theorizing "the environment" to be able to re-theorize organizations. Instead of understanding "the environment" from an organizational viewpoint, we need to understand "the organization" from an environmental viewpoint.

Now we confront the challenge of creating an ecologically sustainable society with a critical mass providing its protection and nourishment. We must understand that the future is now (Birch, 1993). Moreover, we should comprehend our natural environment as both the indispensable supplier and most valued customer of our human activities—organizational and otherwise—the critical source of both life and the quality in our lives (Kinlaw, 1993).

The key players in achieving some sort of environmental sustainabilty are those of governments, consumers, and organizations. Governments need to better devise and implement appropriate economic policies; consumers must be willing to change their consumption patterns; and organizations must reexamine and alter their traditional roles in the environment, including their fostering of expanding consumption and consumerism. Organizations have the knowledge, resources, and power capable of making positive changes in the earth's ecosystems. So environmental sustainability needs to be integrated into the very logic of organizations and sustainability ought be an integral part of an organization's effectiveness (Shrivastava, 1995). Alongside reform, in order to minimize the negative ecological impact of many organizational activities, organizations themselves must be redesigned and restructured (Gladwin, 1992). This includes encouraging the interorganizational alliances discussed in chapter III as a better usage of limited resources.

It is also critical to move away from simplistic notions of organizations and consumers destroying our planet, or the basic polarized view that we must chose between business and the environment. Instead, we must accept the complexity of the interaction process, believing that our consumer society, efficient at delivering consumer wants, can deliver environmental protection as consumer demands for it grow; that regulatory compliance and liability containment are adequate practices; and that organizations can gain strategic competitive advantage through environmental excellence and establishing trust and credibility with their customers and other stakeholders (Perkins & Lepper, 1995).

Furthermore, while a major source of environmental problems can be laid at the door of many organizational practices, it is also the case that with their fiscal, technological, and management resources, organizations are our major source for solving those very problems (Hart, 1997). A simple, single example—how the basic act of recycling brought the Hyatt Regency Chicago's garbage-collection bill down to $2,000 per month from the former $12,000—can demonstrate the value of activities at the easy end of the business-environment relationship (Kinlaw, 1993).

Gradually many organizations in the 1990s have been moving from grudging compliance with environmental regulations to including environmentalism as part of strategic management and everyday organizational operations. The move to active organizational environmental management has arisen from factors such as:

- recognizing industry as holding the key to successful environmental management;
- seeing industry as benefiting from a healthier and more prosperous environment; and
- acknowledging that such constructive management can improve organizational performance and competitive position (Cannon, 1994).

Piasecki (1995) sees this evolutionary change in terms of organizations moving through phases of denial, external blame, self-blame, and finally, that of problem solving. For many, policy, strategy, and practice have been changed. Others, such as Union Carbide and Exxon, have had to learn from crises. The most successful are able to point to the link between such organizational environmentalism and the bottom line; and the best, to ensure good environmental behavior means good business practices and integrate this into strategy, organization behavior, and organizational learning and knowledge management. Their efforts and success demonstrate that government and industry are not necessarily enemies; and that there is no direct and malicious conflict between the environment and the economy.

The critical forces pushing this changed orientation are many and varied. They include legal compliance and avoidance of fines, costs, personal liability, and imprisonment; the need to stay ahead of regulations; a more informed society; international codes for environmental performance; the rise of stakeholder activism; environmentally conscious investors; the concerns of professional associations; globalization of markets; international politics; consumer preference; growing competitive pressures (maintenance of growth and profitability and minimization of environmental degradation); and the desire of many qualified people to work in organizations that have a constructive relationship with the environment (Kinlaw, 1993; Dechant & Altman, 1994).

The crucial environment tasks for modern organizations are numerous, including: environmental protection; waste management; product integrity; worker health; media and government relations; risk, liability, and insurance management; crisis management; and public and community relations. More specifically, they need to devise new missions, goals, and strategies; conserve inputs such as energy and raw materials; create environmentally friendly products and packaging; have more efficient and cleaner production systems; manage and minimize wastes and polluting emissions; and advance green organization structures, systems, cultures, and competencies. They must do so in terms of environmentally sustainable development, embedded in understanding the limits of the natural environment to support growth; not stopping all economic growth, but rather questioning conventional forms of that growth and replacing these with ecologically sound forms—the only viable option available to us, as indicated earlier (Shrivastava, 1996).

Kinlaw (1994) moves beyond sustainable development based on concepts of equity among people, stewardship of nature, limits on nonrenewable resources, community and cooperation, and the interrelationships among all natural ecosystems and human activity. He uses the concept of "sustainable performance," business compatible with nature, describing the basics for business practice for continuation into the indefinite future. For him, sustainable development is the macro large-scale description of how society and the environment must work together in terms of national and international policies; while sustainable performance is concerned with the micro small-scale description of how each business and organization can translate the concept of sustainable development into practical organizational applications. The latter affirms that, in order for nations to survive, business, based on profit, must survive.

His advice on sustainable performance is built on the concept of a partnership with the environment, one that sustains both the environment and an organization's bottom line, and works around achieving a series of milestones. It requires changes in all aspects of an organization and is based in having sustainable-performance policy, baselines, training, improvement projects, environmental technology development, auditing and reporting systems, environmental coalitions, and renewal of management and human resource systems. The distinguishing characteristics of such an approach are profit and performance. The primary goal is not development but total quality and continuous improvement of organizational processes, products, and services required in order to achieve environmental enhancement, long-term profit, and competitive positioning.

Those warring in the environmental drama are government, industry, and a range of public-interest groups, many of who are focused on a black and white approach to the issue of being green. Actually this either/or mentality that works in an adversarial climate, pitting being green against being competitive is wrong, claim Porter and van der Linde (1995). Instead, they argue, that in a dynamic competitive world, rather than the static one epitomized by much economic theory, it is possible to be green and competitive in terms of resource productivity. Evidence drawn, for example, from the Dutch Flower Industry, Dow Chemicals, 3M, Hitachi, and Du Pont, suggests that well-designed environmental standards actually stimulate innovations that can decrease the total cost of a product or better its value. Competitive advantage no longer simply exists in having resources (e.g., lower cost inputs such as labor and raw materials)—it resides in using resources productively through innovation. Improved resource productivity means increased organizational competitiveness rather than less. What organizations that can equate environmentalism with productivity do, is to change from the mind-set of pollution control to that of pollution prevention, source reduction, or resource inefficiency. They focus on resource productivity, giving a real assessment of the opportunity costs of pollution—wasted effort and resources, and lowered product value for customers. The end result is a combination of process and product benefits arising from innovation-based environmental solutions. This only occurs, however, if an organization moves beyond regulatory firefighting toward environmental strategic management (Piasecki, 1995). As Shrivastava (1996, p. vii) suggests:

> ...environmentally responsible action is as good for the bottom line, for employee welfare, and for the long-term survival of corporations as it is necessary for resolving the Earth's ecological problems. Corporations should green themselves not simply to be ethical or to yield to political pressures. Instead...greening today is a competitive, ecological, economic, political, and social necessity.

Perhaps our first step should be toward a better understanding of ecological problems emanating from organizational activities and how organizations might play such a critical role in achieving ecological sustainability (Shrivastava, 1995). This can give us a better basis for adopting the more realistic approach of the sustain-centric paradigm and we can move forward in innovative ways, including devising ways of making sustainable behavior an escalating source of competitive advantage (Makower, 1994).

Certainly there are many benefits organizations can achieve from working toward ecological sustainability such as:

- continuing to operate
- reducing costs
- competitive advantage opportunities in "green" markets (locally and globally)
- being industry leaders
- aiding total quality management
- having a strategy for long-term profitability
- achieving better community relations
- improving the corporate image and reputation
- providing a better proactive legal basis
- reducing long-term environmental risks
- benefiting the ecosystem and environment within communities where organizations operate
- aligning with ethically desirable and politically unavoidable norms (Shrivastava, 1996).

Or, more broadly (Cook cited in Piasecki, 1995, p. 60), "When one changes by strategy, good deeds and good numbers are one and the same."

In order to promote industry innovation, resource productivity, and global competitiveness, one needs to follow some principles of regulatory design such as (Porter & van der Linde, 1995, p. 124):

- focus on outcomes, not technologies;
- enact strict rather than lax regulation;
- regulate as close to the end user as practical, while encouraging upstream solutions;
- employ phase-in periods;
- use market incentives;

- harmonize or converge regulations in associated fields;
- develop regulations in sync with other countries or slightly ahead of them;
- make the regulatory process more stable and predictable;
- require industry participation in setting standards from the beginning;
- develop strong technical capabilities among regulators; and
- minimize the time and resources consumed in the regulatory process itself.

Benefits accruing from such environmental competitive advantage also include the ability to attract and retain certain high-quality employees to an organization's workforce, those concerned about an organization's environmental performance and identity; the capacity to prevent or better manage environmental disasters such as Exxon-Valdez; avoid the potential harmful effects of concerned and active stakeholders; attract and retain consumers for products and services; and escape some of the problems of regulation. These result from best-practice efforts such as having a mission statement and corporate values promoting environmental advocacy; providing an organizational framework for better managing environmental initiatives; having green process/product design; entering into environmentally focused stakeholder partnerships; and ensuring adequate and appropriate internal and external education initiatives (Dechant & Altman, 1994).

Still, perhaps, a different view altogether needs to be adopted today. Most organization studies assume a traditional anthropocentric approach. Yet, alongside a new questioning of the belief in the progress of modern industrial development, gradually writers are urging that we regard nature as having a moral standing in its own right and that we don't see it existing merely as a resource for human welfare. We need to reconceptualize organizational environments in terms of an economic biosphere—consisting of the ecology of the planet Earth, alongside the world and more local economic, social, political, and other relevant contexts. Concern for nature must be core in a company's vision and then permeate its values, mission, inputs, throughputs, and outputs. This also entails effective stakeholder communication and measuring organizational performance in a way that includes environmental performance. Fundamentally, it resides in an ecocentric value system (Shrivastava, 1996):

- that regards humans as part of a community and focuses on community interest, interdependence, and web-like relationships;
- accepts nature as a living system, part of our human community, and symbiotic; and
- that sees the relationship of humans to nature in terms of harmonious coexistence, and aims to renew and conserve nature.

In short, organizations must move beyond mere market and profit concerns to a wider regard for environment and community.

While not without their critics, some of the already recognized programs and approaches for sustainability, as practiced by organizations such as 3M, IBM, BMW, Du Pont, Dow Chemicals, Proctor & Gamble, The Body Shop, Siemens, Deutsche Bank, Lufthansa, Esprit, include:

- total quality environmental management
- life-cycle analysis
- product stewardship
- ecoefficiency
- pollution prevention and waste-management strategy
- environmental risk and liability management
- environmental banking and investment
- environmental accounting
- environmental impact assessment
- environment audit
- environmental officer
- environmental and social reporting
- environmental sponsoring
- environmental information system
- environmental ethic or philosophy
- environmental labeling
- environmental codes of conduct
- responsible care
- environmental public relations and marketing
- green industrial architecture
- environmental awards (Jennings & Zandbergen, 1995).

The real cost benefit of such practices and how far they succeed in reality is often rather difficult to accurately assess.

Others (Booz-Allen & Hamilton cited in Piasecki, 1995, p. 11) evaluate best practice from such organizations and outline the characteristics of their environmental management programs:

1. Clear, articulated corporate policies and practices.
2. Organizational structures which support two-way communication between corporate functions and field units.
3. Effective information management and compliance systems.
4. Top-level support and commitment.
5. Integration of environmental issues into all facets of planning.
6. Risk assessment and risk management practices.

In the last decade a variety of environmental management codes have been developed, such as the Coalition for Environmentally Responsible Economies' (CERES) principles, and the international environmental management standard, ISO 14000. While these require organizations to have environmental management systems, to audit progress toward goals set, and to engage external stakeholders in their environmental programs, they do not, generally, have specific environmental performance standards that organizations must meet. However, when combined with legislated environmental regulations, such private, self-regulation promises a useful complement in safeguarding the environment more effectively. They shift some costs to the private sector, move beyond the scope of regulation, and may strengthen corporate legitimacy. Importantly, they are about fostering long-term changes in how organizations consider the environment and how they integrate environmental aims with other business objectives (Nash & Ehrenfeld, 1996).

Ladd Greeno (1994) suggests that, to ensure excellence in environmental management, an organization must have senior, including CEO, commitment and support, and address the following critical tasks:

• Positioning—outlining the organization's environmental, health, and safety management position (its baseline, where it wants to go, and methods of getting there, including audits, benchmarking, and the like). Critical here are clear, constant top management commitment and support; high reporting levels for environmental, health, and safety personnel; resources commensurate with the company's posture, in both quantity and quality; ongoing awareness and training programs; line responsibility for EHS performance; and continuous improvement. Decisions on where the organization wishes to be are, naturally, affected by organizational culture, the reality of the organization's situation, external factors such as regulation and consumer demands, and the need to continually reevaluate expectations in relation to changing demands.

- Learning—ensuring a personal knowledge base and an organizational data bank that includes information on the organization's environmental practice and performance. Measurement feeds individual and corporate environmental learning.
- Communication—using both formal and information communication approaches, both face-to-face and mediated, not only internally, but also with external organizational constituents and other organizations.
- Personal involvement—the critical role played by the CEO or delegated environmental champion, in developing and implementing excellence in environmental management.
- Catalyzing progress—through senior executive, such as committing to change, progress, and integrating environmental management into the very way the organization thinks about and does business.

Some of the literature's key recommendations for managers is well summarized by Collins (1995) who suggests that we:

- put in place both market-driven and process-driven sustainability strategies that are cost effective;
- have top management commitment;
- use organization changes as opportunities to improve environmental performance;
- reward environmental information gathering;
- have widespread rather than narrow (i.e., residing in individuals alone) environmental responsibilities;
- have dialogue with environmental experts;
- form relationships with environmental organizations;
- develop environmental problem solutions at the source;
- use a flexible conceptual framework for environmental matters;

- understand the political context of environmental issues; and
- make the organization's environmental programs a source of competitive advantage.

Other strategies to achieve a sustainable environment are recommended by Throop, Starik, and Rands (1993):

- Use "real" technology that does more or the same with less, is less wasteful and less destructive (closed-system technologies, renewable power sources, conservation/efficiency, and appropriate substitutes).
- Preempt regulation (fitting into the environment, restraining activities, preventing others from damaging the environment).
- Practice the collective imperative (involve stakeholders, cooperate within industry).
- Create an environmentalist organizational culture.

Ladd Greeno and Robinson (1992) outline the vital essentials for achieving high performance environmental management in terms of defining commitment and posture; measuring performance; recognizing what's wrong in current approaches; building long-term strategy; and integrating and ingraining an environmental mind-set. Their experience suggests that failure occurs where environmental affairs are outside critical processes; a fire-fighting mentality prevails; decision makers are isolated from staff; the tail wags the dog; environmental issues are left only to specialists; financial and human resources are limited; decisions are based on hindsight rather than foresight; culture is a barrier to excellence; poor measurement of environmental performance is in place; and where little motivation exists for implementing environmental excellence.

Successful environmental management approaches must be complemented by what has been termed "sustainable communication," communication that (Harrison, 1992, p. 244):

- manages expectations;
- acknowledges poor past performance as a serious matter;
- looks for options that make sense to all stakeholders;
- presents evidence to support positions and ideas;
- asks and tries to answer questions;
- focuses on core publics to create relationships;

- treats stakeholders as customers who need to be understood;
- interacts with stakeholders at their respective levels of awareness, with a consistent commitment; and
- is always open.

On the other hand, it remains the case that, even if such organizations are doing good in the sense of being more socially and ecologically responsible, they are generally still driving age-old business "virtues" such as more production, expansion, advertising, increased consumption, and use of resources—these degrade the environment and uphold traditional consumerism. So economic growth can never be totally environmentally benign but governments, organizations, and other key stakeholder groups can help ensure the possibility of greener growth (Cairncross, 1992; Hawken, 1993).

SEXUALITY, GENDER, AND DIVERSITY

If diversity in the natural environment is important, so too is that in our social environment, an issue that has been fought over long and hard. Today, while there is growing interest in diversity as a business consideration, it is rarely regarded as a vital strategic priority (Robinson & Dechant, 1997), however broadly the term is conceptualized.

The term "sex" involves biological characteristics while that of "gender" is used in a social context—as a scheme for categorizing individuals using biological differences as the basis for assigning social differences. In organizations sex differences influence how people behave while gender differences influence how they react to others in such settings (Powell, 1993). Significantly,

> Gendered processes are often resources in organizational control and transformation. Underlying these processes, and intimately connected to them, is a gendered substructure of organization that links the more surface gender arrangements with the gender relations in other parts of the society. Ostensibly gender neutral, everyday activities of organizing and managing large organizations reproduce the gendered substructure within the organization itself and within the wider society (Acker, 1992, p. 259).

Furthermore, in traditional hierarchies and control mechanisms, we find power, emotion, and sexuality recurring as key themes (Hearn, 1993).

The organizational world has always been gendered—"his," "hers," and "ours," although it has only been recently regarded as an issue to be explored. This is also true of organizational sexuality— illustrated by sexual relationships (heterosexual and homosexual), calendars, humor, and bodily states (e.g., pregnancy and premenstrual tension), and with a growing recognition of the powerful sexual and emotional politics that make up everyday organizational life (Parkin, 1993). Indeed Burrell (1984, 1992) argues that desexualization, repression, or outright expulsion of sexuality, have been key management goals in both the modern and postmodern organizations. He points to the language of organization failure being linked to sexual satisfaction as undermining effective administration—phrases such as "it's buggered," "what a cock-up," and "it's fucked." Consequently, desexualization has been considered vital in order to increase production processes.

The sexuality of organization life, nevertheless, remains and Powell (1993) argues this occurs along a number of fronts that make up the sexual construction of organizations. For example:

- visible—open sexual liaisons, dress and appearance, display, harassment, and other explicit sexual behavior;
- secret—secret sexual relationships; secret records; secret rules and policies; and
- unseen—unseen sexual behavior, sexual perceptions and desires, and sexual fantasies.

Language, as suggested above, also houses much of an organization's sexuality, both oral and written. Male sexual narrative tends to dominate most organizations, evident, for example, in terminology such as "policy thrusts," "scoring," and "rising to the challenge." However, overall, it is women's sexuality rather than that of men that is, as history reveals, considered dangerous to organizational discipline (Parkin, 1993; Cockburn, 1991).

Gender discrimination continues in organizational life, in spite of some strides being made by women, especially professional women in the workplace (Schwartz, 1992; Alvesson & Billing, 1992). This occurs in relation to salaries, performance appraisal, selection procedures, and the like (Bhatnagar & Swamy, 1995). It also continues generally in terms of managerial stereotypes, despite some increase in the numbers of women managers and in the ongoing debate about potential differences in female and male managers. With regards the latter, research evidence demonstrates that global measures of managerial behavior do not reveal sex differences overall. However, androgynous managers are considered optimum, being the most flexible and adaptable in balancing male and female characteristics and, therefore, having a wider array of responses available to organizational situations (Powell, 1993).

Hearn, Sheppard, Tancred-Sheriff, and Burrell (1989) rightly point out the similarity of organization and sexuality as both being social constructions mired within specific historical and spatial relations and being reflections of each other in the public domain. And while both in the theoretical and popular management literature, sexuality and gender issues have generally been ignored, in recent years the increased debates on EEO, sexual harassment, and AIDS in the workplace have changed the picture. Sexual behavior and gender concerns have become much more visible, public, and organizational.

The notions of sexuality and gender lead into a concern with organizational diversity—a multifaceted, multicultural (in the broad sense) community. Many calls for valuing diversity in the contemporary organization are being made, centered on the idea of managing personnel from diverse cultural backgrounds. Cox and Blake (1991) explore the dimensions of managing cultural diversity as follows:

- mind-sets about diversity—perceptions of it as a problem or opportunity;
- cultural differences—promoting knowledge, acceptance, and taking advantage of opportunities;
- organization culture—valuing differences;
- education programs—education at all school and management levels;
- human resource issues—recruitment, training, and evaluation;
- higher career involvement of women—dual career families, blurring work and family, harassment; and
- heterogeneity in race/ethnicity/nationality—effects on cohesiveness, group identity, and the role of prejudice.

They argue that the key competitive advantages in managing cultural diversity may be summarized in terms of:

- the cost advantage of a well-integrated workforce;
- the resource acquisition advantage of attracting the best personnel;
- a marketing advantage through using the cultural backgrounds of personnel (domestically and internationally);
- increased creativity from a diversity of perspectives and challenging traditional approaches;
- better problem solving from heterogeneity in decision and problem-solving groups; and
- increased system flexibility through a less deterministic and less standardized system.

Attracting, motivating, and retaining people from a diversity of cultural backgrounds can lead to competitive advantage if well managed. What is required is leadership commitment, education and training, appropriate human resources systems and practices, culture change, and ongoing audit and development. The multicultural organization that results is one based on (Cox & Blake, 1991, p. 52):

(1) Pluralism: reciprocal acculturation where all cultural groups respect, value, and learn from one another; (2) full structural integration of all cultural groups so that they are well represented at all levels of the organization; (3) full integration of minority culture-group members in the informal networks of the organization; (4) an absence of prejudice and discrimination; (5) equal identification of minority—and majority—group members with the goals of the organization, and with opportunity for alignment of organizational and personal career goal achievement; (6) a minimum of inter-group conflict which is based on race, gender, nationality, and other identity groups of organization members.

This is a very different scenario to the monolithic organization where assimilation is the goal, where minimal structural integration occurs, where prejudice and discrimination is rife; or the plural organization that also focuses on assimilation, where only partial structural integration occurs, and, while there is more progress on prejudice and discrimination, they continue to exist (Cox, 1991).

The flip side to cultural diversity is the issue of organizational fairness—overcoming inequalities, discrimination, barriers, and disadvantages to diverse cultural groups in the broadest sense—women, minorities, the disabled, and others (Cannon, 1994). This is a growing area of academic research and concern for practitioners, developing to incorporate the broader notion of organizational justice, as discussion earlier in this chapter, on ethics, indicated.

Issues such as those outlined in this chapter are important in their own right. They are, however, also significant in that they affect the organization's overall image. This is critical, given that (Cheney, 1991, pp. 14 & 23):

> Large bureaucratic organizations are in the business of identity management; their controlling members must be concerned about how to (re)present the organization as a whole *and* how to connect the individual identities of many members to that embracing collective identity....*Identity* is a preoccupation of contemporary Western society, and the *management of multiple identities* is a preoccupation of contemporary organizational life.

Certainly public and media scrutiny of organization performance in the environmental domain has forced many companies to reconsider the issue of corporate image. This also goes with other public attitudes concerning an organization's reputation in terms of ethics, justice, integrity, diversity, and the like. A sort of catch-22 situation exists in many places, where a real commitment to the issues covered does not exist and basic practices are followed only in order to prevent legal action or in order to maintain some credibility of organizational image in the eyes of many stakeholders.

Major organizations, driven by these numerous stakeholders, pursue a variety of communication strategies for creating, maintaining, and developing their corporate image or identity. Such strategies include use of corporate consulting firms specializing in image or identity management.

One recent tactic is seen in the growth of corporate philanthropy, tied inextricably to corporate strategies of increasing name recognition, raising employee productivity, increasing loyalty, overcoming regulatory problems, accessing markets, and so on— efforts to increase competitive advantage. Business is being encouraged to help in solving social problems and, alongside just cash donations, is offering help in the guise of managerial advice, technological support, and employee volunteers for diverse community projects. As corporate citizens, such philanthropic businesses are aligning self-interest with the broader public good. A few key examples are the Ronald McDonald House program working in several countries, American Express helping the Hungarian government set up its tourism industry, and the worldwide work of IBM (Smith, 1994).

These approaches are part of the broader picture of stakeholder management as evident in the strategy portfolios of many organizations. How deep real concerns actually go about the environment and diversity often, however, only emerge over time, or when corporate cleverness is overcome by crisis and tragedy in a more immediate manner.

Chapter VII

Some Strategies and Techinques for Managing in a Changing Environment

The future isn't what it used to be (Anonymous).

If we are to develop a full stakeholder model, management's function must become the coordination of the conflicting interests of these stakeholders rather than the controlling of them. The logic is not one of containing stakeholder interest, but trying to accomplish them through corporate activity (Deetz, 1995, pp. 25 and 26).

The continuing challenge for executives…is not technology, but the art of human—and humane—management (Drucker, Dyson, Handy, Saffo, & Senge, 1997, p. 19).

MANAGING STAKEHOLDERS

As outlined in chapter I, stakeholders, as individuals or groups, can have a significant impact on an organization's activities and vice-versa. Given the turbulence and complexity of organizational environments, the diversity of stakeholder groups and competing claims, it is critical that management must identify, develop appropriate relationships with, and assess conflicting demands. In short, it must manage its stakeholders, especially its primary but also increasingly its secondary ones, in order to meet its own goals.

The answers to the following key questions can provide the requisite information for best managing stakeholders (Carroll, 1989):

- Who are the organization's stakeholders—primary and secondary?
- What are their stakes—identify the nature/legitimacy of stakes; the power of a group's stakes; specific groups within a generic group?

- What opportunities and challenges are presented to the organization?
- What responsibilities (economic, legal, ethical, philanthropic) does the organization have to all its stakeholders?
- What strategies or actions should the organization take to best deal with stakeholder challenges and opportunities—direct/indirect; offensive/defensive; accommodate, negotiate, manipulate, or resist overtures; a single course of action or a combination of approaches?

Savage, Nix, Whitehead, and Blair (1991) suggest the following steps in managing internal, external, and interface stakeholders. First, like Carroll (1989) above, they point to the need to identify the organization's key stakeholders. Second, diagnose the stakeholder's potential for threat in order to avoid surprises—a "worst case" scenario; and potential for cooperation as a "best case" scenario, allowing for more than defensive or offensive strategies—even the possibility of cooperation. Some of the key factors to be considered include:

- whether or not the stakeholder controls key resources needed by the organization;
- how powerful is the stakeholder (more, equal, or less powerful than the organization);
- is the stakeholder likely to take action and, if so, is it to be supportive or non-supportive of the organization; and
- is the stakeholder likely to form any coalition and, if so, is it to be with other stakeholders or with the organization?

Generally, the stakeholder's power increases with the dependency of the organization; such power and its relevance in relation to a specific issue determines the stakeholder's capacity for threat; and the higher is the willingness of the stakeholder to cooperate, the more dependent it is on the organization.

Third, the authors suggest the following management strategies, according to potential for threat or cooperation and stakeholder types:

- The supportive stakeholder (e.g., board, managers, employees, and parent company) is low on potential for threat and high on potential for cooperation—involve in relevant issues in order to increase cooperative potential.

- The marginal stakeholder (e.g., consumer interest groups, stockholders, professional associations) is not highly threatening or especially cooperative except insofar as interest is activated by a narrow range of specific issues—monitor interests.
- The non-supportive stakeholder (e.g., competitive organizations, governments, unions, media) is high on potential threat and low on potential cooperation—use a defensive strategy, reducing the dependence on which the stakeholder's interest in the organization is based.
- The mixed blessing stakeholder (e.g., clients, employees in short supply, organizations with complementary assets) has equally high potential to threaten or cooperate—collaborate in order to make it more difficult to oppose the opposition (e.g., joint ventures or even mergers).

Having formulated what are the appropriate strategies to use in order to enhance or change current relationships with key stakeholders and improve the situation for the organization, the final step is to ensure effective implementation of these strategies. One can also consider transforming the stakeholder relationship from the less favorable to a more favorable one and manage the stakeholder appropriately under its "new" type. But stakeholder management must become integral to the organization's strategy, with specific goals established and realized for the organization's relationships with current and potential stakeholders.

Mitroff (1983) proposes a multiple approach to uncovering and identifying stakeholders:

- imperative—identifying stakeholders who feel strong enough about an organizations policies or actions that they will act on their feelings—use policy slogans and exploring actions against the policy system;
- positional—identifying stakeholders occupying formal positions in a policy-making structure (internal or external to the organization)—use government organizational charts and legal documents;

- reputational—identifying critical stakeholders—use knowledgeable or important people to nominate others they believe have a stake in the system;
- social participation—identifying stakeholders participating in a specific policy issue arena—use membership of specific organizations or committees;
- opinion-leadership—identifying those shaping the opinions of stakeholders—use editors of journals, media figures, and the like;
- demographic—identifying policy impact on specific groups—use characteristics such as age, sex, race, and the like; and
- organizational—identifying those having important relationships within specific sectors—select a focal organization in a policy system.

Stakeholders, then, need assessment in terms of their properties—their purposes and motivations, beliefs, and the resources they command (e.g., physical, material, symbolic, power, etc.). Management of the relationships can then be considered in terms of maintaining current or changing future relationships through conversion (e.g., persuasion, bargaining, problem solving); opposing (using resources, destroying or forming coalitions with others); absorbing aspects through cooptation; coalescing through coalition formation; avoiding or ignoring; appeasing; surrendering to the stakeholders; developing an intense relationship; or becoming the stakeholder through a merger or the like.

The changing nature and structure of our organizations into the next decade, as discussed in this book, means that the normal demarcations between internal and external stakeholders is also blurring and so the management of both sets has seen converging practices. Harrison and St. John (1996) point out that justification for managing stakeholders today moves beyond a normative approach alone, suggesting that it is the right thing to do per se and behavior which accepts business responsibility to society. It now includes an instrumental one that recognizes the real increased value for the organization based on payoffs such as better ability to predict/control the organization's external environment; more new products and services; better operating efficiency; less damage by stakeholders (e.g., boycotts and strikes); less conflict and legal problems; better regulation; more trust; greater organizational flexibility; and an enhanced corporate image.

They suggest the following guidelines for managing and partnering with external stakeholders. First, one should establish the strategic importance of particular stakeholders though assessing:

- the stakeholders' contribution to the environmental uncertainty facing the organization;
- the stakeholder's ability to reduce environmental uncertainty for the organization; and
- the strategic choices of managers in the organization.

Having done this, the next step is to devise tactics for managing and partnering one's stakeholders. The following examples demonstrate the basis for their recommended approaches:

- Suppliers—management tactics include purchasing departments; encouraging competition among them; sponsoring new suppliers; threatening vertical integration; and long-term contracts. Partnering tactics include supplier involvement on design teams; integrating ordering systems with manufacturing; joint development of new products and applications; combined information systems; coordinated quality control; and simultaneous production.
- Activist Groups—management tactics involve internal programs satisfying demands; political/public relations approaches offsetting or protecting against negative publicity; and financial donations. Partnering tactics incorporate consulting on sensitive issues; joint ventures for research or research consortia; appointing group representatives onto boards and committees; and jointly sponsoring public relations efforts.

The real essence, here, lies in moving beyond just traditional stakeholder management approaches, practices essentially about buffering and facilitating stakeholder demands, to incorporating a proactive partnering approach that increases control and flexibility in an environment of uncertainty. The mind-set must move from building higher boundaries to building interdependency. In this sense, then, there is a clear distinction between the management of stakeholders in gaining consensus of sorts for organizational success—a control approach; and that of management on behalf of stakeholders, with stakeholders regarded as partners in the organization's destiny—an empowerment approach (Dunn & Brady, 1995).

MANAGING THE ENVIRONMENT

There are a variety of approaches to managing the environment in terms of how intrusive an organization is in its environment—ranging from the passive acceptance of environmental information, to a much more aggressive approach inquiring into environmental information and, sometimes, even attempting to manipulate or actually construct the environment:

- Active enacting organizations—regard the environment as unanalyzable and use experimentation, testing, coercion, inventing the environment plus learn by doing.
- Active discovering organizations—regard the environment as analyzable and use formal search, questioning, surveys, data gathering, and active detection.
- Passive undirected viewing—assume the environment is unanalyzable and use constrained interpretations, nonroutine informal data, hunch, rumor, plus change opportunities.
- Passive conditioned viewing—assume an analyzable environment and interpret within traditional boundaries, using passive detection, routine, and formal data (Hardy, 1994).

Harrison and St. John (1996) outline the more traditional ways in which organizations have responded to environmental demands and opportunities. They:

- ignore or evade external demands or pressure;
- accede to those portions of demands that least threaten organization routines;
- adjust work procedures or flows to take account of changes in the availability of resources or the demand for services;
- limit the impact of pressure groups by assigning responsibility for dealing with them to functions or units (e.g., customer relations) that are isolated from the rest of the organization and have limited impact on it; and

- monitor external developments to reduce surprises and disruptions and to facilitate planning.

Rather than merely reacting, ways are suggested to allow organizations to intervene in their environments:

- lobby and manoeuvre for political support;
- use economic power to influence external groups (e.g., boycotts);
- advertise to shape demand or attitudes;
- cooperate with other organizations to share resources, reduce competition, and shape other environmental conditions; and
- create structural ties with other organizations (contracts, mergers, purchases) that increase control over the environment.

Building on the work of others, Carroll (1989) suggests a useful approach to understanding and managing the changing environment, including the following:

- Scanning the environment—focused on proactively identifying precursors or indications of possible environmental change and issues, and alerting management to same. Early irregular scanning has, in our current environment, given way to much more periodic and even continuous scanning, with a concomitant increase in the sophistication of techniques, approaches, and results, and resources committed.
- Monitoring environmental trends—focused on following specific trends and events in order to confirm/disconfirm patterns or trends. Results lead to forecasts, continually monitoring of trends, or future scanning of specific patterns as identified.
- Forecasting environmental changes—focused on the future-oriented stage of information gathering, offering realistic projections of direction, scope, speed, and intensity of environmental change. This provides the basis for strategic planning in the context of economic, technological, social, and political components of the environment.
- Assessment for organizational implications—focused on analyzing and understanding the information gathered in the other stages, its meaning for management, and the implications

for the organization as a whole in terms of probability and impact.

The heavy emphasis on forecasting and control are evident in a traditional approach that highlights the need to plan with scenarios and employ a wide variety of approaches such as some of the following forecasting techniques:

- Trend extrapolation—a popular method, using a visual inspection of the curves or trends plotted on a chart, and based on the view that future trends will develop in the same direction and at the same rate as past trends unless there is a clear indication of change.
- Trend impact analysis—a way of examining relationships between a trend and events or other trends that could affect it.
- Cross-impact analysis—methods used to identify and determine the significance of relationships and interactions between specific events.
- Econometric modes—are based on regression analysis and can provide data of a national or regional nature.
- Delphi techniques—where a panel of experts are polled for their opinions on predetermined topics in an ongoing reiterative manner until some sort of consensus is reached.

Another approach, made popular by Naisbitt's *Megatrends* (1982) and Naisbitt and Aburdene's *Megatrends 2000* (1990), is trend watching. As Merriam and Makower (1988) put it, this involves accessing news media, counting and recording issues and events, and using the data compiled to form predictions about what may happen over the next one to five years. They make a distinction between the megatrends approach that counts numbers of articles about an issue, and the trend watching approach that measures (in column inches or broadcast minutes) the total volume of coverage the media chooses to give that issue.

Some prefer to conceptualize the best way of reading the environment in terms of competitive intelligence, considered by many as a critical competency for managing in a changing environment. While intelligence itself is an enormous topic that goes back in military history, business intelligence is a more recent phenomenon. Here the practice is part organizational foundation for developing strategies and tactics and involves a heavy concentration on assessing competitors. It consists of (Prescott, 1995, p. 73): "a continuously evolving integration of both formalised and informal processes by which organizational members assess key trends, emerging discontinuities, the evolution of industry structure, and the capabilities and behaviors of current and potential competitors to assist in maintaining or developing a competitive advantage."

What is critical today, as Martinsons (1994) puts it, is to avoid drowning in data and having access to timely, relevant, and meaningful information for decision making. Developments in technology have aided this, to some extent, although an appropriate strategic business intelligence system is required within which to use the advantages of sophisticated data gathering now available. The competitive intelligence information process itself is used to avoid surprises, imitate successes, and set up benchmarking, rather than specifically to outsmart opponents. It entails information on operating procedures and policies, marketing, products, finances, personnel, and a culture profile. Information overload must be avoided through effective filtering, storage, and retrieval of only relevant intelligence.

He also emphasizes that, rather than limiting such intelligence work to one organizational unit, the concept of data gathering ought to be embedded throughout the organization's culture and personnel. Nevertheless, it is important to have intelligence analysts, specialists in the area, a champion in terms of senior management, and a coordinator to ensure the effectiveness of the process. These people guide the process in terms of information sources—publications, databases, internal and indirect sources, and the like. They also ensure intelligence ethics, appropriate delivery of the end results, ongoing evaluation of the organization's intelligence system, and the safeguarding of organization secrets where necessary. In so doing, the constructive link between use of corporate intelligence and organizational success is more likely to be ensured.

Managing in a changing environment means having some sort of understanding of the future, something not possible in a specific sense but feasible in terms of most likely future events, scenarios if you like. Messages are available in the environment suggesting likely future directions. Managers forewarned are forearmed and able to prepare strategically, both offensively and defensively—capturing opportunities and dealing with problems and threats more strategically. This is not the concrete control dreamt about in the past emphasis on rigid planning but rather a tool to help us anticipate, understand, and manage in an increasingly uncertain and complex present and future. Strategic direction and choice must be based soundly in a grasp of external environmental concerns.

Through environmental scanning, as described by Stoffels (1994), we can capture organizational intelligence concerning current and future environments and the change variables likely to impact on organizational processes. While there is no foolproof method of foretelling precise future events accurately all the time, there are ways and means of assessing the most likely patterns and scenarios through reading the clues and cues given by that environment. Scanning, for both large and small organizations, provides a way of learning about emerging environmental changes in time to instil changes required for organizational survival and success, and lessens the potential for destructive surprises. While this does not guarantee accuracy of prediction, so doing helps increase our sensitization and preparedness for an uncertain future. Such practice must be based in adequate resources, and be central and integrated with strategy and operations throughout the organization.

It aids strategic management and competitiveness by providing early warning signals and by alerting us to what we know and, just as importantly, all that we do not know and cannot control. This then feeds into exploring the internal environment of the organization and ensuring it is viable in terms of structure, processes, and behavior, to deal with the changing reality of its external surround. Not surprisingly it is a core platform for the sort of anticipatory, flexible, and opportunistic management required in our turbulent postindustrial society (Ansoff, 1984).

One useful guide for a scanning strategy is outlined in the following (Stoffels, 1994):

1. Set the Environmental Focal Zone: allocation of scanning resources across the five dimensions of operational, financial, technological, competitive and stakeholder.

2. Range Settings of Scanning:

        a. Plausibility—the focus should be on characterizing high payoff (probability x impact) events from the future probable, possible, and improbable environments. Exploring improbable events with very high impacts is critical.

    b.   Time—the organization should respond strategically to environmental input in time frames suitable. However the ideal time horizons are five-10 years for corporations; 10-20 years for government; and more than 20 years for consultants, although actual horizons are usually much less (Fahey, King, & Narayanan, 1981).

    c.   Geography—consider not only local and national environments but also those beyond.

3. Environmental information collection format—the intensity of the scanning process must adjust to the information needs of the organization. The intensity of information data collection is affected by the following:

    a.   Continuity of monitoring related to frequency or periodicity—regular, irregular, or continuous. Decisions have to be based on cost-benefit considerations here, and there are indeed many benefits of continuous scanning (e.g., fewer missed opportunities or threats, better integration into the organizational processes).

    b.   Methods of monitoring where consideration must be given to how structured and intense the approach might be—broad ranging, or narrow and specific.

    c.   Formalism of monitoring modes relating to the sources for environmental information.

In this approach the scanning process per se, consists of three major aspects:

    a.   Gathering inputs and generating information:

- set scanning and information strategy
- gather clues about the future
- abstract, distill, and report information
- maintain, audit, and refine baseline knowledge about "what is."

b. Synthesizing and evaluating emerging issues:

- classify and correlate, combine and integrate, analyze, document and query
- develop scenarios
- evaluate, assess, and rank issues and exposures
- identify key issues.

c. Communicating environmental insights:

- relate environmental vision to near-term task environment and feed into unit plans
- relate environmental vision to strategic position and feed into organizational strategy.

Some of the problems and obstacles mentioned as occurring in such scanning include the real difficulties of:

- interpretation of data received;
- not moving beyond the scanning to action;
- setting too narrow agendas for data collection;
- not measuring actual rates of change;
- using unstructured thinking that lacks organizational credibility;
- most organizations being focused on immediate productivity;
- managers being preoccupied with operations;
- scanning carried out in a fragmented way;
- having information and issue overload; and
- focusing on what is, rather than on what might be.

It is also recommended that both structure and human resources need effective management for environmental intelligence gathering. The formula Stoffels (1994) actually advocates is to have:

a. An external environmental council consisting of representatives from the functions, strategic business units, and other constituencies within the organization. This membership can clearly give input from every significant area of the organization and, importantly, can communicate back in appropriate ways to its own constituencies. This body unifies the idea and functions of environmental scanning through sustaining the locus of scanning activities; representing distinct organizational contexts; providing specialized communication interfaces; coordinating organization-wide environmental knowledge; monitoring environmental adaptation; and measuring accountability. Inputs would occur through a variety of means including from all levels of the organization and from specialist units such as R&D, market research, issues management, and the like. In order to avoid myopia, some external perspective may be gainfully employed through use of consultants and commissioned studies. Industry joint scanning processes may also contribute.

b. Support means some sort of infrastructure consisting of one or more support staff and resources, including library considerations. Having a separate scanning department is not advisable because it abrogates responsibility for scanning from a much wider array of individuals and subunits in the organization.

c. The executive champion links the work of the professional levels doing the scanning work with those engaged in corporate strategy and the executive level. He or she sponsors, provides resources, authorizes work, and communicates with senior executives about the work of the scanning council. This person also leads the way in developing a scanning culture, making all organizational members sensitive to environmental signals and able to communicate these effectively to the appropriate places in the organization for action.

d. The scanners at every level of the organization need to be able to think broadly rather than in narrow confines, to be divergent rather than convergent thinkers. They should be able to reframe their environmental thinking in gathering and evaluating information and to make full use of their intuitive capacities.

Lenz and Engledow (1986) urge the need to consider just how formalized and narrowly located should an organization's environmental analysis actually be. Like Stoffels's (1994) approach mentioned above, they suggest experience reveals that there are real problems associated with designing environmental analysis units, positioning them in the context of an organization, and integrating them into strategic decision processes. Chief among the many stumbling blocks are those of resistance from existing power structures, the real nature of executive support, and the genuine capacity of such specific units to make tangible contributions to important management decisions. It is, therefore, critical for management to reflect on whether one houses scanning and analysis in just one center or disperses it and if one decides on the former:

- How environmental analysis units are organized and staffed, and where they are positioned within the structure of the organization?
- What are the centrally important contingencies when deciding on the organizing and positioning of environmental analysis units?
- In guiding environmental scanning and analysis activities, just what conceptions of the organizational environment are used?
- What are the benefits and problems associated with various ways of organizing an environmental analysis unit?

One must also have an extensive knowledge of the key sources for environmental information. These include mass media—broadcast and print; business periodicals and specialist publications; consultants; government publications; academic journals; professional associations; popular literature, and the like. The central issue is to choose sources that will alert management to what is likely to happen rather than confirming the past or immediate present. So the emphasis should be on approaches that include reading science fiction, futures journals, and making use of long-term opinion polling, experts, and so on (Mendel, 1978).

Analysis of such databases developed requires intuition, creativity, and a variety of qualitative (such as brainstorming) and quantitative (such as econometric modeling) analytic and forecasting techniques. These are too numerous to be discussed here but are outlined well in the literature of the field including the work of Stoffels (1994), already mentioned, and the many journals such as *Technological Forecasting and Social Change, Long Range Planning*, and the *International Journal of Forecasting*.

ISSUES MANAGEMENT

The complement to such environmental scanning is found in the practice of issues management. Ewing (1987) maintains that, at heart, issues management is concerned with public policy research, foresight, and planning. Yet it moves beyond narrow issues of government/business relations and public affairs and enables the management of the enterprise as a whole. Issues management then deals with groups external to the organization engaged in the public policy process that may impact on an organization's future; and how the organization deals with its need to be part of the public policy process.

According to Stoffels (1994), the issues management area of organizational life broadens that of scanning to include those activities wherein the organization concentrates its efforts at managing external elements such as the political, social, and regulatory aspects. Such efforts include forming positions on sensitive public and policy issues; communicating current issues; managing public communication; advocacy activities; and having input to the organization's scanning activities by searching for emerging issues.

Issues management is important to managing a changing environment in being a process that analyzes and prioritizes what issues are relevant to an organization, devises ways of responding to such issues, and then evaluates and monitors outcomes. A narrow approach focuses on public issues, while a broader approach encompasses strategic issues and the strategic management process, much in line with what has been described in the earlier sections of this chapter. The former explores public/social issues, whereas the latter includes all issues and is much more an integral part of overall organizational strategy. The process provides the organization with much more control and a broader array of options and strategies. The approach as outlined by Carroll (1989) for this public policy management strategy follows a similar approach to that discussed previously:

- Identification of issues—often called environmental scanning or social forecasting, focused on scanning the environment and identifying emerging issues of potential relevance to the organization; includes ongoing data gathering from a range of publications, subscription to a trend information services, and so on.

- Analysis of issues—dissecting, grouping, in order to better understand the characteristics of an issue and its potential implications for a variety of organizational stakeholders.
- Ranking or prioritizing of issues—forming issues into a hierarchy of importance to the organization, related to probability of occurrence, impact on the company, and the like.
- Formulating and implementing responses—devising a response design in order to deal with the issue(s) in an appropriate strategic manner; and implementation as a focus after formulation of suitable plans (includes resources required, structures, timing, etc.)
- Evaluating, monitoring, and controlling—constant evaluation of an organization's response to the issue, ensuring actions are according to plans; monitoring of stakeholders' opinions through some form of audit; feeding back information acquired in order to help better manage the overall process.

MANAGING CRISIS

Environmental scanning and issues management, alone, cannot totally prevent organizations sometimes having to confront crises of varying dimensions and types. A crisis here can be defined "as a disruption that physically affects a system as a whole and threatens its basic assumptions, its subjective sense of self, its existential core" (Pauchant & Mitroff, 1992, p. 12).

Crises today are major surprise situations having potentially damaging results for our organizations, including increased stress levels, loss of customer support, and a tarnished corporate image and reputation. A crisis can arise from numerous events such as product injuries, sudden market shifts, regulatory changes, hostile takeover attempts, and environmental catastrophes. Crises can be the result of organizational action or inaction, factors in the external environment, and natural disasters.

Yet, while it is difficult to prevent natural disasters, we do know that many other man-made crises are potentially preventable. Nowadays, there seems to be a certain inevitability about linking the modern organization and crisis. While all ages have undergone traumas of one sort or another, the turbulence and crises faced by organizations and society in general seems to have escalated to a scale previously unfamiliar. Organizations have to deal much more frequently than before with disruptive incidents—financial, labor, environmental, and the like, that pose real threats to their productivity or even their ongoing survival.

The major crises from Bhopal to Exxon-Valdez and Tylenol have demonstrated the real vulnerability to crises that many organizations face in the closing decade of the twentieth century. Little wonder, then, that some organizations now see the wisdom in planning strategically to prevent, and, given the impossibility of eliminating all crises, to manage with crises.

Even on a smaller scale today, most organizations, especially major corporations, cannot escape the necessity of having strategic contingency plans in place for dealing with a variety of potential crises relating to products, production, safety and health concerns, and other critical organizational processes, especially those that may impact on the corporate image. While there are numerous approaches to measuring an organization's successful recovery from crisis, one critical measure is the extent to which customers are willing to deal with an organization again and how they perceive its crisis management and response profile.

While there are numerous events in an organization's history, such as the launch of new products or anniversaries, it is when we come to how crises are handled that the real identity or character of an organization is truly revealed. Therefore, the significance of crisis management should not be underestimated.

Certainly internationally it is clear that the frequency and scale of crises seems to be increasing. Yet while all our business organizations carry insurance coverage, how many actually cover themselves with adequate, systematic, and strategically integrated crisis management programs? Overwhelmingly, the literature in the field, alongside the real-world events that have occurred in the 1980s and 1990s, point to inadequate crisis management preparation by organizations. Moreover, these also suggest (e.g., Pauchant & Mitroff, 1992) that, unlike the case of natural disasters, the human-induced crises are, at least, more preventable.

One need not, of course, go looking for the mega or media grabbing types of crisis. Meyers and Holusha (1986, p. 9) in the late 1960s, in quieter times, did then point out "nine distinct types of business crisis—public perception, sudden market shift, product failure, top management succession, cash, industrial relations, hostile takeover, adverse international events, and regulation and deregulation." More recently, Mahon and Cochran (1991) usefully suggest the following four forces working toward crises:

- organizational action or inaction leading to managerial and technical errors, or failures in standard operating procedures;
- long-term, generally foreseeable trends in the external environment;
- external actions and situations that are not the fault of the organization but rather where some outside agent is trying to "get" the organization; and
- natural disasters such as floods, hurricanes, earthquakes, and the like.

Booth (1993) points out that different types of crisis affect organizations differentially. The ones he focuses on are a sort of evolutionary or "creeping" crises; periodic threats or loss; and the more immediately drastic crisis relating to sudden threat or loss, spelling danger to the whole organization.

Two of the leading researchers and writers in the field, Pearson and Mitroff (1993) propose the following crisis types:

1. Technical/Economic:

- external economic attacks—extortion, bribery, boycotts, hostile takeovers;
- external information attacks—copyright infringement, loss of information, counterfeiting, rumors;
- mega damage—environmental accidents;
- breaks—recalls, product defects, plant defects, computer breakdowns, poor operator/errors, poor security;

2. Human/Social:

- occupational health diseases;
- perceptual—damage to reputation;
- psycho—terrorism, copycats, onsite and offsite sabotage/tampering, executive kidnappings, sexual harassment, rumors.

Whatever the type or dimension, not surprisingly, then, seeing crisis management as an integral part of strategic management, overall, is now emphasized as a critical practice in recent research (Smith & Sipika, 1993). And we do, from analysis of past experience, have in the international literature, some guidelines, both on how we should approach the issue and about the practice of crisis management. Consistently, however, the literature in the field, alongside the real-world events that have occurred in the 1980s and 1990s, as suggested earlier, do point to the ongoing inadequate preparation and missed opportunities by organizations for effective and efficient crisis management.

Crisis situations are not only complex but also ambiguous and there are no guaranteed prescriptions for their management. As Lagadec (1991, pp. xiv-xv) puts it: "crises exploit those miracle solutions that are supposed to deflate them—indeed, they feed off them with an application matched only by their perverseness." The fact that multiple research perspectives are required to understand crisis management—for example, from technology risk, sociology, geography, international relations, psychology, administration, and management—suggests its difficulty as a field. Additionally, crisis management is not about producing a set of plans alone but rather about preparing the organization to think creatively about the apparently unthinkable in order that the best possible decisions can be made in times of crisis (Pearson & Mitroff, 1993).

Some broad guidelines are, nevertheless, available. Generally, authorities see best practice crisis management as anticipating and preventing crisis and minimizing any destructive effects resulting from a crisis occurring. They point to the critical issue of crisis management planning being an integral part of organizational life, reflecting the organization's philosophy rather than being superimposed upon it. It must be tied to an organization's strategic decision rather than its operational levels.

Moreover, the multidisciplinary, multifaceted, but integrated response offers the optimum approach. This is vital, given the very diversity of the perspectives and interests of the differing publics and stakeholders that make for crisis management often being a complex and difficult process (Shrivastava, 1989).

Having a crisis management plan incorporating a focus on the communication processes and technologies—before, during, and after crisis—is a sound organizational investment. This is particularly so if we take a stakeholder approach as outlined in the first and present chapters: not only does it aid in anticipating problems but it also minimizes crisis damage, enhances control, expedites recovery, and offers confidence to management, employees, consumers, and other stakeholders. We need to be prepared to deal with the unanticipated and unusual. We must also contemplate the cost of crisis management plans and safeguards, versus the actual costs of crisis itself.

Pearson and Mitroff (1993) provide a list of preventative actions:

- Audits—legal/financial, legislation, reduction of inventories, environmental impact audits;
- External information/communication—issues management, warning systems, government relationships, 800 numbers, share plans, media training, behavioral profiling;
- Internal repair/design—improved safety, plant design, product packaging, inspection, organizational chain of command; and
- Internal emotional preparation—whistleblowers, emotional training, employee classes, behavioral profiling.

For them, it is critical to understand and utilize the five phases of crisis management: signal detection, preparation/prevention, containment/damage limitation; recovery; and learning from the experience of a crisis. They also provide a useful crisis management (CM) strategic checklist (Pearson & Mitroff, 1993, p. 58):

1. Strategic Action:

- integrate CM into strategic planning processes
- integrate CM into statements of corporate excellence
- include outsiders on the board and on CM teams
- provide training and workshops in CM
- expose organizational members to crisis simulations
- create a diversity or portfolio of CM strategies

2. Technical and Structural Actions:

- create a CM team
- dedicate budget expenditures for CM
- establish accountabilities for updating emergency policies/ manuals

- computerize inventories of CM resources (e.g., employee skills)
- designate an emergency command control room
- assure technological redundancy in vital areas (e.g., computer systems)
- establish working relationship with outside experts in CM

3. Evaluation and Diagnostic Actions:

- conduct legal and financial audit of threats and liabilities
- modify insurance coverage to match CM contingencies
- conduct environmental impact audits
- prioritize activities necessary for daily operations
- establish tracking system for early warning signals
- establish tracking system to follow up past crises or near crises

4. Communication Actions:

- provide training for dealing with the media regarding CM
- improve communication lines with local communities
- improve communication with intervening stakeholders (e.g., police)

5. Psychological and Cultural Actions:

- increase visibility of strong top management commitment to CM
- improve relationships with activist groups
- improve upward communication (including "whistleblowers")
- improve downward communication re: CM programs/ accountabilities
- provide training re: human and emotional impacts of crises
- provide psychological support services (e.g., stress/anxiety/ management)
- reinforce symbolic recall/corporate memory of past crises/ dangers.

Crisis and Communication

Effective communication is a critical strategic factor in crisis management—internal, external, and interorganizational. This is especially so because an organization's image and credibility is on the line during crisis. As Lukaszewski (1988, p. 318) points out: "communications expertise must cut across all levels of crisis management....Carefully structured internal and external communication strategies must be implemented."

Communication is crucial throughout the crisis life cycle—before a problem, identifying a problem, remedying and relieving the problem, and learning to prevent future problems. Its critical role is suggested because communication is two way—the organization receiving and generating communication; communication is inextricably linked to strategy, organizational decision making and planning; communication plays a central role in issues and public affairs management; expertise in public communication is vital in reducing uncertainty, anxiety, and potential damage to the corporate image and reputation; and dealing with the mass media involves a critical ongoing exercise of communication competence at all times.

So a critical aspect of any crisis management plan is the communication dimension:

> Crisis communications built on well-established relationships with key audiences stand a better chance of protecting, even enhancing, company reputations in times of difficulty. The real success stories are told by organizations to whom effective corporate communications is an intrinsic part of their day-to-day business activities. A company which decides to start communicating during a crisis will have little chance of establishing credibility....Enlightened management understand the importance of an open communication policy (Aspery, 1993, p. 16).

Crisis puts any organization's normal communication systems and processes under enormous additional pressure, often leading to the sort of disinformation that is frequently characteristic of the early phases of crisis management. Consequently, crisis communication plans per se focus on communication responsibility and variable audiences or stakeholders for consideration. These may include, for example, the mass media, shareholders, employees, clients, emergency services, the public, contractors, and so on. Such plans need to ensure that the organization provides adequate information to key stakeholders throughout all phases of crisis management and that it has in place all the communication media and processes necessary.

Keeping the organization's reputation untarnished relates to the level of credibility it has in an ongoing sense, unrelated to crises. Once a crisis hits, how the organization deals with the crisis is paramount, although those organizations with ongoing credibility, a good reputation, and who act in a socially responsible manner, tend to fare better overall. The views of external agencies such as the media and regulatory bodies also have an impact (Siomkos & Shrivastava, 1993).

In most of the literature we find recommendations for some type of crisis management group, usually involving very senior organizational personnel such as the MD, finance, HR, and communication managers who are at the pinnacle of a cascading chain of responsibilities within the organization and who are both qualified and competent to communicate disaster communications. The more pragmatic literature also emphasizes the need for honesty (especially accepting responsibility if this is the case in the crisis), openness and timeliness in crisis responses.

Communication planning should include scenarios for before, during, and after crisis processes. The before communication processes should ensure adequate communication about crisis communication, with appropriate circulation of communication plans and the like. During crisis processes may include dealing with the media and the public in general, communicating with employees and relatives and other stakeholders involved. The after processes involve continued communication with staff and other stakeholders, including counselling as appropriate; continued liaison with the media; and setting in place a whole array of learning mechanisms for the organization.

Potent crisis planning allows also for the centralization and control of information flows during an actual crisis, providing for appropriate communication flows among interested players, allowing for speedy translation of the imagined to the real. This includes failsafe, secure, and alternate communication processes, providing the opportunity to better manage the crisis effectively. Necessarily, such communication and information flows are only possible in effectively designed organizations given that (Smith & Sipika, 1993) an organization's structure and culture remains a central factor in affecting its ability to respond to crisis events.

Equally important is the recent emphasis on interorganizational relationships during crisis management. The area of interorganizational communication has been relatively under-researched (More & Ross Smith, 1992) in the past. Nathan and Mitroff (1991) have explored the issue from negotiated order theory as it applies to crisis management and the need for cooperative strategy among numerous organizations. Interestingly, their research early on found that the majority of organizations, certainly in product-tampering crises, believed that they could work alone. The authors argue (p. 165) instead that a collaborative approach to managing a variety of crisis is warranted and that, "At a minimum, organizations should be able to identify all the parties likely to become involved in a crisis and how each should be expected to respond under sometimes severe time pressures."

The whole arena of external information and communication is also important as a preventative measure. Pauchant and Mitroff (1992) emphasize here processes such as issues management, warning systems, media training, 800 numbers, government relationships and the like. So, too, is the considered use of supportive communications technology (Rice, 1990).

Thus, generally, though only one dimension of crisis management overall, communication is a highly significant, central, yet often neglected, facet. Aside from this broad belief, we need to tailor our communication solutions according to specific situations and variables including (Seymour, 1991): the scope of the crisis, the target audience, the content of messages (objective, sensitivity, urgency, frequency, amount), the sensitivity of the information from a credibility or competitive strategy standpoint, the urgency of disseminating information, organizational resources available, and type of crisis (especially attribution of guilt or innocence). Choosing the appropriate medium is also important in terms of reach, timing, and so on.

Organizational problems affecting crisis communication include deficient accident prevention systems, inappropriate crisis management information, limited credibility and fragile legitimacy. Into a crisis situation, inappropriate communication like the following is dysfunctional: an embarrassed silence, downplaying, denial, stereotype responses, inadequate information, concealment and deceit, and absence of impositions of responsibility (Lagadec, 1987).

Another issue relating to communication and crisis management, overall, is that of organizational power and politics. While crisis management should never be merely the province of CEO or senior executives, we need to remember that it does, however, involve:

...questions about power and how it is used. Handling a crisis is first and foremost a matter of making judgements, redefining standards, establishing options, defining strategies, remodelling power relationships, and sticking with a position—all this when the conventional framework has become completely obsolete (Lagadec, 1991, p. xiv).

Crisis and Culture

Organizational crisis can be like a sudden and perhaps brutal type of organization audit—often in no more than a moment's notice, what was left unprepared turns into a complex problem and all that is unhealthy in the organization is instantly revealed. Crisis opens any breeches in the organization's defenses, creating an instant vision of reality and often creating a type of vacuum (Lagadec, 1991).

Not surprisingly, then, the internal dynamics of the organization are the key to crisis prevention or preparedness, management, and recovery. Many agree that managers need to link crisis management with changing culture, communication, and organization design. Certainly critical, in terms of susceptibility to crisis, is the culture of the organization in all its many manifestations—values, attitudes, beliefs, and the like. Mitroff, Pauchant, and Shrivastava (1989, p. 271) argue culture as one, if not the most important of variables in crisis management:

> Certain cultures not only value but actively encourage the process of learning; others actively discourage it. Indeed, it had become clear to us that the culture of an organization was one of the most important variables, perhaps the most important one, in explaining what, if anything, an organization did in the area of CM.

Therefore, this suggests that a crisis-prone culture is basic to precipitating catastrophe. In addition, the managerial culture in place before a crisis occurs affects the capacity for the organization to survive the crisis experience (Smith & Sipika, 1993). Rigid mental sets determine the organization's level of preparedness, its capacity to respond, and its ability to learn and recover from crises.

Ongoing research by Mitroff, Pauchant, Finney, and Pearson (1989), and Mitroff and Pearson (1993) demonstrates that, while important in one sense, formal plans and procedures don't necessarily tally with crisis management action, nor that just having a formal set of crisis plans and procedures will mean one is sufficiently prepared. Indeed, often the process of planning, of thinking and learning is more important and here is where corporate culture is central. Using an onion model of CM they claim (Mitroff et al., 1989, p. 273):

> ...the factors which constitute the core are often the most decisive. In a phrase, if the core of an organization is in trouble—or in common parlance, "rotten"— then the surface activities (behavior, policies) of an organization will count for little. The organization can put together formal crisis manual after crisis manual and issue formal directive after directive and still little of a positive nature will result. At best, it will have the illusion of preparation and control. In other words, the health of the entire onion is often no better than that of its core...successful CM is a matter of performing well across all the levels.

For them, the core of corporate culture/identity especially as it relates to crisis management focuses on three issues: self-centeredness/narcissism; defensive mechanisms; and fatalism/passivity. So we find that:

- crisis-prone organizations are more narcissistic/self-centered than prepared organizations; and have unhealthy narcissism to ward off bad self-feelings while prepared organizations have healthy narcissism related to a positive self-regard for the organization, its employees, and society.
- prone organizations see crisis as something that happens essentially to them—inwardly focused, while with prepared ones crisis happens to them and all stakeholders.
- prone organizations use various defense mechanisms to protect their inflated self-image and ward off the reality of crises; prepared organizations make far less use of defense mechanisms.
- fatalism allows prone organizations to avoid guilt and to justify doing little or nothing; prepared organizations use the strategy far less and, instead, believe in strategic action, in accepting guilt and anxiety created by crisis in order to respond more effectively.
- prepared organizations adopt both technical and behavioral actions to prepare for and manage crises.
- prepared organizations go further than the routine motions of CM—for example, they have early warning systems, better and flexible structures, top management support for CM, simulate

and train for crises, and see CM as an integrated vital part of all business practices.

Here we see links to the learning organization, knowledge management, devising appropriate structures, and adopting different mind-sets, as explored in the earlier chapters of this book.

Mitroff (1988) himself had suggested, previously, that there ought to be five phases of crisis management: signal detection, preparation/ prevention, containment/damage limitation; recovery; and learning. Pauchant, Mitroff, and Lagadec (1991) complement this by offering five "families" of crisis management: (1) strategic efforts; (2) technical and structural efforts; (3) efforts in evaluation and diagnosis; (4) communication efforts; and (5) psychological and cultural efforts. Therefore, crisis management clearly requires an enormous amount from organizations, often akin to reengineering of some kind. Certainly it demands far greater than what is generally assumed, that is public relations, media training, and the like.

For example, Pauchant, Mitroff, and Lagadec (1991) propose that in effective and systematic crisis management planning many basic assumptions, ideologies, and frames of reference are challenged. These can include the general corporate philosophy, ideas of corporate excellence, and being able to see the organization as both a productive and destructive system. As in the earlier comments on existentialism in chapter IV, in order to reduce our deep anxiety over challenges to basic assumptions, we often resort to using a variety of powerful defense mechanisms.

What their research suggests is that in crisis-prepared organizations crisis management is considered overall as a moral and strategic necessity rather than as a cost. In addition, senior personnel in such organizations focus not only on the optimistic dimensions of organizational life, such as success and growth, but also consider issues such as decay, death, and organizational failure. In other words they have developed the capacity to imagine the worst as a basis for managing crisis or, even better, trying to prevent it.

So for crisis management we need more flexibility and learning systems that permit improved understanding of both the internal and external environments of organizations. This includes the capacity to reframe, to challenge basic organizational views through which such understanding is constructed (Morgan, 1997; Bolman & Deal, 1997; Powell, 1991).

More recently, Greening and Johnson's research (1996, p. 25) suggested that not only organizational strategies but also the characteristics of top-management teams were related to the capacity to avoid crises, or to be very responsive to potentially threatening events:

> ...firms that are better able to avoid crisis events have top-management teams with a higher level of functional team heterogeneity, higher education levels, shorter organizational tenures, and more tenure heterogeneity. These characteristics serve as proxies for deeper underlying cognitive processes such as more complex thinking, quality decision making, dialectical inquiry, and multiple perspectives in solving potential catastrophic problems.

In spite of the clear warnings the crisis management research provides to organizations, however, practice falls far short of the ideal:

- In 1989 researchers showed that less than half of the Fortune 1000 corporations surveyed had a crisis management team or had any type of crisis management plan in place to deal with a major crisis or catastrophe. They found that most employers believed that crisis could not happen to their organization and two-thirds that, in order to instigate crisis planning, their organization would have to actually undergo a major crisis. Some executives, not recognizing the high financial and human costs of crisis, simply could not conceive of how they could fit crisis management into their present processes because of current practices, including commitment to the bottom line and the short term (Mitroff et al., 1989).

- In 1992 evidence showed that fewer than 10 to 15 percent of the major organizations in North America and Europe had currently developed significant crisis management programs. In a survey of the Fortune 500 companies, many organizations did not match crisis management preparations with vulnerabilities; that while generally organizations supported the idea of crisis management, the requisite support systems were not in place, they lacked communication coherence, and programs were in very early stages of development (Pauchant & Mitroff, 1992).

- In 1993 work showed how generally unprepared, inexperienced, and defensive were organization leaders in the face of problems generated by organizational crisis. Few organizations, even in high-risk areas, had seriously tried to develop an integrated culture for reinforcing and motivating staff and management toward promoting crises prevention systems and mind-sets. Managers were limited in being able to assess the nature of risks adequately, ignoring risks of which they were aware, and not using crisis management systems when they were available. Overall, few organizations had a management style and culture that enabled an anticipatory view of the future where both likely and unlikely options are considered and, instead, followed a largely reflexive strategy, seeing the future in terms of the present and the past (Booth, 1993).

• In 1995 an Australian study (More, 1995) found fairly similar results to those above, with the major trends suggesting ongoing inadequate preparation and resources commitment.

So, apparently, managers generally find it difficult to consider inherent risks in their organizations. Not that they are necessarily unaware of the mega crises around the globe, but they cannot match such crisis management issues to their own organizations. As Roberts and Libuser (1993) put it, many supposedly typical organizations are really capable of contributing to great harm but remain unwilling or incapable of seeing this possibility. Unfortunately, many such organizations are precisely those where small perturbations develop into major catastrophes. Furthermore, given the recent recessionary climate, with resource pressures, downsizing, and the like, crisis management activities compete with many other organizational initiatives, which are perceived as more important in many instances. The short term again wins out here over the longer term.

Clearly then, not enough organizations have an adequate crisis management mind-set and processes in place. This means that not only do they not prepare for the dysfunctional dimensions of crisis but they are not aware of the positive aspects of preparation or the real role that crises per se play in contemporary and future organizational life (Denis, 1991). Indeed, the most potent finding arising out of the crisis management research and literature of the 1980s and 1990s is that crisis-prepared organizations have precisely the critical competencies required in the difficult 1990s and beyond. These include thinking skills, mind-sets, structures, and the like, necessary (as outlined earlier in this book) for gaining a competitive edge in our global economy (Mitroff, Pauchant, & Shrivastava, 1989).

MANAGING DIFFERENT

Reading Mr. Malcolm Muggeridge's brilliant and depressing book, *The Thirties*, I thought of another cruel trick I once played on a wasp. He was sucking jam on my plate, and I cut him in half. He paid no attention, merely went on with his meal, while a tiny stream of jam trickled out of his severed oesophagus....Only when he tried to fly away did he grasp the dreadful thing that had happened to him. It is the same with modern man. The thinking that has been cut away is his soul, and there was a period—twenty years perhaps—during which he did not notice it (Orwell cited in Piasecki, 1995, p. 7).

Ultimately, despite the limits upon what people can control, it is still up to people to act, and in acting they do more than predict the future, they invent it (Moss Kanter et al. 1992, p. 18).

Recently, Geus (1997) has highlighted the notion of "the living company"—one that has a personality allowing for harmonious evolution in a lengthy, successful history. Through research he found four key variables that such successful organizations have in common: financial conservatism; environmental sensitivity; understanding of identity; and a tolerance for new ideas. These lead to an emphasis on valuing people rather than assets; flexible controls; learning opportunities; and the notion of community.

Conversely, we have been told about the neurotic organization which Kets de Vries and Miller (1984) suggest becomes so in relation to its top leadership styles—dramatic, depressive, paranoid, compulsive, and schizoid. And while they describe how some mixes can be functional, they also illustrate the dysfunctional nature of many. Kets de Vries and associates (1991) have developed this psychodynamic research from the clinical perspective of a psychoanalyst, continuing to show how "...rational approaches to management, which assume that human beings can be managed solely by logical, means-to-ends modes of organization, are mistaken." (1993, p. xiv) and how executives, instead of always being rational, can be driven by emotions, aspirations, or fantasies that affect the very management of their organizations from day to day.

We have also been warned about the addictive organization, about obsession with work at the expense of all else in a fully rounded life.

While many, such as Peters and Austin (1985), urge us on to pay the high cost of excellence with the lure of rewards, such as a sense of purpose and self-respect, others question such drive and fixation and warn that addiction, in the form of workaholism and other organizational forms is, instead, a fatal disease for both individuals and organizations:

> Organizations can be involved in the addictive system in many ways. To the extent that they are addicts, we are all affected and the society is affected. Ultimately, organizations that are addicts have a serious obligation to become healthy, for they have wide networks that spread the disease. Through it all, we should remember that they are not bad organizations getting good, they are sick trying to get well. They are hurting at many levels and are in need of recovery (Schaef & Fassel, 1988, p. 176).

Such addiction, complementing the struggle for survival in a changing environment can result in ruthlessness, dishonesty, immorality, risk aversion, rigidity, tight control, short-term quick fixes, and self-destruction. Destructive, dysfunctional images of organizations cannot provide the macro environment required for the real source of enduring competitive advantage—that of people as an organization's vital assets. As Pfeffer (1995, p. 55) puts it:

> Achieving competitive success through people involves fundamentally altering how we think about the workforce and the employment relationship. It means achieving success by working with people, not by replacing them or limiting the scope of their activities. It entails seeing the workforce as a source of strategic advantage, not just as a cost to be minimized or avoided. Firms that take this different perspective are often able to successfully outmanoeuvre and outperform their rivals.

In valuing the organization's human assets and giving up our traditional control mechanisms, we move toward a different attitude base. Here we have organizations involving full citizens as adults rather than parent-child, control-controlled relationships. Individuals take on new responsibility and accountability in an environment that eschews the false need for traditional control, consistency, and predictability that requires the control mind-set of management as parents and others as children. To achieve this we need:

- organizations where individuals think and act like owners;
- reintegration of the management of work with the doing of work;

- the open construction and wide distribution of quality information;
- to build our social structures in terms of growth from the bottom rather than enforcement from the top; and
- frequent explicit discussion of the ends sought and major values guiding decisions (Deetz, 1995).

Problems for renewal, creativity, and appropriate perspectives for managing in a changing environment abound. It is critical that we be mindful of these. Renewal does require destruction but not the dysfunctional destruction that is all too often evident in the contemporary organization. It is also important to consider a different conception of organization—to fill out its frame with dynamism just as we ought fill out our own with joy. In moving away from traditional control and rationality in both we ought take note of the words of Tom Peters (1992) when he urges us toward liberation management. He recommends that we consider effective organizations as not built on the pyramid model but rather on that of a carnival in Rio, full of dynamism and craziness in order to thrive in our turbulent times. He urges the best use of technology for alliances, links, networks, communication, and community, and for the flexibility and staying power of the small cockroach, along with the requisite personal responsibility of postmodernism in a world of paradox.

Consequently, a rising number of people are calling for new management and leadership paradigms into the twenty-first century. They propose different approaches, ones more broadly based in ethical, spiritual, and humanitarian concerns, without ignoring the economic arguments for individuals and organizations to survive and prosper.

They demand also the development of new competencies— understanding diverse contexts, reading the environment, managing complexity, managing proactively, developing new insight into leadership, valuing people as key resources, fostering creativity/ learning/innovation; and using information technology as a tool for functional transformation (Morgan, 1988). Many of these we have covered in this book but we must be watchful for the ongoing alterations in competencies required for changing times and circumstances into the next century.

Furthermore, whether one calls it new-age management or not, there is a growing belief in the need for better organizational meaning creation and for more sense of community in contemporary organizational life. Many such calls end up illuminating the reality of managing organizational paradox (Nichols, 1994; Handy, 1994). Yet this need to create a sense of community, to anchor the organization parts into a permeable rather than rigid whole, is a view that continues to be echoed throughout the more recent literature (Bohl, Slocum, Luthans, & Hodgetts, 1996).

Given this urge toward community, what the new organizational environment may require is less concern with fighting competitors— many of whom will indeed be unknown, and more focus on anticipating market trends and rapid response to customers' needs. It will not be the organization's product line but its core capabilities and senior-level strategic thinking that will be the critical weapons. The self-image of the organization will thus shift toward one of a set of shared resources and competencies capable of rapid, effortless, and proactive mobilization in a myriad of ways in order to meet customer needs in an anybody, anyplace, anytime, anyway, future environment. Not surprisingly, then, the current obsession with downsizing and outsourcing are also being reconsidered in light of developing human resources in the future environment, recognizing the pivotal nature of people for competitive advantage, for learning and knowledge management. So insourcing and employability may take over but will work only if internal human resources are able to compete successfully with the outside and match the real needs of the organization as determined by its environment. This must include the transfer of decision making to those closest to the customers in an organization design that is much more flexible than in the past—boundaryless (internal and external) in the broad sense, or virtual, networked, and horizontal in the specific. It will also include competencies in managing partnerships and alliances, perhaps even with competitors. Importantly, the new organizational environment requires individuals themselves to change:

- to develop empathy in relationships with all stakeholders;
- to become "double-loop" learners;
- to adopt systemic thinking, seeing the macro not only the micro level of organizational experience;
- to move from traditional leadership roles, focused on control, to that encompassing catalyst, coordinator, conscience, and coach; and

- to have a degree of humility in understanding the limitations of our own values, experiences, and knowledge (Bohl et al., 1996).

Thus, recognizing the inadequacy of a purely economic view of organizational life alone, with its attendant stress on profitability, managerial control, and value-neutral rationality, we can move beyond many of the traditional formulas for managing in a changing environment. We can adopt a broader stakeholder model of organizational life, accepting different forms of ownership and adopting appropriate forms of communication, negotiation, and rationality to support such an extended vision and enhance competitive advantage in novel ways (Deetz, 1995).

Furthermore, we ought reflect on that crucial environment within our organizations and ourselves. We need to explore some of the ways in which we wish to live, the role of organizations in such scenarios (Gladwin, Kennelly, & Krause, 1995), and making better sense of our lives and those of our organizations through ongoing questioning and renewal (Hurst, 1995). With responsibility for managing our own lives, we must develop the capacity to deal with disappointment and to be able to devise congruence between our own internal and external environments. We must also strengthen our own self-reflective, empathic, and listening capacities and come to accept the existence of different ways of seeing and understanding (Kets de Vries, 1993).

Finally, we need to take the path inward and confront management of ourselves in a changing environment. As Gardener (1991) urges, we must stop business getting in the way of our learning and growing, of making us function below our real potential. We should guard against, indeed prevent, the secret ailments of organizational life—boredom and staleness, complacency, rigidity, and imprisonment in one's own comfortable habits and opinions. Moreover, it is critical to make time to look inward and overcome the tendency to be fugitives from ourselves, remembering that, after all, it is ourselves that we meet at the end of every road.

Managing in a changing environment, then, calls for a manifold journey—exploring the micro and the macro, the inner and outer, and then some—not easy, but if well trod then surely fruitful, both for the individual and the organization, for both the present and the future that we may devise.

References

Acker, J. (1992). Gendering organizational theory. In A. Mills & P. Tancred (Eds.), *Gendering organizational analysis* (pp. 248-260). Newbury Park, CA: Sage.

Adler, N., & Bartholomew, S. (1992). Managing globally competent people. *Academy of Management Executive, 6* (3), 52-65.

Agor, W. (1989). *Intuition in organizations.* Newbury Park, CA: Sage.

Alexander, E. (1995). *How organizations act together.* Luxembourg: Gordon and Breach Publishers.

Albrow, M. (1992). Sine ira et studio—or do organizations have feelings? *Organization Studies, 13* (3), 313-329.

Allende, I. (1988). *Eva luna.* New York: Alfred A. Knopf.

Alvesson, M., & Billing, Y. (1992). Gender and organization: Toward a differentiated understanding. *Organization Studies, 13* (1), 73-103.

Alvesson, M., & Willmott, H. (Eds.) (1992). *Critical management studies.* London: Sage.

Anonymous. (1995, September 9). Holding the hand that feeds. *Economist, 336,* 65.

Ansoff, H. (1984). *Implanting strategic management.* Englewood Cliffs, NJ: Prentice-Hall.

Apte, M. (1985). *Humour and laughter. An anthropological approach.* Ithaca, NY: Cornell University Press.

Argyris, C. (1982). *Reasoning, learning, and action: Individual and organizational.* San Francisco: Jossey-Bass.

Argyris, C. (1990). *Overcoming organizational defenses: Facilitating organizational learning.* Needham, MA: Allyn & Bacon.

Argyris, C. (1991, May-June). Teaching smart people how to learn. *Harvard Business Review,* 99-109.

Argyris, C. (1993). *Knowledge for action. A guide to overcoming barriers to organizational change.* San Francisco: Jossey-Bass.

Argyris, C., & Schon, D. (1996). *Organizational learning.* Reading, MA.: Addison Wesley.

Arlow, P. (1992, August). What are stakeholders and can we manage them? Paper presented at the meeting of the Academy of Management.

Arthur, M., Claman, P., & DeFillipp, R. (1995). Intelligent enterprise, intelligent careers. *The Academy of Management Executive, 9* (4), 7-20.

Ashworth, B., & Humphrey, R. (1995). Emotion in the workplace: A reappraisal. *Human Relations, 48,* 97-125.

Aspery, J. (1993). Planning for the inevitable. *Management Services, 39* (2), 16-17.

Badaracco, J., Jr. (1991). *The knowledge link: How firms compete through strategic alliances.* Boston, MA: Harvard Business School Press.

Barsoux, J. (1991, June). Is business a laughing matter? *Director*, 65-68.

Barsoux, J. (1993). *Funny business*. London: Cassell.

Barsoux, J. (1996). Why organisations need humour. *European Management Journal, 14* (5), 500-508.

Bartlett, C., & Ghoshal, S. (1995, May-June). Changing the role of top management: Beyond systems to people. *Harvard Business Review*, 132-142.

Bateson, G. (1979). *Mind and nature: A necessary unity*. New York: Dutton.

Behling, O., & Eckel, N. (1991). Making sense out of intuition. *Academy of Management Executive, 5* (1), 46-54.

Bergquist, W. (1993). *The postmodern organization*. San Fancisco: Jossey-Bass Publishers.

Bergquist, W. Betwee, J., & Meuel, D. (1995). *Building strategic relationships*. San Francisco: Jossey-Bass Publishers.

Bhatnagar, D., & Swamy, R. (1995). Attitudes toward women as managers: Does interaction make a difference? *Human Relations, 48* (11), 1285-1307.

Birch, C. (1993). *Confronting the future* (Rev. ed.). Victoria; Australia: Penguin.

Blackler, F. (1995). Knowledge, knowledge work and organizations: An overview and interpretation. *Organization Studies, 16* (6), 1021-1046.

Bloor, G., & Dawson, P. (1994). Understanding professional culture in organizational contexts. *Organization Studies, 15* (2), 275-295.

Bohl, D., Slocum, J., Jr., Luthans, F., & Hodgetts, R. (1996). Ideas that will shape the future of management practice. *Organizational Dynamics, 25* (1), 7-14.

Bolman, L., & Deal, T. (1997). *Reframing organizations* (2nd ed.). San Francisco: Jossey-Bass.

Booth, S. (1993). *Crisis management strategy*. London: Routledge.

Braham, J. (1988). Lighten up. *Industry Week, 236* (5), 50-52.

Brass, D., & Burkhardt, M. (1993). Potential power and power use: An investigation of structure and behavior. *Academy of Management Journal, 36* (3), 441-470.

Bresnen, M. (1996). An organizational perspective on changing buyer-supplier relations: A critical review of the evidence. *Organization, 3* (1), 121-146.

Brooking, A. (1996). *Intellectual capital*. London: International Thompson Business Press.

Brouthers, K., Brouthers, L., & Wilkinson, T. (1995). Strategic alliances: Choose your partners. *Long Range Planning, 28* (3), 18-25.

Brown, A. (1995). Managing understandings: Politics, symbolism, niche marketing and the quest for legitimacy in IT implementation. *Organization Studies, 16* (6), 951-969.

Bureau of Industry Economics (1995). *Beyond the firm. An assessment of business linkages and networks in Australia*. Report 67. Canberra: AGPS.

Burrell, G. (1984). Sex and organisational analysis. *Organization Studies, 5* (2), 97-118.

Burrell, G. (1992). The organization of pleasure. In M. Alvesson & H. Willmott (Eds.), *Critical management studies* (pp. 66-89). London: Sage.

Burrell, G., & Morgan, G. (1979). *Sociological paradigms and organisational analysis*. London: Heinemann.

Burton, J. (1995). Composite strategy: The combination of collaboration and competition. *Journal of General Management, 21* (1), 1-23.

Cairncross, F. (1992). *Costing the earth*. Boston, MA.: Harvard Business School Press.

Cannon, T. (1994). *Corporate responsibility*. London: Pitman.

Cantwell, J., & Barrera, P. (1995). Intercompany agreements for technological development: Lessons from international cartels. *International Studies of Management & Organization, 25* (1, 2), 75-95.

Carlin, B., Dowling, M., Roering, W., Wyman, J., Kalinoglou, J., & Clyburn, G. (1994). Sleeping with the enemy: Doing business with a competitor. *Business Horizons, 37* (5), 9-15.

Carroll, A. (1989). *Business & society*. Cincinatti, OH: South-Western Publishing Co.

Cauley De La Sierra, M. (1995). *Managing global alliances*. Wokingham, England: Addison-Wesley.

Chan Kim, W., & Mauborgne, R. (1997, July-August). Fair process: Managing in the knowledge economy. *Harvard Business Review*, 65-75.

Chattell, A. (1995). *Managing for the future*. London: Macmillan.

Cheney, G. (1991). *Rhetoric in an organizational society. Managing multiple identities*. Columbia, OH: University of South Carolina Press.

Chesbrough, H., & Teece, D. (1996, January-February). When is virtual virtuous? Organizing for innovation. *Harvard Business Review*, 65-73.

Chia, R. (1996). Teaching paradigm shifting in management education: University business schools and the entrepreneurial imagination. *Journal of Management Studies, 33* (4), 409-428.

Clark, T., & Salaman, G. (1996). The management guru as organizational witchdoctor. *Organization, 3* (1), 85-107.

Clarkson, M. (1995). A stakeholder framework for analyzing and evaluating corporate social performance. *Academy of Management Review, 20* (1), 92-117.

Clegg, S. (1990). *Modern organizations. Organization studies in the postmodern world*. London: Sage.

Clegg, S., Hardy, C., & Nord, W. (Eds.) (1996). *Handbook of organization studies*. London: Sage.

Clippinger, J. (1995). Visualization of knowledge: building and using intangible knowledge assets. *Planning Review, 23* (6), 28-31, 46.

Clutterbuck, D. with Dearlove, D., & Snow, D. (1992). *Actions speak louder*. London: Kogan Page.

Coates, J., Jarratt, J., & Mahaffie, J. (1990). *Future work*. San Francisco: Jossey-Bass.

Cockburn, C. (1991). *In the way of women: Men's resistance to sex equality in organizations*. Ithaca: ILR Press.

Cohen, S. (1993). New approaches to teams and teamwork. In J. Galbraith, E. Lawler, III, & Associates (Eds.), *Organising for the future* (pp. 194-226). San Francisco, Jossey-Bass

Coleman, J. (1992). All seriousness aside: The laughing-learning connection. *International Journal of Instructional Media, 19* (3), 269-276.

Collins, D. (1995). The complexity of fresh air. In J. Post (Ed.), *Research in corporate social performance and policy* (Supplement 1, pp. 369-381). Greenwich, CT: JAI Press.

Coopey, J. (1995). The learning organization. Power, politics and ideology. *Management Learning, 26* (2), 193-213.

Cosier, R. (1960). Laughter among colleagues: A study of the functions of humour among the staff of a mental hospital. *Psychiatry, 23* (1), 81-95.

Covey, S. (1992). *Principle-centered leadership.* London: Simon & Schuster.

Cox, T. (1991). The multicultural organization. *Academy of Management Executive, 5* (2), 34-47.

Cox, T., & Blake, S. (1991). Managing cultural diversity: implications for organizational competitiveness. *Academy of Management Executive, 5* (3), 45-56.

Crossan, M., Tiemessen, I., Lane, H., & White, R. (1995). Diagnosing organizational learning. Unpublished manuscript.

Crowley, L., & Karim, M. (1995). Conceptual model of partnering. *Journal of Management in Engineering, 11* (5), 33-39.

Culpan, R. (Ed.) (1993). *Multinational strategic alliances.* New York: International Business Press.

Daft, R., & Huber, G. (1987). How organizations learn: A communication framework. In S. Bacharach (Ed.), *Research in the sociology of organizations* (Vol 5, pp. 1-36). Greenwich, CT: JAI Press.

Davis, S., & Botkin, J. (1994, September-October). The coming of knowledge-based business. *Harvard Business Review,* 165-170.

De Meuse, K., & McDaris, K. (1994, February). An exercise in managing change. *Training and Development,* 55-57.

Dechant, K., & Altman, B. (1994). Environmental leadership: From compliance to competitive advantage. *Academy of Management Executive, 8* (3), 7-20.

Decker, W. (1987). Managerial humour and subordinate satisfaction. *Social Behaviour and Personality, 15* (2), 225-232.

Deetz, S. (1993). The negotiative organization: Building responsive and responsible workplaces. Working paper, Center for Negotiation and Conflict Resolution, Rutgers University.

Deetz, S. (1995). Transforming communication, transforming business: Stimulating value negotiation for more responsive and responsible workplaces. *International Journal of Value-Based Management, 8* (3), 255-278.

Denis, H. (1991). The complexity of technological disaster management: Technical, sociopolitical and scientific issues. *Industrial Crisis Quarterly, 5* (1), 1-18.

Dess, G., Rasheed, A., McLaughlin, K., & Priem, R. (1995). The new corporate architecture. *Academy of Management Executive, 9* (3), 7-20.

Dodgson, M. (1993). Organizational learning: A review of some literatures. *Organization Studies, 14* (3), 375-394.

Drucker, P. (1989). *The new realities.* London: Mandarin.

Drucker, P. (1992, September-October). The new society of organizations. *Harvard Business Review,* 95-104.

Drucker, P. (1993). *Post-capitalist society.* Oxford: Butterworth-Heinemann.

Drucker, P., Dyson, E., Handy, C., Saffo, P., & Senge, P. (1997, September-October). Looking ahead: Implications of the present. *Harvard Business Review,* 18-32.

Duncan, R. (1972). The characteristics of organizational environments and perceived environmental uncertainty. *Administrative Sciences Quarterly, 17* (3), 313-326.

Duncan, W. (1984). Perceived humour and social network patterns in a sample of task-oriented groups: A re-examination of prior research. *Human Relations, 37* (11), 895-907.

Duncan, W. (1985). The superiority theory of humour at work. *Small Group Behaviour, 16* (4), 556-564.

Duncan, W., & Feisal, J. (1989). No laughing matter: Patterns of humour in the workplace. *Organizational Dynamics, 17* (4), 18-30.

Duncan, W., Smeltzer, L., & Leap, T. (1990). Humor and work: Applications of joking behavior to management. *Journal of Management, 16* (2), 255-278.

Dunn, C., & Brady, F. (1995). From rules to relationship: A review of the search for an ethical justification of stakeholder interests. *Proceedings of the International Association for Business and Society, Austria, 6,* 47-52.

Dwyer, T. (1991). Humour, power, and change in organizations. *Human Relations, 44* (1), 1-19.

Ebers, M. (Ed.) (1997). *The formation of inter-organizational networks.* Oxford: Oxford University Press.

Eccles, T. (1994). *Succeeding with change.* London: McGraw Hill.

Eisenhardt, K., Kahwajy, J., & Bourgeois III. (1997, July-August). How management teams can have a good fight. *Harvard Business Review,* 77-85.

EIU/IBM. (1996). *Research report. The learning organisation. Managing knowledge for business success.* New York: The Economist Intelligence Unit.

Eliot, T. (1965). Choruses from "The Rock." *Collected Poems, 1909-1962.* New York: Harcourt, Brace & World.

Elise Walton, A. (1995). Staging discontinuous change. In D. Nadler, R. Shaw, A. Elise Walton, & Associates (Eds.), *Discontinuous change* (pp. 82-96). San Francisco: Jossey-Bass.

Emery, F., & Trist, E. (1973). *Towards a social ecology: Contextual appreciations of the future in the present.* New York: Plenum Books.

Ernst, D., & Thomas, D. (1996). Coffee and one way to Boston. *McKinsey Quarterly, 1,* 164-175.

Evan, W. (1993). *Organization theory. Research and design.* New York: Macmillan Publishing Co.

Ewing, D. (1993). The corporation as a just society. In M. Ray & A. Rinzler (Eds.), *The new paradigm in business* (pp. 205-212). New York: Tarcher/Perigree Books.

Ewing, R. (1987). *Managing the new bottom line.* Homewood, IL: Dow Jones-Irwin.

Fahey, L., King, W., & Narayanan, V. (1981). Environmental scanning and forecasting in strategic planning: The state of the art. *Long Range Planning, 14* (1), 32-39.

Feigelson, S. (1989). Mixing mirth and management. *Supervision, 50* (11), 6-8.

Field, L., & Ford, B. (1995). *Managing organisational learning. From rhetoric to reality.* Melbourne: Longman.

Fine, G. (1984). Humorous interaction and the social construction of meaning: Making sense in a jocular vein. *Studies in Symbolic Interaction, 5,* 83-101.

Fineman, S. (Ed.) (1993). *Emotion in organizations.* London: Sage.

Fineman, S. (1993). Organizations as emotional arenas. In S. Fineman (Ed.), *Emotion in organizations* (pp. 9-35). London: Sage.

Flam, H. (1993). Fear, loyalty and greedy organizations. In S. Fineman (Ed.), *Emotion in organizations* (pp. 58-75). London: Sage.

Fombrun, C., & Kumaraswamy, A. (1991). Strategic alliances in corporate communities: The evolution of telecommunications 1980-1988. *Japan and the World Economy, 3,* 243-259.

Ford, R., & Fottler, M. (1995). Empowerment: A matter of degree. *Academy of Management Executive, 9* (3), 21-28.

Foucault, M. (1980). *Power/knowledge: Selected interviews and other writings 1972-1977.* Brighton: Harvester Press.

Frederick, W. (1995). *Values, nature, and culture in the American corporation.* New York: Oxford University Press.

Freedman, D. (1992, November-December). Is management still a science? *Harvard Business Review,* 26-38.

Freeman, R. (1984). *Strategic management: A stakeholder approach.* Boston: Pitman.

Friedman, M. (1985). The social responsibility of business. Reprinted in C. McCoy, *The management of values* (pp. 253-260). Boston: Pitman.

Frisch-Gauthier, J. (1961). Le rire dans les relations de travail. *Revue Francaise de Sociologie, 2* (4), 292-303.

Fry, R., & Srivastva, S. (1992). Continuity and change in organizational life. In S. Srivastva & R. Fry (Eds.), *Executive and organizational continuity. Managing the paradoxes of stability and change* (pp. 1-24). San Francisco, Jossey-Bass.

Galbraith, J., & Lawler, E., III. (1993). Conclusion: Effective organizations: Using the new logic of organizing. In J. Galbraith, E. Lawler, III, & Associates. *Organising for the future* (pp. 285-300). San Francisco: Jossey-Bass.

Galbraith, J., Lawler, E., III, & Associates. (1993). *Organising for the future.* San Francisco: Jossey-Bass.

Gardener, J. (1991). Personal renewal. *The McKinsey Quarterly, 2,* 71-81.

Gatewood, R., & Carroll, A. (1991). Assessment of ethical performance of organizational members: A conceptual framework. *The Academy of Management Review, 16* (4), 667-690.

Gergen, K. (1992). Organization theory in the postmodern era. In M. Reed & M. Hughes (Eds.), *Rethinking organization. New directions in organization theory and analysis* (pp. 207-226). London: Sage.

Geus, A. (1997, March-April). The living company. *Harvard Business Review,* 51-59.

Ghoshal, S., & Bartlett, C. (1994, January-February). Changing the role of top management: Beyond structure to process. *Harvard Business Review,* 86-96.

Ghoshal, S., & Bartlett, C. (1996). Rebuilding behavioral context: A blueprint for corporate renewal. *Sloan Management Review, 37* (2), 23-36.

Giddens, A. (1991). *Modernity and self-identity.* Cambridge: Polity Press.

Gladwin, T. (1992). *Building the sustainable corporation: Creating environmental sustainability and competitive advantage.* Washington, DC: National Wildlife Federation.

Gladwin, T., Kennelly, J., & Krause, T. (1995). Shifting paradigms for sustainable development: Implications for management theory and research. *Academy of Management Review, 20* (4), 874-907.

Goleman, D. (1995). *Emotional intelligence.* New York: Bantam Books.

Gomes-Casseres, B. (1994, July-August). Group versus group: How alliance networks compete, *Harvard Business Review,* 62-74.

Goodman, J. (1991). Laughing all the way to the learning bank. *Computerworld, 25* (7), 95.

Goodstein, L., & Burke, W. (1991). Creating successful organization change. *Organization Dynamics, 19* (4), 805-826.

Gouillart, F., & Kelly, J. (1995). *Transforming the organization.* New York: McGraw-Hill.

Greening, D., & Johnson, R. (1996). Do managers and strategies matter? A study in crisis. *Journal of Management Studies, 33* (1), 25-51.

Grint, K. (1994). Reengineering history: Social resonances and business process reengineering. *Organization, 1* (1), 179-201.

Gross, T., Pascales, R., & Athos, A. (1993, November-December). Rereinvention roller-coaster: Risking the present for a powerful future. *Harvard Business Review,* 97-108.

Gulati, R. (1995). Does familiarity breed trust? The implications of repeated ties for contractual choice in alliances. *Academy of Management Journal, 38* (1), 85-112.

Hagedoorn, J. (1993). Understanding the rationale of strategic technology partnering: Interorganizational modes of cooperation and sectoral difference. *Strategic Management Journal, 14* (5), 371-385.

Hakansson, H., & Snehota, I. (1995). *Developing relationships in business networks.* London: Routledge.

Hall, R. (1992). The strategic analysis of intangible resources. *Strategic Management Journal, 13,* 135-144.

Hammer, M., & Champy, J. (1993). *Reengineering the corporation. A manifesto for business revolution.* Sydney: Allen & Unwin.

Handy, C. (1990). *The age of unreason.* London: Arrow Books.

Handy, C. (1994). *The age of paradox.* Boston, MA: Harvard Business School Press.

Handy, C. (1995, May-June). Trust and the virtual organization. *Harvard Business Review,* 40-50.

Handy, C. (1997). *The hungry spirit.* London: Hutchinson.

Hannan, M., & Freeman, J. (1989). *Organizational ecology.* Cambridge, MA: Harvard University Press.

Harari, O. (1994). Colluding with competitors is a dead end. *Management Review, 83* (10), 53-55.

Hardy, C. (1994). *Managing strategic action.* London: Sage.

Harper, S. (1992). The challenges facing CEOs: Past, present, and future. *Academy of Management Executive, 6* (3), 7-25.

Harrigan, K. (1995). The role of intercompany cooperation in integrated strategy: Strategic alliances and partnering. In P. Shrivastava (Ed.), *Advances in strategic management* (Vol 11, pp. 5-20). Greenwich, CT: JAI Press.

Harrington, S. (1991). What corporate America is teaching about ethics. *Academy of Management Executive, 5* (1), 21-30.

Harrison, E. (1992). Achieving sustainable communication. *The Columbia Journal of World Business, 27* (3-4), 243-247.

Harrison, J., & St. John, C. (1996). Managing and partnering with external stakeholders. *Academy of Management Executive, 10* (2), 46-60.

Hart, S. (1997) Beyond greening: Strategies for a sustainable world. *Harvard Business Review,* 66-76.

Hawken, P. (1993). *The ecology of commerce: A declaration of sustainability.* New York: Harper Business.

Hawkins, P. (1994). Organizational learning. Taking stock and facing the challenge. *Management Learning, 25* (1), 71-82.

Hearn, J. (1993). Emotive subjects: Organizational men, organizational masculinities and the (de)construction of "emotions." In. S. Fineman (Ed.), *Emotion in organizations* (pp. 142-166). London: Sage.

Hearn, J., Sheppard, D., Tancred-Sheriff, P., & Burrell, G. (1989). *The sexuality of organization.* London: Sage

Herring, J. (1994). Business intelligence aspects of alliances. *Directors & Boards, 18* (2), 50-52.

Herzberg, F. (1968). *Work and the nature of man.* London: Crosby Lockwood Staples.

Hiebeler, R. (1996). Benchmarking: Knowledge management. *Planning Review, 24* (2), 22-29.

Heifetz, R., & Laurie, D. (1997, January-February). The work of leadership. *Harvard Business Review,* 124-134.

Hill, C., & Jones, T. (1992). Stakeholder-agency theory, *Journal of Management Studies, 29* (2), 131-154.

Hirschhorn, L., & Gilmore, T. (1992, May-June). The new boundaries of the "boundaryless" company. *Harvard Business Review,* 104-115.

Hochschild, A. (1983). *The managed heart.* Berkeley: University of California Press.

Hofstede, G. (1991). *Cultures and organizations. Software of the mind.* London: McGraw-Hill.

Hofstede, G. (1993). Cultural constraints in management theories. *Academy of Management Executive, 7* (1), 81-94.

Holden, R. (1993). *Laughter. The best medicine.* London: Thorsons.

Hosking, D., & Fineman, S. (1990). Organizing processes. *Journal of Management Studies, 27* (6), 583-604.

Hosseini, J., & Brenner, S. (1992). A stakeholder theory of the firm: A methodology to generate value matrix weights. *Business Ethics Quarterly, 2* (2), 99-118.

Howard, R. (1992, September-October). The CEO as organizational architect. *Harvard Business Review,* 107-121.

Howarth, C., Gillin, M., & Bailey, J. (1995). *Strategic alliances.* Melbourne: Pitman.

Huber, G., & Glick, W. (Eds.) (1993). *Organizational change and redesign.* New York: Oxford University Press.

Hunter, L., Beaumont, P., & Sinclair, D. (1996). A "partnership" route to human resource management? *Journal of Management Studies, 33* (2), 235-257.

Hurst, D. (1995). *Crisis & renewal. Meeting the challenge of organizational change.* Boston: Harvard Business School Press.

Huxham, C. (Ed) (1996). *Creating collaborative advantage.* London: Sage.

Isaacs, W. (1993). Taking flight: Dialogue, collective thinking, and organizational learning. *Organizational Dynamics, 22* (2), 24-39.

Itami, H., & Roehl, T. (1987). *Mobilizing invisible assets.* Cambridge, MA: Harvard University Press.

Jackall, R. (1988). *Moral mazes: The world of corporate managers.* New York: Oxford University Press.

Jagtenberg, T., & McKie, D. (1997). *Eco-impacts and the greening of postmodernity.* London: Sage.

James, H., Jr., & Weidenbaum, M. (1993). *When businesses cross international borders. Strategic alliances and their alternatives.* Westport, CT: Praeger.

Jennings, P., & Zandbergen, P. (1995). Ecologically sustainable organizations: An institutional approach. *Academy of Management Review, 20* (4), 1015-1052.

Jones, G. (1995). *Organizational theory.* Reading, MA: Addison-Wesley.

Jones, M. (1996). Missing the forest for the trees. *Business & Society, 35* (1), 7-41.

Kahn, W. (1989). Toward a sense of organizational humour: Implications for organizational diagnosis and change. *The Journal of Applied Behavioral Science, 25* (1), 45-63.

Katz, D., & Kahn, R. (1978). *The social psychology of organizing* (2nd ed.). New York: Wiley.

Katzenbach, J., & The RCL Team. (1997). *Real change leaders.* London: Nicholas Brealey.

Kaye, M. (1996). *Myth-makers and story-tellers.* Sydney, Australia: Business & Professional Publishing.

Keidel, R. (1994). Rethinking organizational design. *Academy of Management Executive, 8* (4), 12-28.

Ketterer, R., & Chayes, M. (1995). Executive development: Finding and growing champions of change. In D. Nadler, R. Shaw, A. Elise Walton, & Associates (Eds.), *Discontinuous change* (pp. 190-216). San Francisco: Jossey-Bass.

Kets de Vries, M. (1990). The organizational fool: Balancing a leader's hubris. *Human Relations, 43* (8), 751-770.

Kets de Vries, M. (1993). *Leaders, fools, and impostors.* San Francisco: Jossey-Bass.

Kets de Vries, M. (1994). The leadership mystique. *The Academy of Management Executive, 8* (3), 73-89.

Kets de Vries, M., & Associates. (1991). *Organizations on the couch.* San Francisco: Jossey-Bass.

Kets de Vries, M. , & Miller, D. (1984). *The neurotic organization.* San Francisco: Jossey-Bass.

Kiernan, M. (1993). The new strategic architecture: Learning to compete in the twenty-first century. *Academy of Management Executive, 7* (1), 7-21.

King, N., & Anderson, N. (1995). *Innovation and change in organizations.* London: Routledge.

Kinlaw, D. (1993). *Competitive & green. Sustainable performance in the environmental age.* Amsterdam: Pfeiffer & Company.

Knights, D., Murray, F., & Willmott, H. (1993). Networking as knowledge work: A study of strategic interorganizational development in the financial services industry. *Journal of Management Studies, 30* (6), 975-995.

Kofman, F., & Senge, P. (1993). Communities of commitment: The heart of learning organizations. *Organizational Dynamics, 22* (2), 5-23.

Kotter, J. (1995, March-April). Leading change: Why transformation efforts fail. *Harvard Business Review,* 59-67.

Kouzes, J., & Posner, B. (1990). *The leadership challenge.* San Francisco: Jossey-Bass.

Kurtzman, J. (1996, April). A mind is a terrible thing to waste. *Chief Executive, 112* (20).

Ladd Greeno, J. (1994). Corporate environmental excellence and stewardship: Five critical tasks of top management. *Total quality Environmental Management, 3* (4), 479-499.

Ladd Greeno, J. , & Robinson, S. (1992). Rethinking corporate environmental management. *The Columbia Journal of World Business, 27* (3-4), 223-232.

Lagadec, P. (1987). Communications strategies in crisis. *Industrial Crisis Quarterly, 1,* 19-26.

Lagadec, P. (1991). *Preventing chaos in a crisis* (J. Phelps, Trans.). London: McGraw Hill.

Larkin, T., & Larkin, S. (1994). *Communicating change.* Sydney: McGraw Hill.

Lawler, E., III (1993). Creating the high-involvement organization. In J. Galbraith, E. Lawler, III, & Associates (Eds.), *Organizing for the future* (pp. 172-193). San Francisco: Jossey-Bass.

Leigh, A. (1988). *Effective change.* London: Institute of Personnel Management.

Lenz, R., & Engledow, J. (1986). Environmental analysis units and strategic decision-making: A field study of selected "leading-edge" corporations. *Strategic Management Journal, 7* (1), 69-89.

Lessem, R. (1992). Foreword. In S. Urban & S. Vendemini (Eds.), *European strategic alliances. Cooperative corporate strategies in the new Europe* (R. Ingleton, Trans.) (pp. 1-8). Oxford: Blackwell.

Levinthal, D., & March, J. (1993). The myopia of learning. *Strategic Management Journal 14,* 95-112.

Lewin, A., & Stephens, C. (1993). Epilogue. Designing postindustrial organizations: Combining theory and practice. In G. Huber & W. Glick (Eds.), *Organizational change and redesign* (pp. 393-409). New York: Oxford University Press.

Lewin, K. (1951). *Field theory in social science.* New York: HarperCollins.

Lewis, J. (1990). *Partnerships for profit.* New York: The Free Press.

Lewis, J. (1995). *The connected corporation. How leading companies win through customer-supplier alliances.* New York: The Free Press.

Liedtka, J. (1996). Collaborating across lines of business for competitive advantage. *Academy of Management Review, 10* (2), 20-34.

Linstead, S. (1988). "Jokers wild": Humour in organisational culture. In C. Powell & G. Paton. (Eds.), *Humour in society. Resistance and control* (pp. 123-148). New York: St. Martin's Press.

Locke, K. (1992). Emotion management in professional relationships: A study of comedic microperformances. Unpublished manuscript.

Lorange, P., & Roos, J. (1993). *Strategic alliances.* Oxford: Blackwell.

Lukaszewski, J. (1988). Tactical ingenuity: New techniques for surviving corporate crises. *Industrial Crisis Quarterly, 2* (3 & 4), 309-326.

Lundberg, C., & Brownell, J. (1993). The implications of organizational learning for organizational communication—a review and reformulation. *The International Journal of Organizational Analysis, 1* (1), 29-53.

Luthans, F., Hodgetts, R., & Thompson, K. (1990). *Social issues in business* (6th ed.). New York: Macmillan.

Lynch, R. (1993). *Business alliances guide.* New York: John Wiley & Sons, Inc.

Lyotard, J. (1984). *The postmodern condition.* Minneapolis, MN: University of Minnesota Press.

Madhavan, R. (1996). Networks in transition: How industry events (re)shape interfirm relationships. Unpublished manuscript.

Mahon, J., & Cochran, P. (1991). Fire alarms and siren songs: The role of issues management in the prevention of, and response to, organizational crises. *Industrial Crisis Quarterly, 5* (2), 155-176.

Makower, J. (1994). *Beyond the bottom line: Putting social responsibility to work for your business and the world.* New York: Simon & Schuster.

Mallam, P., & Huang, D. (1996). Opportunities in the Asia-Pacific: Investing in relationships. *Intermedia, 24* (3), 23-25.

Manley II, W. with Shrode, W. (1990). *Critical issues in business conduct.* New York: Quorum Books.

Manz, C., & Neck, C. (1991). Inner leadership: Creating productive thought patterns. *Academy of Management Executive, 5* (3), 87-95.

Marcus, A. (1996). *Business and society* (2nd ed.). Chicago: Irwin.

Marks, M., & Shaw, R. (1995). Sustaining change: Creating the resilient organization. In D. Nadler, R. Shaw, A. Elise Walton, & Associates (Eds.), *Discontinuous change* (pp. 97-120). San Francisco: Jossey-Bass.

Marquardt, M., & Reynolds, A. (1994). *The global learning organization.* New York: Irwin.

Marshall, C., Prusak, L., & Spilberg, D. (1996). Financial risk and the need for superior knowledge management. *California Management Review, 38* (3), 77-101.

Martinsons, M. (1994). A strategic vision for managing business intelligence. *Information Strategy: The Executive's Journal, 10* (3), 17-30.

Maslow, A. (1954). *Motivation and personality.* New York: Harper & Row.

Maynard, H., Jr., & Mehrtens, S. (1993). *The fourth wave. Business in the 21st century.* San Francisco: Berrett-Koehler Publishers.

McCaskey, M. (1988). The challenge of managing ambiguity and change. In L. Pondy, R. Boland, Jr., & H. Thomas (Eds.), *Managing ambiguity and change* (pp. 1-16). New York: John Wiley & Sons.

McGill, M., Slocum, J., & Deli, D. (1992). Management practices in learning organizations. *Organizational Dynamics, 21* (1), 5-17.

McKenna, J. (1993, January 18). Change must be managed. *Industry Week,* 50.

McKnight, R., & Thompson, M. (1990, December). Navigating organizational change. *Training and Development Journal,* 46-49.

McWhinney, W. (1992). *Paths of change.* Newbury Park: Sage.

Merriam, J., & Makower, J. (1988). *Trend watching.* New York: AMACOM.

Mendel, J. (1978). The practice of intuition. In J. Fowles. (Ed.), *Handbook of futures research* (pp. 149-161). Westport, CT: Greenwood Press.

Messick , D., & Bazerman, M. (1996). Ethical leadership and the psychology of decision making. *Sloan Management Review, 37* (2), 9-22.

Meyer, A., Goes, J., & Brooks, G. (1993). Organizations reacting to hyperturbulence. In G. Huber & W. Glick (Eds.), *Organizational change and redesign* (pp. 66-11). New York: OUP.

Meyer, J., & Scott, W. (1992). *Organizational environments. Ritual and rationality.* Newbury Park: Sage.

Meyers, G., & Holusha, J. (1986). *Managing crisis.* London: Unwin.

Miles, G., & Preece, S. (1995, October). Strategic alliances and strategy formulation: Challenging the dominant logic of a firm. Paper presented at the meeting of the Strategic Management Society, Mexico City.

Miles, R. (1996). Twenty-first century partnering and the role of ADR. *Journal of Management Engineering, 12* (3), 45-55.

Mink, O., Esterhuysen, P., Mink, B., & Owen, K. (1993). *Change at work.* San Francisco: Jossey-Bass.

Mintzberg, H. (1994, January-February). The fall & rise of strategic planning. *Harvard Business Review,* 107-114.

Mitchell, W., & Singh, K. (1996). Survival of businesses using collaborative relationships to commercialize complex goods. *Strategic Management Journal, 17* (3), 169-195.

Mitroff, I. (1983). *Stakeholders of the organizational mind.* San Francisco: Jossey-Bass.

Mitroff, I. (1988). Crisis management: Cutting through the confusion. *Sloan Management Review, 29* (2), 15-20.

Mitroff, I., & Pearson, C. (1993). *Crisis management.* San Francisco: Jossey Bass.

Mitroff, I., Mason, R., & Pearson, C. (1994). Radical surgery: What will tomorrow's organizations look like? *Academy of Management Executive, 8* (2), 11-21.

Mitroff, I., Pauchant, T., & Shrivastava, P. (1989, May). Can your company handle a crisis? *Business and Health,* 41-44.

Mitroff, I., Pauchant, T., Finney, M., & Pearson, C. (1989). Do (some) organizations cause their own crises? The cultural profiles of crisis-prone vs, crisis-prepared organizations. *Industrial Crisis Quarterly, 3* (3), 269-283.

Mohr, J., & Spekman, R. (1996). Perfecting partnerships. *Marketing Management, 4* (4), 34-43.

Molander, E. (1987). A paradigm for design, promulgation, and enforcement of ethical codes. *Journal of Business Ethics, 6* (8), 619-631.

More, E. (1995). Crisis management and communication in Australian organisations. *Australian Journal of Communication, 22* (1), 31-47.

More, E., & McGrath, M. (1996). *Cooperative Corporate Strategies In Australia's Telecommunications Sector—The Nature of Strategic Alliances.* Canberra, Australia: DIST.

More, E., & Ross Smith, A. (1992). Being green—A communication approach to the N.S.W. green movement. *Australian Journal of Communication, 19* (1), 46-76.

Morgan, G. (1988). *Riding the waves of change: Developing managerial competencies for a turbulent world.* San Francisco: Jossey-Bass.

Morgan, G. (1993). *Imaginization.* Newbury Park: Sage.

Morgan, G. (1997). *Images of organization* (2nd ed.). London: Sage.

Morris, K., & Raben, C. (1995). The fundamentals of change management. In D. Nadler, R. Shaw, A. Elise Walton, & Associates (Eds.), *Discontinuous change* (pp. 47-65). San Francisco: Jossey-Bass.

Moss Kanter, R. (1989, November-December). The new managerial work. *Harvard Business Review,* 85-92.

Moss Kanter, R. (1994, July-August). Collaborative advantage. *Harvard Business Review,* 96-108.

Moss Kanter, R., Stein, B., & Jick, T. (1992). *The challenge of organizational change.* New York: The Free Press.

Mulkay, M. (1988). *On humour. Its nature and its place in modern society.* London: Polity Press.

Mumby, D., & Putnam, L. (1992). The politics of emotion: A feminine reading of bounded rationality. *Academy of Management Review, 17* (3), 465-86.

Nadler, D. (1995). Organizational architecture: Designing for high performance. In D. Nadler, R. Shaw, A. Elise Walton, & Associates (Eds.), *Discontinuous change* (pp. 138-150). San Francisco: Jossey-Bass.

Nadler, D., & Tushman, M. (1990, Winter). Beyond the charismatic leader: Leadership and organizational change. *California Management Review*, 77-96.

Nadler, D., Gerstein, M., Shaw, R., & Associates. (1992). *Organizational architecture.* San Francisco: Jossey-Bass.

Nadler, D., Shaw, R., Elise Walton, A., & Associates. (1995). *Discontinuous change.* San Francisco: Jossey-Bass.

Naisbitt, J. (1982). *Megatrends.* London: Macdonald.

Naisbitt, J., & Aburdene, P. (1990). *Megatrends 2000.* London: Pan Books.

Nash, J., & Ehrenfeld, J. (1996). Code green: Business adopts a voluntary environmental standards. *Environment, 38* (1), (Internet, 1-13).

Nathan, M., & Mitroff, I. (1991). The use of negotiated order theory as a tool for the analysis and development of an interorganizational field. *Journal of Applied Behavioural Science, 27* (2), 163-180.

Nichols, M. (1994, March-April). Does new age business have a message for managers? *Harvard Business Review*, 52-60.

Nonaka, I. (1991, November-December). The knowledge-creating company. *Harvard Business Review*, 96-104.

Nonaka, I. (1994). A dynamic theory of organizational knowledge creation. *Organization Science, 5* (1), 14-37.

Ostell, A. (1996). Managing dysfunctional emotions in organizations. *Journal of Management Studies, 33* (4), 525-557.

Paine, L. (1994, March-April). Managing for organizational integrity. *Harvard Business Review*, 106-117.

Palmer, J. (1994). *Taking humour seriously.* London: Routledge.

Parikh, H., Neubauer, F., & Lank, A. (1994). *Intuition: The new frontier of management.* Oxford: Blackwell.

Park, S. (1996). The interfirm collaboration in global competition. *Multinational Business Review, 4* (1), 94-106.

Parkhe, A. (1995). Partner nationality and the structure-performance relationship in strategic alliances. *Organization Science, 4* (2), 301-324.

Parkhe, A. (1993). Strategic alliance structuring: A game theoretic and transaction cost examination of interfirm cooperation. *Academy of Management Journal, 36* (4), 794-829.

Parkin. W. (1993). The public and the private: Gender, sexuality and emotion. In S. Fineman (Ed.), *Emotion in organizations* (pp. 167-189). London: Sage.

Pascale, R. (1990). *Managing on the edge.* London: Penguin.

Pascale, R. (1993, October). The benefit of a clash or opinions. *Personnel Management*, 38-40.

Pauchant, T., & Associates. (1995). *In search of meaning. Managing for the health of our organizations, our communities, and the natural world.* San Francisco: Jossey-Bass.

Pauchant, T., & Mitroff, I. (1992). *Transforming the crisis-prone organization.* San Francisco: Jossey-Bass.

Pauchant, T., Mitroff, I., & Lagadec, P. (1991). Toward a systemic crisis management strategy: Learning from the best examples in the US, Canada and France. *Industrial Crisis Quarterly, 5* (3), 209-232.

Pearson, C., & Mitroff, I. (1993). From crisis prone to crisis prepared: A framework for crisis management. *Academy of Management Executive, 7* (1), 48-59.

Perkins, B., & Lepper, E. (1995). Foreword. In B. Piasecki (Ed.), *Corporate environmental strategy* (pp. ix-xii). New York: John Wiley & Sons.

Peters, T. (1992). *Liberation management.* London: Macmillan.

Peters, T., & Austin, N. (1985). *A passion for excellence.* New York: Warner Books.

Peters, T., & Waterman, B. (1987). *In search of excellence.* New York: Harper and Row.

Pettigrew, A., & Whipp, R. (1993). *Managing change for competitive success.* London: Blackwell Business.

Pfeffer, J. (1992). *Managing with power.* Boston, MA: Harvard Business School Press.

Pfeffer, J. (1995). Producing sustainable competitive advantage through the effective management of people. *Academy of Management Executive, 9* (1), 55-69.

Pfeffer, J. (1997). *New directions for organization theory. Problems and prospects.* New York: Oxford University Press.

Pfeffer, J., & Salancik, G. (1978). *The external control of organizations.* New York: Harper and Row.

Phillips, N., & Brown, J. (1993). Analyzing communication in and around organizations: A critical hermeneutic approach. *Academy of Management Journal, 36* (6), 1547-1576.

Piasecki, B. (1995). *Corporate environmental strategy.* New York: John Wiley & Sons, Inc.

Pogrebin, M., & Poole, E. (1988). Humour in the briefing room. A study of the strategic uses of humour among police. *Journal Of Contemporary Ethnography, 17* (2), 183-210.

Polanyi, M. (1958). *Personal knowledge.* Chicago: University of Chicago Press.

Polanyi, M. (1966). *The tacit dimension.* London: Routledge.

Pollard, A. (1995). Strategic partnering. *Chief Executive, 108,* 52-62.

Pollock, B. (1994). Partnering: Joining forces through change. *Business Directions, 50,* 24.

Porter, M. (1990). *Competitive advantage of nations.* New York: Free Press.

Porter, M., & van der Linde, C. (1995, September-October). Green and competitive: Ending the stalemate. *Harvard Business Review,* 120-134.

Powell, G. (1993). *Women & men in management* (2nd ed.). Newbury Park, CA: Sage.

Powell, J., & Andresen, L. (1985). Humour and teaching in higher education. *Studies in Higher Education, 10* (1), 79-90.

Powell, T. (1991). Shaken, but alive: Organizational behavior in the wake of catastrophic events. *Industrial Crisis Quarterly, 5* (4), 271-291.

Powell, W. (1990). Neither market nor hierarchy: Network forms of organization. In B. Staw & L. Cummings (Eds.), *Research in organizational behaviour* (Vol 12, pp. 295-336). Greenwich, CT: JAI.

Prescott, J. (1995). The evolution of competitive intelligence. In D. Hussey (Ed.), *Rethinking strategic management* (pp. 71-90). Brisbane: John Wiley & Sons.

Price Waterhouse Change Integration Team (1996). *The paradox principles.* Chicago: Irwin.

Putnam, L., & Mumby, D. (1993). Organizations, emotion and the myth of rationality. In S. Fineman (Ed.), *Emotion in organizations* (pp. 36-57). London: Sage.

Quinn, B. (1993). Managing the intelligent enterprise: Knowledge and service based strategies. *Planning Review, 21* (5), 13-16.

Quinn, B., Anderson, P., & Finkelstein, S. (1996, March-April). Managing professional intellect: Making the most of the best. *Harvard Business Review,* 71-80.

Rai, A., Borah, S., & Ramaprasad, A. (1996). Critical success factors for strategic alliances in the information technology industry: An empirical study. *Decision Sciences, 27* (1), 141-155.

Ralf, M., Hughes, J., & Cox, A. (1995, October). Developing purchasing leadership: Competing on competence. *Purchasing & Supply Management,* 37-42.

Ray, M., & Rinzler, A. (Eds.) (1993). *The new paradigm in business.* New York: Tarcher/Perigree Books.

Reardon, K., & Spekman, R. (1994). Starting out right: Negotiation lessons for domestic and cross-cultural business alliances. *Business Horizons, 37* (1), 71-79.

Reed, M., & Hughes, M. (1992). *Rethinking organization. New directions in organization theory and analysis.* London: Sage.

Reger, R., Mullane, J., Gustafson, L., & DeMarie, S. (1994). Creating earthquakes to change organizational mindsets. *Academy of Management Executive, 8* (4), 31-46.

Reichers, A., Wanous, J., & Austin, J. (1997). Understanding and managing cynicism about organizational change. *Academy of Management Executive, 11* (1), 48-59.

Rice, R. (1990). From adversity to diversity: Applications of communication technology to crisis management. In T. Housel (Ed.), *Advances in telecommunications management* (Vol 3, pp. 91-112). Greenwich, CT: JAI Press.

Rigby, D., & Buchanan, R. (1994). Putting more strategy into strategic alliances. *Directors & Boards, 18* (2), 14-19.

Ring, P., & Van de Ven, A. (1994). Developmental processes of cooperative interorganizational relationships. *Academy of Management Review, 19* (1), 90-118.

Roberts, K., & Libuser, C. (1993). From Bhopal to banking: Organizational design can mitigate risk. *Organizational Dynamics, 21* (4), 15-26.

Robinson, G., & Dechant, K. (1997). Building a business case for diversity. *Academy of Management Executive, 11* (3), 21-31.

Ryan, M. (1995). Human resource management and the politics of knowledge: Linking the essential knowledge base of the organization to strategic decision making. *Leadership & Organization Development Journal, 16* (5), 3-10.

Saint-Onge, H. (1996). Tacit knowledge: The key to the strategic alignment of intellectual capital. *Planning Review, 24* (2), 10-14.

Sankar, C., Boulton, W., Davidson, N., Snyder, C., & Ussery, R. (1995). Building a world-class alliance: The Universal card—TSYS case. *Academy of Management Executive, 9* (2), 20-29.

Savage, T., Nix, T., Whitehead, C., & Blair, J. (1991). Strategies for assessing and managing organizational stakeholders. *Academy of Management Executive 5*, (2), 61-75.

Schaef, A., & Fassel, D. (1988). *Addictive organization.* New York: Harper & Row.

Schein, E. (1996). *Organizational learning: What is new?* Working paper, MIT Sloan School of Management.

Schwartz, F. (1992, March-April). Women as a business imperative. *Harvard Business Review*, 105-113.

Senge, P. (1990). *The fifth discipline.* New York: Doubleday.

Senge, P. (1993). Transforming the practice of management. *Human Resource Development Quarterly, 4* (1), 5-32.

Seymour, M. (1991). Crafting a crisis communications plan. *Directors and Boards, 15* (4), 26-27.

Sheppard, B., Lewicki, R., & Minton, J. (1992). *Organizational justice.* New York: Lexington Books.

Shrivastava, P. (1989). Managing the crisis at Bhopal. In U. Rosenthal, M. Charles, & P. Hart (Eds.), *Coping with crises* (pp. 92-176). Springfield, IL: Charles C. Thomas.

Shrivastava, P. (1994). Castrated environment: Greening organizational Studies. *Organization Studies, 15* (5), 705-726.

Shrivastava, P. (1995). The role of corporations in achieving ecological sustainability. *Academy of Management Review, 20* (4), 936-960.

Shrivastava, P. (1996). *Greening business. Profiting the corporation and the environment.* Cincinnati, OH: Thomson Executive Press.

Simons, R. (1995, March-April). Control in an age of empowerment. *Harvard Business Review*, 80-88.

Siomkos, G., & Shrivastava, P. (1993). Responding to product liability crises. *Long Range Planning, 26* (5), 72-79.

Smeltzer, L., & Leap, T. (1988). An analysis of individual reactions to potentially offensive jokes in work settings. *Human Relations, 41* (4), 295-304.

Smith, C. (1994, May-June). The new corporate philanthropy. *Harvard Business Review*, 105-116.

Smith, D., & Sipika, C. (1993). Back from the brink—post-crisis management. *Long Range Planning, 26* (1), 28-38.

Solomon, R. (1992). *Ethics and excellence.* New York: Oxford University Press.

Spears, L. (Ed.) (1995). *Reflections on leadership.* New York: John Wiley & Sons.

Spekman, R., Isabella, L., MacAvoy, T., & Forbes, T., III (1996). Creating strategic alliances which endure. *Long Range Planning, 29* (3), 346-357.

Stace, D., & Dunphy, D. (1994). *Beyond the boundaries.* Sydney, Australia: McGraw-Hill.

Stacey, R. (1991). *The chaos frontier: Creative strategic control for business.* Oxford: Butterworth-Heinemann.

Stacey, R. (1992). *Managing chaos*. London: Kogan Page.

Stacey, R. (1993). *Strategic management and organisational dynamics*. London: Pitman.

Stacey, R. (1996). Emerging strategies for a chaotic environment. *Long Range Planning, 29* (2), 182-189.

Stafford, E. (1994). Using co-operative strategies to make alliances work. *Long Range Planning, 27* (3), 64-74.

Starke, L. (1993). The five stages of corporate moral development. In M. Ray & A. Rinzler (Eds.), *The new paradigm in business* (pp. 203-204). New York: Tarcher/Perigree Books.

Stein, R., & Pinchot, G. (1995). Building an intelligent organization. *Association Management, 47* (11), 32-39.

Stewart, T. (1994). Your company's most valuable asset: Intellectual capital. *Fortune, 130* (7), 68-74.

Stoffels, J. (1994). *Strategic issues management. A comprehensive guide to environmental scanning*. Oxford: Elsevier.

Strassman, P. (1994, Winter). Choosing the right change path. *California Management Review*, 29-51.

Strassman, P. (1996, January 30). The value of computers, information and knowledge. *Internet*.

Strebel, P. (1993). New contracts: The key to change. *European Management Journal, 11* (4), 397-402.

Strebel, P. (1994, Winter). Choosing the right change path. *California Management Review*, 29-51.

Thornburg, L. (1994). Accounting for knowledge. *HR Magazine, 39* (10), 50-56.

Throop, G., Starik, M., & Rands, G. (1993). Sustainable strategy in a greening world: Integrating the natural environment into strategic management. In R. Lamb (Ed.), *Advances in strategic management* (Vol 9, pp. 63-92). Greenwich, CT: JAI Press.

Tiemessen, I., Crossan, M., Lane, H., & Inkpen, A. (1995). International joint ventures: Learning how to learn in Mexico. Unpublished manuscript.

Tiemessen, I., Lane, H., Crossan, M., & Inkpen, A. (1996). Knowledge management in international joint ventures. Unpublished manuscript.

Trevino, L., & Nelson, K. (1995). *Managing business ethics*. New York: John Wiley & Sons.

Ulian, J. (1976). Joking at work. *Journal of Communication, 26* (3), 129-133.

Urban, S., & Vendemini, S. (1992). *European strategic alliances*. Co-operative corporate strategies in the new Europe (R. Ingleton, Trans.). Oxford: Blackwell

Van de Ven, A., & Walker, G. (1984). The dynamics of interorganizational coordination. *Administrative Science Quarterly, 28*, 598-621.

Vedder, J. (1992). How much can we learn from success? *Academy of Management Executive, 6* (1), 56-66.

Vinton, K. (1989). Humour in the workplace: It is more than telling jokes. *Small Group Behaviour, 20* (2), 151-166.

Walsh, J., & Ungson, G. (1991). Organizational memory. *Academy of Management Review, 16* (1), 57-91.

Want, J. (1993). Managing radical change. *Journal of Business Strategy, 14* (3), 21-28.

Warnock, P. (1989). Humour as a didactic tool in adult education. *Lifelong Learning, 12* (8), 22-24.

Wathne, K., Roos, J., & Von Krogh, G. (1995). The impact of trust and experience on knowledge transfer in a cooperative context. Unpublished manuscript.

Weick, K. (1979). *The social psychology of organizing.* Reading, MA: Addison-Wesley.

Wells. P., & Cooke, P. (1991). The geography of international strategic alliances in the telecommunications industry. *Environment and Planning, 28,* 87-106.

Wicks, A. (1996). Overcoming the separation thesis. *Business & Society, 35* (1), 89-118.

Wolff, M. (1994). Building trust in alliances. *Research-Technology Management, 37* (3), 12-15.

Wood, D. (1991). Corporate social performance revisited. *The Academy of Management Review, 16* (4), 691-718.

Wouters, C. (1989). The sociology of emotions and flight attendants: Hochschild's "Managed Heart." *Theory, Culture & Society, 6* (1), 95-123.

Yoshino, M., & Rangan, U. (1995). *Strategic alliances. An entrepreneurial approach to globalization.* Boston: Harvard Business School Press.

Zald, M. (1996). More fragmentation? Unfinished business in linking the social sciences and the humanities. *Administrative Science Quarterly, 41* (2), 251-261.

Zemke, R. (1991). Humour in training; Laugh and the world learns with you—maybe. *Training, 28* (8), 26-29.

Zemke, R., & Zemke, S. (1994). Partnering: A new slant on serving the internal customer. *Training, 31* (9), 37-43.

Zijderveld, A. (1983). Trend report: The sociology of humour and laughter. *Current Sociology, 31* (3), 1-100.

Zuboff, S. (1995). The emperor's new information economy. In W. Orlikowski, G. Walsham, M. Jones, & J. DeGross (Eds.), *Information technology and changes in organizational work* (pp. 13-17). London: Chapman & Hall.

Author Index

Acker, J., 190
Adler, N., 23
Agor, W., 118, 119
Albrow, M., 114
Alexander, E., 87
Allende, I., 12
Altman, B., 182, 185
Alvesson, M., 101, 114
Anderson, N., 38
Anderson, P., 137, 143, 159, 162
Andresen, L., 123
Ansoff, H., 206
Apte, M., 134
Argyris, C., 48, 106, 112, 113, 146, 150
Arlow, P., 10
Arthur, M., 140
Ashworth, B., 114
Aspery, J., 218
Athos, A., 20
Austin, J., 39, 48
Austin, N., 227

Badaracco, J., Jr., 65, 66, 75, 78, 95, 99, 138, 143, 146, 152, 153, 155, 165
Bailey, J., 99
Barrera, P., 99
Barsoux, J., 122, 127, 134
Bartholomew, S., 23

Bartlett, C., 13, 17, 19, 23, 35, 61, 160
Bateson, G., 48
Bazerman, M., 175
Beaumont, P., 71, 89
Bergquist, W., 1, 26, 27, 28, 29, 30, 32, 34, 35, 48, 49, 59, 61, 66, 67, 79, 83, 85, 87, 90, 91, 97, 99
Betwee, J., 66, 67, 79, 83, 85, 87, 90, 91, 97, 99
Bhatnagar, D., 191
Billing, Y., 191
Birch, C., 180
Blackler, F., 140, 145, 148, 150, 165
Blair, J., 10, 198
Blake, S., 192, 193
Bloor, G., 20, 150
Bohl, D., 229, 230
Bolman, L., 23, 103, 223
Booth, S., 214, 225
Borah, S., 79, 97, 99
Botkin, J., 138
Boulton, W., 76, 99
Bourgeois, III, 46
Brady, F., 202
Braham, J., 133
Brass, D., 150
Bresnen, M., 93
Brooking, A., 139
Brooks, G., 34

Brouthers, K., 77
Brouthers, L., 77
Brown, A., 111, 143
Brown, J., 148, 150
Brownell, J., 105, 146
Buchanan, R., 97
Bureau of Industry Economics, 95
Burke, W., 59
Burkhardt, M., 150
Burrell, G., 111, 121, 192
Burton, J., 71

Cairncross, F., 190
Cannon, T., 181, 193
Cantwell, J., 99
Carlin, B., 84, 99
Carroll, A., 170, 174, 197, 203, 211
Cauley de La Sierra, M., 90, 99
Champy, J., 15
Chan Kim, W., 179
Chattell, A., 1
Chayes, M., 42, 43
Cheney, G., 194
Chesbrough, H., 15
Chia, R., 104
Claman, P., 140
Clark, T., 13, 22
Clarkson, M., 168, 173
Clegg, S., 4, 101
Clippinger, J., 136, 158
Clutterbuck, D., 170, 175
Clyburn, G., 84, 99
Coates, J., 177
Cochran, P., 214
Cockburn, C., 191
Cohen, S., 61, 64
Coleman, J., 123
Collins, D., 188
Cooke, P., 74
Coopey, J., 105, 148, 151
Cosier, R., 124, 129
Covey, S., 42
Cox, A., 71, 77

Cox, T., 192, 193
Crossan, M., 109, 112, 137, 147,
    153, 155
Crowley, L., 79
Culpan, R., 67, 78, 95

Daft, R., 105, 158
Davidson, N., 76, 99
Davis, S., 138
Dawson, P., 20, 150
De Meuse, K., 55
Deal, T., 23, 103, 223
Dearlove, D., 170, 175
Dechant, K., 182, 185, 190
Decker, W., 126
Deetz, S., 9, 197, 228, 230
DeFillipp, R., 140
Deli, D., 106, 108, 161
DeMarie, S., 36, 41, 59
Denis, H., 225
Dess, G., 13, 65
Dodgson, M., 111, 136, 148, 149
Dowling, M., 84, 99
Drucker, P., 4, 16, 21, 104, 142, 197
Duncan, R., 6, 123, 129
Duncan, W., 122, 123, 128, 130,
    131
Dunn, C., 202
Dunphy, D., 25, 30, 32, 36, 47, 53,
    57
Dwyer, T., 129, 131
Dyson, E., 197

Ebers, M., 72
Eccles, T., 37, 46, 51, 52, 57
Ehrenfeld, J., 187
Eisenhardt, K., 46
EIU/IBM, 138, 152, 162, 163, 164
Eliot, T., 135
Elise Walton, A., 25, 33, 44, 46
Emery, F., 4
Engledow, J., 209
Ernst, D., 97, 99

Esterhuysen, P., 25, 42, 58
Evan, W., 8
Ewing, D., 179, 211

Fahey, L., 207
Fassel, D., 227
Feisal, J., 122, 123, 128, 130, 131
Field, L., 144, 149, 151, 162
Fine, G., 123
Fineman, S., 114, 116, 117, 119, 120
Finkelstein, S., 137, 143, 159, 162
Finney, M., 221, 222, 224
Flam, H., 115
Fombrun, C., 69, 74
Forbes, T., III, 72, 87, 92, 97
Ford, B., 144, 149, 151, 162
Ford, R., 18
Fottler, M., 18
Foucault, M., 49
Frederick, W., 178
Freedman, D., 21
Freeman, J., 8
Freeman, R., 9
Friedman, M., 10
Frisch-Gauthier, J., 129
Fry, R., 38, 52

Galbraith, J., 1, 62
Gardener, J., 230
Gergen, K., 50
Gerstein, M., 145
Geus, A., 226
Ghoshal, S., 13, 17, 19, 23, 35, 61, 160
Giddens, A., 120
Gillin, M., 99
Gilmore, T., 17, 160
Gladwin, T., 167, 171, 179, 180, 230
Glick, W., 26, 28
Goes, J., 34
Goleman, D., 114, 116

Gomes-Casseres, B., 155
Goodman, J., 121, 133
Goodstein, L., 59
Gouillart, F., 28, 35
Greening, D., 224
Grint, K., 16, 21, 22
Gross, T., 20
Gulati, R., 87
Gustafson, L., 36, 41, 59

Hagedoorn, J., 82
Hakansson, H., 68, 73, 78, 94, 153
Hall, R., 138
Hammer, M., 15
Handy, C., 16, 21, 167, 197, 229
Hannan, M., 8
Harari, O., 77, 99
Hardy, C., 4, 50, 202
Harper, S., 2
Harrigan, K., 61, 76, 96
Harrington, S., 173
Harrison, E., 189
Harrison, J., 199, 202
Hart, S., 180
Hawken, P., 168, 190
Hawkins, P., 105
Hearn, J., 190, 192
Heifetz, R., 42
Herring, J., 77
Herzberg, F., 16
Hiebeler, R., 138, 142, 146, 149, 151, 157, 164
Hill, C., 10
Hirschhorn, L., 17, 160
Hochschild, A., 114
Hodgetts, R., 168, 229, 230
Hofstede, G., 20, 134
Holden, R., 122, 125
Holusha, J., 213
Hosking, D., 116
Howard, R., 13, 14
Howarth, C., 99
Huang, D., 99

Huber, G., 26, 28, 105, 106, 158
Hughes, J., 71, 77
Hughes, M., 101
Humphrey, R., 114
Hunter, L., 71, 89
Hurst, D., 230
Huxham, C., 68

Inkpen, A., 109, 112, 137, 153, 155
Isaacs, W., 107, 112, 157, 162
Isabella, L., 72, 87, 92, 97
Itami, H., 146, 149

Jackall, R., 115
Jagtenberg, T., 179
James, H., Jr., 98
Jarratt, J., 177
Jennings, P., 186
Jick, T., 25, 31, 32, 39, 45, 56, 66,
    226
Johnson, R., 224
Jones, G., 6
Jones, M., 171
Jones, T., 10

Kahn, R., 5
Kahn, W., 123, 124, 128, 134
Kahwajy, J., 46
Kalinoglou, J., 84, 99
Karim, M., 79
Katz, D., 5
Katzenbach, J., 122
Kaye, M., 49
Keidel, R., 13, 22, 62
Kelly, J., 28, 35
Kennelly, J., 167, 171, 179, 230
Kets de Vries, M., 30, 116, 124,
    226, 230
Ketterer, R., 42, 43
Kiernan, M., 2, 19
King, N., 38
King, W., 207
Kinlaw, D., 180, 181, 182

Knights, D., 143
Kofman, F., 149
Kotter, J., 59
Kouzes, J., 42
Krause, T., 167, 171, 179, 230
Kumaraswamy, A., 69, 74
Kurtzman, J., 138

Ladd Greeno, J., 187, 189
Lagadec, P., 215, 223
Lane, H., 109, 112, 137, 147, 153,
    155
Lank, A., 118
Larkin, S., 47
Larkin, T., 47
Laurie, D., 42
Lawler, E., III, 1, 62, 64
Leap, T., 122, 129
Leigh, A., 38, 41
Lenz, R., 209
Lepper, E., 180
Lessem, R., 67
Levinthal, D., 165
Lewicki, R., 179
Lewin, A., 63
Lewin, K., 31, 53
Lewis, J., 69, 70, 73, 77, 79, 83, 84,
    85, 87, 89, 91, 99
Libuser, C., 225
Liedtka, J., 13, 15, 22
Locke, K., 124
Lorange, P., 99
Lukaszewski, J., 218
Lundberg, C., 105, 146
Luthans, F., 168, 229, 230
Lynch, R., 65, 66, 68, 74, 75, 78, 79,
    93, 96
Lyotard, J., 49

MacAvoy, T., 72, 87, 92, 97
McCaskey, M., 4
McDaris, K., 55
McGill, M., 106, 108, 161

McGrath, M., 87, 99
McKenna, J., 54
McKie, D., 179
McKnight, R., 54
McLaughlin, K., 13, 65
McWhinney, W., 26, 31
Madhavan, R., 73
Mahaffie, J., 177
Mahon, J., 214
Makower, J., 184, 204
Mallam, P., 99
Manley, W., II, 169, 171, 173
Manz, C., 102
March, J., 165
Marcus, A., 12
Marks, M., 38, 42, 47
Marquardt, M., 105, 145, 156, 158, 161
Marshall, C., 135, 137, 139, 144, 146, 148, 149, 156, 165
Martinsons, M., 205
Maslow, A., 16
Mason, R., 1
Mauborgne, R., 179
Maynard, H., Jr., 167
Mehrtens, S., 167
Mendel, J., 210
Merriam, J., 204
Messick, D., 175
Meuel, D., 66, 67, 79, 83, 85, 87, 90, 91, 97, 99
Meyer, A., 34
Meyer, J., 8
Meyers, G., 213
Miles, G., 78, 94
Miles, R., 99
Miller, D., 226
Mink, B., 25, 42, 58
Mink, O., 25, 42, 58
Minton, J., 179
Mintzberg, H., 24
Mitchell, W., 95, 98

Mitroff, I., 1, 9, 14, 199, 214, 215, 216, 219, 220, 221, 222, 223, 224, 226
Mohr, J., 89, 90
Molander, E., 177
More, E., 87, 99, 219, 225
Morgan, G., 11, 28, 102, 111, 223, 228
Morris, K., 41, 51
Moss Kanter, R., 25, 31, 32, 39, 45, 56, 66, 86, 151, 155, 226
Mulkay, M., 121, 123
Mullane, J., 36, 41, 59
Mumby, D., 116, 117
Murray, F., 143

Nadler, D., 25, 29, 33, 34, 44, 145
Naisbitt, J., 204
Narayanan, V., 207
Nash, J., 187
Nathan, M., 219
Neck, C., 102
Nelson, K., 173, 176
Neubauer, F., 118
Nichols, M., 229
Nix, T., 10, 198
Nonaka, I., 138, 141, 143, 145, 162
Nord, W., 4

Ostell, A., 115
Owen, K., 25, 42, 58

Paine, L., 167, 174
Palmer, J., 131
Parikh, H., 118
Park, S., 66
Parkhe, A., 82, 99
Parkin, W., 191
Pascale, R., 46
Pascales, R., 20
Pauchant, T., 28, 120, 121, 212, 213, 220, 221, 222, 223, 224

Pearson, C., 1, 14, 214, 215, 216, 221, 222, 224
Perkins, B., 180
Peters, T., 13, 22, 227, 228
Pettigrew, A., 7, 30, 43, 53
Pfeffer, J., 4, 5, 9, 150, 227
Phillips, N., 148, 150
Piasecki, B., xiii, xxx, 181, 183, 184, 187, 226
Pinchot, G., 158, 159, 163
Pogrebin, M., 125
Polanyi, M., 141
Pollard, A., 99
Pollock, B., 69
Poole, E., 125
Porter, M., 98, 183, 184
Posner, B., 42
Powell, G., 190, 191, 192, 223
Powell, J., 123
Powell, W., 73
Preece, S., 78, 94
Prescott, J., 205
Price Waterhouse Change Integration Team, 12
Priem, R., 13, 65
Prusak, L., 135, 137, 139, 144, 146, 148, 149, 156, 165
Putnam, L., 116, 117

Quinn, B., 137, 143, 159, 162

Raben, C., 51
Rai, A., 79, 97, 99
Ralf, M., 71, 77
Ramaprasad, A., 79, 97, 99
Rands, G., 189
Rangan, U., 67, 70, 74, 76, 78, 92, 93, 95, 98, 99
Rasheed, A., 13, 65
Ray, M., 168
The RCL Team, 122
Reardon, K., 73, 89, 90, 91
Reed, M., 101

Reger, R., 36, 41, 59
Reichers, A., 39, 48
Reynolds, A., 105, 145, 156, 158, 161
Rice, R., 220
Rigby, D., 97
Ring, P., 67, 85, 88
Rinzler, A., 168
Roberts, K., 225
Robinson, G., 190
Robinson, S., 189
Roehl, T., 146, 149
Roering, W., 84, 99
Roos, J., 99, 163
Ryan, M., 151

Saffo, P., 197
St. John, C., 199, 202
Saint-Onge, H., 137, 146, 149, 157
Salaman, G., 13, 22
Salancik, G., 5, 9
Sankar, C., 76, 99
Savage, T., 10, 198
Schaef, A., 227
Schein, E., 105, 147, 162
Schon, D., 112, 146
Schwartz, F., 191
Scott, W., 8
Senge, P., 48, 137, 149, 151, 152, 157, 197
Seymour, M., 220
Shaw, R., 25, 33, 38, 42, 47, 145
Sheppard, B., 179
Sheppard, D., 192
Shrivastava, P., 179, 180, 182, 183, 184, 185, 215, 219, 221
Shrode, W., 169, 171, 173
Simons, R., 16, 160
Sinclair, D., 71, 89
Singh, K., 95, 98
Siomkos, G., 219
Sipika, C., 215, 219, 221
Slocum, J., 106, 108, 161, 229, 230

Smeltzer, L., 122, 129
Smith, A., 219
Smith, C., 195
Smith, D., 215, 219, 221
Snehota, I., 68, 73, 78, 94, 153
Snow, D., 170, 175
Snyder, C., 76, 99
Solomon, R., 172
Spears, L., 45
Spekman, R., 72, 73, 87, 89, 90, 91, 92, 97
Spilberg, D., 135, 137, 139, 144, 146, 148, 149, 156, 165
Srivastva, S., 38, 52
Stace, D., 25, 30, 32, 36, 47, 53, 57
Stacey, R., 9, 12, 25, 26, 37, 50, 101, 102, 111
Stafford, E., 97
Starik, M., 189
Starke, L., 177
Stein, B., 25, 31, 32, 39, 45, 56, 66, 226
Stein, R., 158, 159, 163
Stephens, C., 63
Stewart, T., 135, 139, 155, 164
Stoffels, J., 6, 9, 206, 208, 209, 210, 211
Strassman, P., 165
Strebel, P., 25, 40, 55
Swamy, R., 191

Tancred-Sheriff, P., 192
Teece, D., 15
Thomas, D., 97, 99
Thompson, K., 168
Thompson, M., 54
Thornburg, L., 164
Throop, G., 189
Tiemessen, I., 109, 112, 137, 147, 153, 155
Trevino, L., 173, 176
Trist, E., 4
Tushman, M., 29, 33, 34, 44

Ulian, J., 129
Ungson, G., 110, 152
Urban, S., 69, 86, 90, 92, 93, 95, 98, 99
Ussery, R., 76, 99

Van de Ven, A., 67, 74, 85, 88
van der Linde, C., 183, 184
Vedder, J., 22
Vendemini, S., 69, 86, 90, 92, 93, 95, 98, 99
Vinton, K., 126
Von Krogh, G., 163

Walker, G., 74
Walsh, J., 110, 152
Wanous, J., 39, 48
Want, J., 25, 33
Warnock, P., 132
Waterman, B., 13, 22
Wathne, K., 163
Weick, K., 9, 110
Weidenbaum, M., 98
Wells, P., 74
Whipp, R., 7, 30, 43, 53
White, R., 147
Whitehead, C., 10, 198
Wilkinson, T., 77
Willmot, H., 101, 114
Willmott, H., 143
Wolff, M., 88
Wood, D., 168, 169
Wouters, C., 116
Wyman, J., 84, 99

Yoshino, M., 67, 70, 74, 76, 78, 92, 93, 95, 98, 99

Zald, M., 104
Zandenbergen, P., 186
Zemke, R., 95, 132
Zemke, S., 95
Zijderveld, A., 131
Zuboff, S., 63

Subject Index

Adaptive learning (*see* Single-loop learning)
Agency and stakeholder theory, 10
Alliance (*see* Organizational alliance relationships)
American Express, 194
American Productivity & Quality Center, 164
Architecture (organizational), 61, 144-145
AT&T, 132

Baring, 136
Bechtel, 137
BMW, 186
The Body Shop, 186
Boundaries,
 new needs for knowledge management, 165
 psychological replacing traditional, 160
 spanning, 5
BP, 137

Challenger disaster, 173
Change,
 alternatives, 33
 conditions for feasibility, 37
 discontinuous, 35
 eras, 32
 forms, 32
 incremental and strategic, 33
 management, 30, 46-49
 as a political process, 49, 51
 as process versus event, 58
 reactive and anticipatory, 33-34
 resistance, 38-42, 63
 sources, 31
 Ten Commandments guideline, 56-57
 types, 32-34
 typology, 34
 as waves, 167-168
 (*see also* Transformation of organizations)
Change-capability, 25
Coalition for Environmentally Responsible Economies' principles (CERES), 187
Collaboration and cooperation, 68, 148, 163
 adaptation, 69
 advantage, 66, 71, 93-95
 and competition, 70
 coordinated, 70
 difficulties, 22, 76, 95-97
 functional, 69-70
 need for trust, 87-89
 with other organizations, 65
 within an organization, 64
 (*see also* Organizational alliance relationships)

Communications,
   central to alliances, 90
   and change management, 46-49
   humor and difficult messages,
      124
   sustainable, 189
Continuity, and organizational
      health, 52
Control,
   and accountability, 159
   levels, 16-17
   and psychological boundaries, 17
Corporate image, 21
Crisis management, 212-221
   communications, 218
   five phases, 223
   integrated program, 213
   like "brutal audit", 221
   onion model, 222
   research statistics, 224-225
   strategic checklist, 216-217
Culture,
   and differences in humor,
      133-134
   and knowledge, 146-150
   pluralism versus assimilation,
      193
   variables in nations, 20-21

Deconstructionism, and communi-
      cation, 48
Desert Storm, 42
Deutsche Bank, 186
Dialogue-learning (*see* Triple-loop
      learning)
Double-loop learning, 107, 161,
      229
   and error detection/correction,
      112-113
Dow Chemicals, 164, 183, 186
Dramaturgy, 116
Du Pont, 132, 183, 186
Dutch Flower Industry, 183

Edvinsson, Leif, 139, 164
Emotional intelligence, 19
   collective within organizations,
      114, 115
Empowerment, 17-19
   and limits, 18
Environment in organizations,
   changes, 26
   focal zone, 206
   and forecasting, 203, 204
   macro and micro perspectives,
      xv, 15, 31
   major types in organizations, 4-9
   pressures, 8
   as social construct, 9
   and uncertainty, 6
Equilibrium dynamics and change,
      38
Esprit, 186
Ethics,
   improving decision making, 175
   and management, 167, 177
   and social responsibility, 169,
      171-172
   stages of corporate moral devel-
      opment, 178
   and stakeholders, 9, 168
   theorems for syntheses with
      responsibility, 178
   training, 172
Exxon, 181
   Valdez crisis, 185, 213

Failures, in change management,
      58-59

Gender,
   discrimination, 191
   and rationality versus emotional-
      ity, 116
   versus sex, 190
Generative learning (*see*
      Double-loop learning)
Greenleaf, Robert, 45

Harvey-Jones, John, 13
Hierarchies, 2
Hitachi, 183
Hughes Corporation, 137, 164
Humor (*see* People)
Humor consultants, 132-133
Hyatt Regency Chicago, 181

IBM, 41, 132, 186, 195
Imaginization, 103
International environmental management standards (ISO 14000), 187
International Journal of Forecasting, 210
Intuition in organizations, 117
  and decision making, 118
  impediments, 119
  levels, 118-119

Kidder Peabody, 136
Knowledge management, 75, 135-136, 137, 157-158
  globalization, 138-139, 153
  impediments, 149
  and measurement, 163-165
  and organizational change, 135
  and strategic alliances, 94
  support structure requirements, 158-160, 165
  (*see also* Organizational alliance relationships)
Knowledge Management Assessment Tool (KMAT), 164
Kodak, 132

Leadership, 27-30, 42-45
  in alliances, 87, 92-93
  charismatic, 29-30, 42
  importance of senior management ethics, 177
  instrumental, 44
  integrative role, 29

  and "knowledge engineers," 162
  servant-leader approach, 45
  and vision, 34
  (*see also* Organization entities)
Learning perspective organizational types,
  Knowing Organization, 108
  Learning Organization, 109, 162-163
  Thinking Organization, 108
  Understanding Organization, 108
The "living company," 226
Long Range Planning, 210
Lufthansa, 186

McKinsey & Co., 162
The "managed heart," 115, 120
Management,
  areas of change, 2-3
  and intellectual capital, 136, 139, 144, 157
  Japanese, 137
  liberation, 228
  new-age, 228
  rewards and frustrations, 3-4
  as "strategic termites," 103
  and study of humor, 122
  of transition, 41-42
Marks, Rodney, 133
"Mastery Play," 124-125
Metallgesellschaft, 136
Metcalf, C.W., 133
Moss Kanter, Rosabeth, 12

New mind-sets, xvi

Organization,
  challenges, 3
  and diversity, 192
  ecology, 5, 179
  economic view, xiv, 10, 230

existential underpinnings,
119-120
historical roots of complexity, 26,
27
as information-processing entities, 111
knowledged-based types,
140-141
liability of traditional approach,
1
need for contention, 46
old versus new style, 62
as open learning system, 5
as organism, 5
as rational entities debate,
116-117, 226
as social construct, 111, 115-116
success factors, 2
(*see also* Architecture; Environment; Learning perspec-
tive)
organizational types; Transformation
Organization entities,
knowledge/learning center, 14,
19, 105, 148
leadership institute, 14
operations center, 14
recovery/development center, 14
service/spiritual center, 14
Organizational alliance relationships, 65, 66
with competitors, 84
critical elements, 79-80
customer-supplier alliances, 84
during crisis management,
219-220
evolution, 72-73
as expensive exercises, 97
and knowledge links, 153-154
and knowledge management,
152
networks, 73-74

paradox, 98
structural arrangements, 82-84
theoretical explanations, 67
Organizational culture, 19-21,
160-163
and change, 45-46
Organizational learning, 19,
105-106
interpretive path, 106
limiting factors, 112
process, 155-156
systems-structural path, 1
types, 106-109, 109
(*see also* Learning perspective
organizational types)
Organizational memory, 19, 45, 49,
110
Organizational processes management frames,
human resource frame, 103
political frame, 104
structural frame, 103
symbolic frame, 104

Paradigm-shifting versus analytical
problem-solving skills, 104
Partnering, 69-72
building compatible culture, 91
effective partnerships, 79-82
(*see also* Organizational alliance
relationships)
People,
and humor as organizational
resource, 121-122,
127-128, 129
issues in strategic alliances,
81-82, 85-86
knowledge workers, 142-143
as solutions, 16
Peters, Tom, 13
Pinto car disaster, 173
Porter, Michael, 12

Power,
    dynamics in alliances, 89-90
    and high price of egalitarianism,
        51
    and knowledge, 150-152, 163
    in organizational life reflected by
        humor, 130-131
    and organizational politics,
        49-50
Price Waterhouse Change Integra-
    tion Team, 12
Proactive change, xiii, xiv, 40-41
    and communication, 47
Proctor & Gamble, 186
Professional cultures, 20, 150
Psychodynamics, and organiza-
        tional behavior analysis,
        115, 226
Purpose-process-people doctrine,
    61

QRS Inc., 126

Reactive change path, 40
Recipe approaches,
    "buzzologies," 53
    magic bullets, 12, 21, 166
    management gurus, xiii, 12-13,
        22
    quick fixes, xv
    simplistic and textbook, 4
Reengineering, 14-15, 62-63
    Hammer, 22
Reframing, 23
    and change, 31, 35
Regulatory design principles,
    184-185
Relational competence, xvi
Resource dependency approach, 8
Rethinking, 23, 62, 63
Reward systems, seniority versus
    productivity, 2

Ronald McDonald House program,
    194

Saab, 22
Science fiction, and future tends,
    210
Siemens, 186
Silicon Valley, 154
Single-loop learning, 106
Situational/contingent model of
    leadership, 28
Skandia, 139, 164
Smith Kline Beecham, 54
Social control, and management, 1
Social responsibility model,
    170-171
Stabilization, 59-60
Stakeholders, 9-10, 178, 198
    and corporate contract changes,
        55-565
    model, 197, 230
    and organizational theory, 11-12
    and a proactive partnering
        approach, 201-202
    versus shareholders, 10
Strategic alliance, 68-69, 70
    four Cs test, 77
    rationale, 74-75
Strategies,
    active environmentalism, 181
    advantage of ethical culture, 172
    and mental models, 102
    public policy management,
        211-212
    stakeholder analysis, 10
    thinking that synthesizes learn-
        ing, 24
    turbulence reduction, 6
    unpredictability as base, 101
Structure,
    as an organizational tool, 13
    barrier free, 14, 65
    and knowledge, 143-146

modular, 14, 65
strategy-structure-systems doctrine, 61
teams for the intelligent organization, 159
virtual, 14, 15-16, 65
(*see also* Architecture)
Success,
critical factors, 53
(*see also* Failures)
Sun Tzu, 42
Sustain-centric paradigm, 171
Sustainable development, 180, 182
benefits, 184
strategies, 189

Technocentric paradigm, 171
Technological Forecasting and Social Change, 210
Technology,
expertise and power issues, 150
and high involvement organizational model, 64
and partnering, 82
as a tool for knowledge management, 158
3M, 183, 186
Three Mile Island disaster, 173
Transformation of organizations, 35
charismatic, 36
developmental transitions, 36
task-focused transitions, 36
tectonic, 37
turnarounds, 36
Transformational behavioral context, 17, 160
Trend watching, 204
Triple-loop learning, 107
Tylenol crisis, 213

Union Carbide, 181
Bhopal crisis, 213
Unlearning, 94, 110, 138

Volvo, 22